WILDERNESS HUNTING
AND WILDCRAFT

Photo by Dr. A. B. Chesterfield.

THE BIG HORN, OR ROCKY MOUNTAIN SHEEP, THE FINEST TROPHY
THAT CAN FALL TO THE RIFLE OF THE AMERICAN SPORTSMAN

WILDERNESS HUNTING
and WILDCRAFT

WITH NOTES ON THE HABITS AND LIFE
HISTORIES OF BIG GAME ANIMALS

BY

LIEUT. COLONEL TOWNSEND WHELEN

ILLUSTRATED WITH PHOTOGRAPHS AND
WITH SKETCHES BY THE AUTHOR

E P B M
ECHO POINT BOOKS & MEDIA, LLC

Published by Echo Point Books & Media
Brattleboro, Vermont
www.EchoPointBooks.com

ISBN: 978-1-62654-123-8

Cover image: *Among the Sierra Nevada Mountains, California*
by Albert Bierdstadt

Cover design by Rachel Boothby Gualco,
Echo Point Books & Media

Editorial and proofreading assistance by Christine Schultz,
Echo Point Books & Media

CONTENTS

INTRODUCTION

"Hunting of big game in the wilderness is, above all things, a sport for a vigorous and masterful people. The rifle-bearing hunter, whether he goes on foot or on horseback, whether he voyages in a canoe or travels with a dog-sled, must be sound of body and firm of mind, and must possess energy, resolution, manliness, self-reliance, and capacity for hardy self-help. In short, the big-game hunter must possess qualities without which no race can do its life-work well; and these are the very qualities which it is the purpose of this club, so far as may be, to develop and foster."—Theodore Roosevelt, in *"American Big Game Hunting."*

"I wish that members of the Boone and Crockett Club, and big-game hunters generally, would make a point of putting down all their experiences with game, and with any other mark-worthy beasts or birds, in the regions where they hunt, which would be of interest to students of natural history; noting any changes of habits in the animals and any causes that tend to make them decrease in numbers, giving an idea of the times at which the different larger beasts became extinct, and the like."—Theodore Roosevelt, in *"Hunting in Many Lands."*

This work treats of the hunting of big game for sport on the continent of North America, of the woodcraft essential to success, and of the habits and life histories of our big game in as much as is of interest and use to the hunter. It comprises my own experiences of a total of approximately sixty months in the game fields, as well as a compilation from the writings of our most virile, observant, and successful hunters. I have consulted all of our best works on the subject, acknowledgment being made from time to time in the text, and in the list of these works in the appendix. I have tried to make the book such that it will be useful to the sportsman and contribute to his success. I trust that it will also encourage the qualities of good sportsmanship among hunters of big game. I am not one of those who believe that it is wrong to kill big game, but the reader will not find herein any record of slaughter with which all too many works of this kind are filled. I believe that one should never kill except as a gentleman and a sportsman. The primordial instinct to kill for food and trophy, the matching of the human brain against the instincts of a wild animal, and the test of manliness which a wilderness demands, will usually be the call which induces one tc take up big game hunting. But I do think that a gentleman will always feel a desire to curb the almost inborn tendency to kill, and that he should limit himself to one or two good heads of each species. If he shoots these in a sportsmanlike way he will have no regrets, and he will learn the delights of the unspoiled places of the earth, and its fauna and flora. He will appreciate the attractiveness of wild life, the glorious scenery, the sense of solitude, the exhilaration of hard exercise in the purest air, and the test of manhood. Thereafter he will be only too glad to confine himself mainly to photography instead of shooting, and to the study of the habits of the game. After one has obtained a trophy, photography and the study of wild life offer far greater promises for reward than merely more shooting and killing. It takes much greater skill to obtain a really good photograph of a wild animal in its native haunts than it does to shoot the same animal, and the picture is quite as good a trophy on one's wall. Also in the study of the habits and the life histories of game of all kinds I feel that the gentleman hunter will obtain great reward, and will contribute much to both science and sport. We know little even today about the habits, life histories and distribution of our wild creatures. Even the most minor instances and experiences may be of great assistance in increasing and corroborating our knowledge on these matters. There are many things about even our more common wild animals and birds that need verification or clearing up. A single incident does not prove a habit, but a dozen or more experiences duly recorded go a long way in verifying a belief or proving it a fallacy.

What I have set forth herein is mainly for the city sportsman, the amateur at the game, the man who takes his hunting in vacation time. The less experience a man has the more good information should he try to obtain from others and carry in his head. We must admit that we constantly learn from the experience of others as laid down in books. Not that I believe that a man can learn to hunt big game successfully from any book. He must have that great teacher, Experience. But a proper text-book will teach him to correctly interpret his experience. It will show him the reason for certain things which he runs up against. It will give him theory, which is always a good servant but a poor master, and so it will shorten his apprenticeship.

The delight of wild scenery, the exhilaration of bodily exercise in pure air, and the ever-varying circumstances of wild and majestic country; the inspiring sense of solitude, broken only by the whistle of the marmot or the laugh of the loon; the intimate communing with Nature in every aspect of sunshine, mist, and storm—all these, and with them the satisfying of that hunter's instinct which is one of the most deeply rooted things in human nature; the delight of pitting the intellect and the senses against the instincts of self-preservation of a really wild animal—that is wilderness hunting.

This work is really a revision and extension of a small booklet entitled "Big Game Hunting," which I wrote and which was published by *Outers' Recreation* in 1923. The scope of that booklet was necessarily limited by its restrictions in size to 100 pages. While I was working on it I became more and more impressed with the need of such a work, not only for the information which it contained, but for its opportunity to present lessons of true sportsmanship and conservation among American boys and men. I also found that I was compelled by reason of my limitation in space to leave unsaid much that I would like to have set forth, and which I believed the book should contain to make it of real value. "Big Game Hunting" has been most useful in the compilation of this work as I have been able to obtain many comments and criticisms on it from our leading hunters and sportsmen, as well as many most valuable suggestions, and have thus been able to correct certain errors which it contained, and add much comprehensive and useful matter. My thanks are due to *Outer's Recreation* for permitting me to incorporate herein much of the matter which appeared in "Big Game Hunting."

My thanks are due to the United States Biological Survey, the United States Forest Service, The New York Zoological Society, and to *Nature Magazine* for some of the photographs used in the illustration of the text. I am also indebted to the

following gentlemen for assistance and advice in the preparation
of the text:

Daniel M. Barringer.	Dr. A. B. Critchfield.
Charles A. Barker.	E. Mallinckrodt, Jr.
Steven Camp.	W. J. Morden.
James L. Clark.	F. H. Riggall.
Stanley H. Clark.	Charles Sheldon.

A. Bryan Williams.

I have also received considerable assistance from the works
of the following:

Vilhjalmur Stefansson.	Major C. H. Stigand.
Ernest Thompson Seton.	Theodore S. Van Dyke.

George Bird Grinnell.

Considerable assistance has also been obtained from articles
which have appeared in the following magazines:

The American Rifleman.	Nature Magazine.
Field and Stream.	Outdoor Life.
Forest and Stream.	Outdoor Recreation.
Journal of Mammalogy.	Rod and Gun in Canada.

"Others may learn much, see much, enjoy much, but the most
and best is known to the man who quits his bed before sunrise, who
spends his nights as well as days by the month and year on mountain
ranges, in forests, and in the wilderness; who bears heat and cold
and hunger, thirst and toil, for the love of Nature; and is pushed by
his passion down into the abysmal depths of Himalayan gorges, African
kloofs, or American cañons, or led up to snowy peaks, to realms of
eternal ice, or over the sun-withered wastes of the earth, to visit
the utmost refuges of beast and bird. The artist is his only rival in
his courtship, the only competitor of the bliss of a sportsman's
paradise. The best artists have something of the sportsman's instinctive longing to see, to touch, to handle, and the best sportsmen have
something of the artistic temperament. Yet, when I think of it,
where is the artist in literature or painting who, like innumerable
sportsmen, despising wealth and fame, have wandered off alone to
spend all their years in Nature's wilds, finding there alone what can
satisfy their love of her delights."—Sir Alfred Pease, in *"The Book of
the Lion."*

CHAPTER I

THE HABITS OF BIG GAME

Without a knowledge of the habits of game it is almost impossible to hunt with real success, and I might say with real sportsmanlike interest. Lacking such information one merely stumbles upon the animals by accident, and unless he is in a country where the game is remarkably plentiful he usually meets with poor success. The experienced guide succeeds in getting game for his patrons because he is familiar with the habits of the game in his locality. He knows in what kind of country to look for them at certain times of the year and day, and he knows to a certain extent what they will generally do under certain circumstances. If the sportsman is to hunt alone he too should have this knowledge. But even when assisted by a guide some understanding of the habits and life histories of our game animals will make the hunt many times more interesting. It will show the why and wherefore of many things the guide does, and oftentimes it adds absorbing interest to a day which might otherwise be a tiresome tramp.

Study of the habits and life histories of wild creatures has been the hobby of some of our most prominent men—Roosevelt, Burroughs, Ford, Edison. We cannot know too much about such matters. The knowledge is good for us from moral and philosophical standpoints, and its scientific value is very great. I have tried to lay down herein what we know of each of our big game animals, supplementing my own meager experiences with the recorded notes of our most trustworthy hunter-naturalists. As a matter of fact we know all too little of such subjects. Any one man's lifetime is all too short, and his opportunites too fleeting to learn much first hand. It is only by compiling the combined experience of a great many accurate observers that we can hope to eventually arrive at a fairly full understanding of the

1

habits, impulses, mind, manners, instinct, and life of our fauna. The recorded experience of one man means little, but when a dozen observers have recorded a fact—set it down accurately as to time, place, date, etc.—then we begin to get something on which we can rely. About the best that can be said for the following notes is that they are a start on which to build, and I sincerely trust that our coming sportsmen and hunters will do their best to add to the structure, brick by brick, until we have a real edifice.

I used to be a diligent reader of the accounts of hunting trips as published almost monthly in our sporting magazines, but I confess that of late years the majority of such stories do not interest me. All too many of them are merely accounts of killings. And yet once in a while I come across a real gem which I clip out and save for its description of the animals, their habits and doings, and the country in which they live, or for its word picture of the unspoiled scenery, and perhaps for the good photographs and maps which leave an accurate record for the sportsmen who come after.

Many of the remarks, ideas, and conclusions as to animals which I have set forth herein, or which are quoted from the writings of other observers, may not meet with the approval of older and more experienced sportsmen, but at the same time they are the results of some experience and observation, and with the present knowledge on these subjects differences of opinion concerning the habits of animals are bound to occur between most sportsmen, no two holding exactly the same views. I will frequently use the words "usually," "often," or "generally," in describing the habits of animals. I think that it is a great mistake to say that any animal *will* do this or that because, the behavior of no two animals is any more alike than that of two human beings. Moreover the same animal may have totally different habits in different localities, and at different times of the year.

In the chapters dealing with each of the animals I have given roughly the range, that is the localities in North America where they exist at the present day. This matter of range is an exceedingly interesting topic to which several of our field naturalists* have given considerable study with remarkable findings, which

* Dr. J. A. Allen, Dr. C. Hart Merriam, and Ernest Thompson Seton.

Photo by Mr. E. Mallinckrodt, Jr.
BIG BROWN BEAR CHARGING, SHOWING TYPICAL ALASKAN BROWN BEAR COUNTRY

findings serve to illustrate in a small measure the almost unlimited promise of reward for investigation on any subject connected with our animals, or indeed with any branch of Natural
History or Science.

The arctic, temperature, and tropical regions of North America may be divided into certain faunal areas, and these faunal
areas will be found to include or to limit the range of almost all
of our animals and non-migratory birds. Thus in the Arctic Region the northern limit of trees marks the southern limit of
range of the polar bear, the polar oxen, and the white fox, and
the northern limit of range of the moose. The great spruce belt
which stretches across Canada from Labrador to the Pacific, and
which circles the upper slopes of the high mountains as far south
as northern Mexico, contains in its sub-faunal areas the range of
the grizzly bear, sheep, and goats, while its southern edge is the
southern limit of range of the moose and caribou. The northern
limit of range of the jaguar is the northern limit of the well-
watered dense forests or jungle of the tropical region, and so on.

It is not to be understood that animals are, or even originally
were plentiful or evenly distributed over the whole of the faunal
area which contains their range. Each individual animal or
band of animals seem to have what may be termed a home range,
a choice locality in which normally they spend their entire lives,
and the geographical range of a species consists of numbers of
these home ranges interspersed throughout the geographical range.
The hunter speaks of these home ranges as "game countries" or
as localities where game is plentiful. Between the home ranges
are found stretches of country, often apparently perfectly suited
to the species, throughout which it does not exist, or exists only
in occasional wandering individuals or bands. The home ranges
of sheep and goats are relatively small, bands frequenting certain
mountains or ranges of mountains, and not being found on other
adjacent ranges where all condition including food are apparently
. suitable. Some animals such as caribou have two home ranges,
each quite large in extent, and they make seasonal migrations
from one to the other. The home range of the flesh eaters as a
class is usually larger than that of the ruminants. Even in the
very small area of game countries which I have personally visited
I can draw maps which will clearly define the home ranges of
certain species, which home ranges are entirely independent of

food conditions. Take for example the valley of the Fraser River north of the main line of the Canadian Pacific Railway in British Columbia. It is a country of high mountains, and the higher slopes of all these mountains are suitable for sheep and goats, and yet ever since white men have been familiar with this region sheep have never been known in the ranges west of the river and south of the town of Lillooet, although they are plentiful north of that town. And goats are extremely rare or absent in the ranges on the east side of the river. Also in the main range of the Canadian Rockies in northwestern Alberta and eastern British Columbia, sheep are plentiful on the east slopes of the mountains down almost to the foothills, but are almost or totally absent on the west side of the main divide.

The home or family life of our animals also offers great possibilities for investigation. Our horned ruminants, for example, do not seem to have any family life, the males being entirely polygamous, and while they run in herds at times there can hardly be said to be any family significance in the herd. On the other hand wolves and beavers unite in real families, and are monogamous.

Seton has indicated a general plan for the treatment or investigation of each species* and has divided the schedule into thirty-nine sections containing some five hundred different questions, answers to which are desirable for each animal. It would be well for the would-be hunter-naturalist to systematize his investigations on the lines of such a schedule, as he thus avoids overlooking matters of importance.

"Keeping records and data will test the care, accuracy, integrity, and honor of the would-be naturalist. And right here let it be clearly understood that the *slightest deviation from truth and accuracy, or a carelessness that leaves a chance for error, destroys the usefulness, reputation, and standing of any naturalist.* An unswerving regard for the truth is the religion of a genuine naturalist, and his whole training is to see straight, think straight, and be straight. The rules of the game are rigorous, and the training and self-discipline make for real character."†

---

* *"Lives of Game Animals,"* Vol. 1, E. T. Seton, 1925.
† Vernon Bailey, Chief Field Naturalist, U. S. Biological Survey.

CHAPTER II

THE THREE NORTH AMERICAN DEER

1. WHITE-TAILED DEER, or Virginia Deer.

2. MULE DEER, or Rocky Mountain Black-Tailed Deer, or Jumping Deer.

3. BLACK-TAILED DEER, or Columbian Black-Tailed Deer, or Coast Deer.

The above are the three principal or main species of the deer of North America. Each of these species, in different localities, may differ slightly from the type, and some of these differences have amounted to enough to justify naturalists in describing them as different species. But in general our deer may be classed under these three heads. They may be identified one from the others by their tails and by the metatarsal glands on the hind legs. the white-tailed deer may also be told from the others by its antlers.

Tails.—The top or upper surface of the tail of the white-tailed deer is dull, rusty red or yellowish brown in summer and bluish gray in winter. The edges and the under side are white. The tail of the mule deer is white except the bunch on the tip, which is black all around. The tail of the black-tailed deer is all black on the upper side, and all white on the under side.

Metatarsal Glands.—On the white-tailed deer these are about 1 inch long, on the mule deer about 5 inches long, and on the black-tailed deer about 2 inches long.

Antlers.—The antlers of the white-tailed deer have one main beam, bending back and then forward when viewed from the side, and the main beam bears the tines behind and above it. The

mule deer and black-tailed deer antlers are an arrangement of
equal forks. That is, instead of one main beam and tines branching out from it, the main beam divides equally to form two
branches or tines, and a branch may divide equally again to form
two tines. These are the typical antlers, the variations from
which are endless.

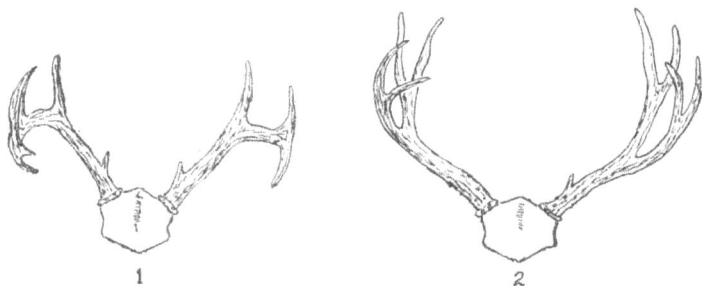

1   2
TYPICAL ANTLERS.   (1) WHITE-TAILED DEER.   (2) MULE AND BLACK-
TAILED DEER

1   2   3
TAILS OF WHITE-TAILED (1), MULE (2), AND BLACK-TAILED (3) DEER

CHAPTER III

THE WHITE-TAILED DEER OR VIRGINIA DEER

Odocoïleus virginianus virginianus, Boddært

Type Locality.—Virginia.

The White-tailed or Virginia Deer is the best known and most widely distributed of our big-game animals. It inhabits at least a portion of all the United States except California and Nevada, although it is extinct in Delaware and scarce in Washington and Oregon. It is perhaps most plentiful in the States of Maine, New York, Pennsylvania, Wisconsin, Michigan, Minnesota, and Texas. In Canada it is most plentiful in Nova Scotia, New Brunswick, Quebec, and Ontario, and is also found in Manitoba and in some parts of the southern portion of British Columbia, but is probably not found or is very scarce in Alberta and Saskatchewan. It is quite common throughout Mexico, but not in Southern California, and various species are found at least as far south as Panama. It is most abundant today in the woods of the northeastern portion of the United States, and in that portion of Canada drained by the Great Lakes and the St. Lawrence River, and also in the valley of the Rio Grande. It flourishes closer to human habitations than any other of our large animals. I have seen deer feeding within twenty-five miles of the city of Boston, Mass.

The white-tailed deer was first described as *Cervus virginianus* by Boddært in 1784, the type locality being Virginia. In all, twenty-two other species and sub-species of this deer have been recognized and described, the majority of them differing very little, however, from the typical Virginia deer.*

---

* List of North American Recent Mammals, 1923—Miller. Smithsonian Institute Bulletin No. 128.

9

The length of the male deer is from 5 to 5½ feet, the height at the shoulders about 3 feet, and the tail about 12 inches long. A northern male white-tailed deer in its prime will weigh from 225 to 300 pounds. The females of the species are somewhat smaller. This deer seems to reach its maximum size today in the States and Provinces from Michigan to New Brunswick. There is no positive record of maximum weight, but quite a number of deer, both bucks and does, have been killed that weighed over 300 pounds dressed. In the southern part of its range the white-tailed deer usually decreases in size and weight.

The color of both the bucks and does is similar. In summer the body is reddish brown, with the belly, under side, and tip of the tail, and inside of the legs and throat white. There is also a whitish band across the nose, and a ring of the same color about the eye. When winter comes the body color changes to grayish (sometimes called bluish) or grayish brown. The fawns when born are reddish-brown with white spots over the body, these spots persisting until the animals are five or six months old, usually disappearing with the winter coat.

The white-tailed deer can easily be distinguished from the other two American deer, the mule deer and the coast black-tailed deer, by the character of its antlers, these having one main beam which first bends outward and backward, then curves forward and perhaps slightly inward at the tips, and bears the tines behind. In white-tailed deer the metatarsal gland on the outer side of the hind shank is about 1 inch long, while in the black-tailed deer it is about 2 inches long, and in mule deer about 5 inches. The tails are also very distinctive, and their differences are shown in the previous chapter. Only the bucks have horns, which are shed each year about January to March.* The new antlers begin to grow at once under the velvet, and are usually full grown by the end of August, at which time the buck rubs the velvet off against trees and bushes. In those localities where the white-tailed deer flourishes best a young buck will grow single-spiked antlers during his second summer. Each succeeding year, given good food conditions, this buck will usually grow one additional

---

* These seasonal notations refer to the northern deer, and are sometimes quite different in the South. For example. in Louisiana the mating season and the birth of the fawns are about two to three months earlier than in Canada, and it is said that in the tropics there are no regular mating, horn shedding, or fawn bearing periods.

branch or tine on each antler up to about four. A four-pronged buck is usually at least five years old and perhaps more. After five or six years as the deer gets old, the horns may get irregular and scrubby. Occasionally we see antlers that are very irregular, with many tines growing in all directions. For example a white-tailed deer has been killed in Texas with 78 points and a spread of 26½ inches. These abnormal antlers are always caused by disease, usually a sexual disturbance, for the antlers are sexual appendages.

The rutting season is usually late in October or early in November, depending a little on the weather. In the southern portions of the United States it may be much earlier. Just before the rut starts the necks of the bucks begin to swell. Before this they have been indifferent to the does and living off by themselves singly, but now their mating instincts begin to be aroused, and they chase the does all over the woods, occasionally battling with other bucks for their possession. At this time Seton says of the bucks, "Their whole nature seems to undergo a corresponding change at this time, and by November they are blind and mad with desire, as well as ready and eager to fight any of their own or other kind that seem to hinder their search for a mate." It is at this season of the year that the hunter is usually most successful in seeing and getting bucks. They are much more abroad in daytime than at other seasons, and are not nearly as secretive and cautious as usual. In 1919 I was hunting with Colonel Honeycutt in New Brunswick. We were still-hunting along the hillside, when we suddenly heard a rustle of leaves back of us and turned around just in time to see a doe chased by a buck coming straight toward us. The doe swerved a little when she saw us and passed about ten feet to one side, but the buck saw nothing but the doe and would have run practically over us had not Honeycutt shot it.

The rut seems to last a month, sometimes two months. With the white-tailed deer it apparently seems to be longer than with any other game. After it is over the bucks, does, and fawns seem to be on much better terms than at other times of the year. Then the bucks often remain with the does and fawns, where before the rut they seem to come together only by accident. Often at this time the deer will gather together in small bands in country where they are plentiful and little disturbed. They wander around on the good feeding grounds storing up fat for the winter.

If the country contains beech trees they are sure to be found looking for the nuts. Then as the snow deepens the little bands are restricted in their roaming, and they settle down to one small locality where they trample trails criss-crossing everywhere in the snow in their search for food.

As winter progresses the bucks shed their antlers. Usually I think the antler loosens and is then knocked off by contact with a bush or tree. Almost at once the new horns start to grow and develop very quickly under the velvet. Towards the end of winter when the snow is deepest and food gets scarce within the forest, the deer often comes down to the lake shores to feed on the branches of the cedars which fringe the lakes in the north woods. They browse on these branches, standing on the ice. In the woods of eastern Canada, New York, and Maine it is a common sight to see a distinct line of cedar branches coming only to within about six feet of the water, marking the high point to which the deer are able to reach in their quest for food.

As the spring and summer come on we find the deer of both sexes frequenting the banks of ponds, lakes, and streams. Probably they come to these places both to escape the plague of mosquitoes and to feed on the pond lilies and succulent water grasses. Then bucks and does may be found on the same shore, but ignoring each other completely.

In the latter part of the summer the buck's antlers reach their full growth, but still under the velvet, and apparently very tender. As at this time the antlers have attained a size that causes them to come occasionally in contact with branches and twigs, the buck appears to nurse them most carefully. He usually retires to the higher ridges to lie up most of the day. Then towards the end of August, as the antlers harden and the blood supply in the velvet ceases, they begin to rub the velvet off against trees and bushes. By the middle of September the antlers are usually bare, but the bucks continue to lead more or less solitary lives until the rut starts. It is this season just before the rut, that is the start of the legal hunting season in most States, that it is usually hardest to obtain shots at bucks. They are then not stirring around much, and are very much on the alert.

Throughout the northern part of the range of the white-tailed deer the fawns come into the world the last part of May or the first part of June. Most observers believe that when young and

WHITE-TAILED DEER

helpless the fawns are devoid of any smell, probably a provision
of nature to guard them against predatory animals until they are
large enough to run with their mothers.   The does suckle the
fawns until about the middle of September.   Charles L. Barker,
a very observant guide of New Brunswick, told me that once he
shot a doe in October that still had milk in her udder.   The
young deer remain with the old doe until the next spring, no doubt
being driven away by the mother when she is getting ready to
bring another fawn into the world.   Twin fawns are quite common among deer; indeed they seem to be the rule rather than
the exception.

Deer are generally supposed to be browsing animals, but this
is not always strictly true everywhere, or at all seasons of the
year.   Charles Barker who has had a lifetime among deer writes
me from New Brunswick: "In the spring and summer deer feed
on all the young shoots and grasses, and are very fond of feeding
on the water grasses and weeds around the edges of lakes and
streams, keeping in the shallow water.   In the fall and winter
they feed on the beech nuts (when there are any), digging down
through several inches of snow in search of them.   Then as the
snow gets deeper they retire to some cedar swamp where they
browse on the leaves of the cedar, the moss that grows on the
evergreen trees (cedar, spruce, and fir), and the needles of the
fir, and lastly on the branches of the whitewood, moosewood, and
dogwood.   In feeding they break the branches so that if one did
not see the tracks he might mistake the fed-over ground for a
moose yard."   Around the settlements it is very common to find
deer feeding on the farms at night, sometimes causing considerable damage to the farmers' crops and garden stuff.   When I was
a boy in the Adirondack Mountains there was an albino buck
confined for several years in a wire enclosure close to where we
lived, and he was fed on oats and hay the same as horses, and
apparently thrived on this diet.   In these same mountains in
summer I have frequently seen deer feeding on the lily pads including leaf, stem, and also the root.   In the far Southwest they
feed much on cactus, and probably find at least a portion of their
water supply in them.

Deer have very keen senses of sight, smell, and hearing.   Almost any noise will put a deer keenly on the alert, seemingly
more so than with any other hoofed animal, and any sound which

is not perfectly natural to its habitat will alarm it and send it off at once. The occasional breaking of a twig, or the rustling of a bush or leaves, which are natural sounds in the woods, will be noticed by deer, and will make them watchful, although they will not usually be alarmed sufficiently to cause them to jump out of their beds. But any unnatural sound, such as striking metal against rock or wood, talking, coughing, sneezing, blowing the nose, will send deer off in a hurry. There are exceptions to this alertness and keenness, however. In some localities where the game laws are rigidly enforced deer get quite tame and careless in the spring and summer. When fishing in the summer in Maine I have frequently come across deer feeding on the shores of lakes and streams, and they would permit one to approach quite close in the canoe without becoming alarmed. If one got too near they would simply walk off into the woods. Also the bucks will do lots of foolish things and lose lots of their caution during the rutting season, which is the period of the year when they can be hunted with the greatest chance of success.

When deer are alarmed they either sneak off with head and tail down (usually when they think that they have not been seen), or else run off with long, graceful bounds, easily clearing bushes and fallen trees. When running thus the most prominent part of the deer in view is the white, bushy tail, held stiffly aloft and swaying from side to side. When a white-tailed deer is alarmed it often blows or whistles. This sound is sometimes a "s-s-sush," like a man rapidly exhaling air from his lungs, and at other times almost a shrill whistle, with every graduation between the two.

There is nothing that will alarm deer more quickly than the scent of man. One whiff of the tainted air and away he goes. Under favorable conditions a man's scent will travel and be smelled by a deer for over a mile. Hence the necessity for hunting deer up wind. But this matter of wind needs a little explanation. The deer is a forest animal, and in thick woods it takes a pretty strong wind to give a decided direction to the air currents down below on the ground among the trees, and to carry scent steadily and a long distance in a certain direction. Scent not only travels with the wind, but also rises like smoke (it scarcely ever descends unless the wind be blowing down a hill), so that one on a hill need not usually bother about deer getting his

scent on the ground below. In thick forests, unless the wind
is quite strong, the air currents and the scent eddy around in
every direction, the scent usually ascending a little so that on
level ground by the time it gets 200 yards or so away it is usually
too high above the ground to be caught by the deer. Under such
conditions one can sometimes travel or hunt fast enough to keep
ahead of his scent, although such fast travel, which is also noiseless enough to be safe in hunting deer, usually requires rather
open ground as well as wet ground to keep the leaves from rustling. But if the deer is uphill, or if the wind is blowing steadily
in his direction he can often scent man a long way. Dangerous
scent will also lie in a man's tracks, or where he has touched trees
or branches, for a long time. I was once going through an open
piece of country, and coming up on a little knoll, stopped to eat
my lunch and to look around. I had been there probably twenty
minutes when, looking back over my trail, about 500 yards off
I saw a doe walking slowly on a course that would take her across
my trail in about 100 yards. I watched her, and as soon as she
reached my tracks, up went her tail, and away she sailed with
leaps twenty feet long.

A deer can hardly distinguish a man from a stump even at
close range so long as the man stands perfectly still. I have
several times had deer run or walk up to within a few feet of me
when I was sitting or standing still. But they will instantly
detect even the slightest motion for quite long distances, and this
even when there are literally thousands of limbs and leaves in the
way, and even when the wind is swaying all these apparent ob-
structions to vision. If a deer is in sight it is not safe to move at
all. Even the slow bringing of the rifle to the shoulder, or the
cautious step to one side to see past some obstruction is very
liable to send the animal off. In approaching the top of a ridge
the hunter cannot afford to raise his head more than is absolutely
necessary to see, and he must do this very slowly. I think that
the still-hunter alarms quite as many white-tailed deer by the
sight of his movements as by sound or wind. I do not think,
however, that deer have very long vision, certainly nothing like
mountain sheep, which is natural as the deer is a forest animal.
Several times I have seen deer five or six hundred yards away
from where I have been walking in plain sight and they have paid
no attention to me.

Tracking is something that a hunter cannot know too much about. Some guides and woodsmen have a wonderful knowledge of tracks, but seldom can explain it or give the whys and wherefores. Others profess a knowledge which they are far from possessing. I have many times seen a man glance at a single, average-size track on bare ground and announce right off that it was a buck. After a rather wide and long experience in hunting deer I feel quite sure that no one can tell the sex to a certainty from a single, average-size track on ground devoid of snow, and the guide who professes to do so is usually either fooling himself or trying to fool his sportsman. But the tracks of a big buck can often be

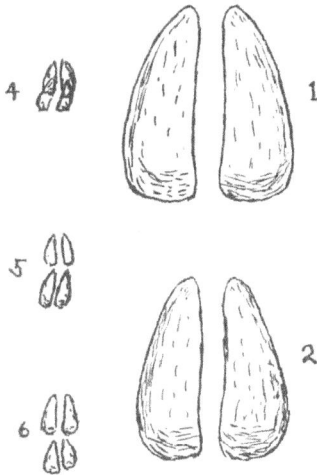

TRACKS OF WHITE-TAILED DEER. THE TRACK OF THE FRONT HOOF (1) IS LARGER THAN THAT OF THE HIND (2). A HEAVY DEER, IN RUNNING WILL SPREAD ITS HOOF AND THE DEW CLAWS MAY SHOW (3). AT A WALK A DEER NORMALLY PLANTS ITS HIND HOOFS IN THE TRACKS OF ITS FRONT HOOFS (4), BUT A YOUNG BUCK OFTEN OVERHASTENS WITH ITS HIND LEGS (5), AND AN OLD BUCK, STIFFENED WITH AGE, LAGS BEHIND (6)

told at once from their size alone, and on snow there are other indications sometimes present that enable one to tell the sex from a single hoof print. Rounded toes are usually but not always an indication of a buck. The two halves of a big buck's hoof will often spread more than in does or young bucks, but this is not an infallible sign. Any deer's hoofs will spread on soft or wet ground, or when it is running, leaping, or going down hill. A very fat deer will spread its hoofs a little on level ground, as will a doe heavy with fawn. In September many bucks get very fat, and a big, spreading track at this time of the year is very liable to be a buck—if it is very large it is practically certain to be. But the trail usually has to be followed for a considerable distance, and one has to keep his eyes skinned for dozens of little details to determine the sex. The front feet of all hoofed animals are slightly larger than the hind feet, and make larger tracks.

An old buck is usually a little stiffened, and his hind feet, instead of printing with or slightly in front of the fore feet at a walk, may print slightly in rear of them. Sometimes from the same cause, bucks have a tendency to drag their legs, and their hoofs make little scratches in front and behind the main prints, disturb the grass and leaves between the tracks, or make long furrows in the snow. Does will almost always step clean, even in snow six inches deep. An old buck when walking will often stop, sometimes two or three times in a hundred yards, to make observations, and he usually does this from some sort of cover; while the does, fawns, and young bucks, unless feeding, travel right along. During the late summer when the bucks are fat, and until the rutting season is well along, their right and left feet are often planted further apart from the center line of the trail than normal—that is they straddle, and this straddle is usually accompanied by a slight toeing out. From the first of September on, a buck's track is often marked by places where he has stopped to rub the velvet off against small trees and bushes. During the rutting season a buck often stops to stamp and hook at bushes, but is not so liable to stop simply to look around. Also during this season he often urinates when he starts off, or when he has been jumped from his bed, and the urine will show on a trail in the snow. In fact the track of a buck during or immediately before the rut usually has frequent traces of urine in or between the tracks. This can seldom be seen except on snow, but it is a sure indication of a buck. (For indications of the age of tracks see chapter on "Woods Hunting.")

If a white-tailed deer is wounded seriously by the hunter he usually goes off with his tail down. All that I have shot and hit have dropped their tails at once, and I have had old hunters tell me that this is invariably the case, but Charles Barker writes me that: "Sometimes a fatally wounded animal will run right away without showing any sign of being hit, and beyond the bunch of hair knocked out by the bullet, will leave no sign of blood for many yards. A deer ninety-nine times out of one hundred claps his tail down when hit, but I have seen them, when shot directly through the lungs, go off with their tails up as though nothing had happened. Hence always go and look for hair."

A deer shot through the heart will not always drop to the shot. About half the time it will run off for twenty-five to a hundred yards or so before falling. It is said that if the deer's lungs are filled when he receives a heart shot he will run, but if he has just exhaled he will fall. If one hits a deer and it runs off, the trail had better be followed at once for not more than 200 yards. If in that distance the deer is not found dead, but blood is found on the trail, the hunter should invariably sit down quietly and rest for at least an hour or, better, two hours if it is not too near nightfall. The chances are that the badly wounded deer will have run less than half a mile, and then have lain down. If one follows it within less than an hour it will be watching its back trail very closely, will surely see or hear the hunter approach, and will be up and off and lead the sportsman a merry chase, if indeed he ever comes up with it again. But if one waits an hour or, better, two hours, the deer will lose a lot of blood and will stiffen up in its bed. The hunter will either come across it lying down, or it will not get up out of its bed until he is quite close, and will do so slowly and stiffly, most likely offering a good, easy shot. The tracking of a wounded deer on snow is a comparatively easy matter. All one has to do is to look out that he does not get the track mixed up with those of other deer. But on bare ground it is a difficult and tedious matter. The trail must be followed almost track by track, always making sure of the last hoof-print before going ahead. If the trail is lost go back to the last sure print and start again. Keep a sharp lookout for blood, it is a great help and encourager. On some ground it is next to impossible to trail an animal, and the only way to follow or come up with the animal is to still-hunt in the general direction in which it went off.

Deer used to be hunted and killed in large numbers by jacking with a headlight at night on the edges of ponds and streams where they were very fond of feeding on the water grasses and pond lilies. I myself hunted deer that way in the Adirondack Mountains back in 1892, but I am glad to say that I did not kill any. But this murderous method is now happily prohibited almost everywhere. In some of the Southern States they are still hunted with hounds, but to my mind there is no more sport in this than there is in similarly hunting rabbits—not as much, for you feel that the deer is worthy of a better chance and a better death.

Photo by Thos. Blagden

Courtesy U. S. Biological Survey

WHITE-TAILED DEER IN ADIRONDACK MOUNTAINS

In Pennsylvania, where, thanks to efficient protection, deer are once more quite plentiful in the wilder mountainous sections, deer are driven by the hunters themselves acting as beaters. The hunting is usually done by clubs, or camps of a number of hunters. Some of the members act as beaters, forming a large semi-circle, and gradually driving a large extent of country towards the hunters who have taken their position on "stands" or runways. It is usually the habit of deer to use the same routes in traveling through a country time after time. These routes are called runways and are known to the local hunters. It is towards these runways that the beaters drive a large section of the country in the hopes that the deer they scare up will run past the hunters who are stationed on these runways. Don't get the idea, however, that a runway is a trail; it may be a valley, a dip between two hills, a piece of country several hundred yards wide, through which it has been found that traveling deer are more liable to pass than through other places.

Still-hunting is the only sportsmanlike method of hunting deer, and it is the most difficult of all forms of hunting, requiring the most skill and experience. (See "Woods Hunting.") A successful still-hunter of white-tailed deer is a past master at woodcraft, and must know the habits of the game in his country. It is the quickness of the deer in detecting motion, and the acuteness of its ears and nose which make this hunting so difficult and so fascinating. These senses have enabled the white-tailed deer to live and survive within sound of the backwoodsman's axe long after the elk and moose have been exterminated. Deer can evade and defy man for months and even years in a circle of woods three miles in diameter, and give us unbounded respect for the senses which enable them to do so. And of these the sight and hearing are the more important to circumvent because it is quite possible to avoid the nose, keen as it is. To avoid the other two successfully and to succeed at still-hunting requires experience, knowledge of the habits of the deer, and snow or wet ground for still-walking, with the greatest care on the part of the hunter, aided by eyes almost as keen as those of the game.

T. S. Van Dyke, author of that classic book on deer, "The Still-Hunter," says: "Still-hunting the wild Virginia deer is the farthest from murder of all that is done with the rifle and gun, the finest game of skill man ever plays, finer even than he plays

against his fellow man.   The intense care, eyesight, and knowledge of the game and woods necessary for much success, make
the hunting of the Virginia deer a joy to thousands who would
not touch a gun for any other purpose, for beside it all other
hunting is tame, and even the pursuit of the black-tail and the
mule deer often ridiculous in simplicity."

CHAPTER IV

THE MULE DEER
OR ROCKY MOUNTAIN BLACK-TAILED DEER,
JUMPING DEER.

Odocoileus hemionus, RAFINESQUE.

TYPE LOCALITY.—Sioux River, South Dakota.

The mule deer is essentially a western animal. It inhabits most of the mountainous and some of the broken plain regions of western North America from about central Mexico to the Peace River and Lake Athabasca in Alberta, and the valley of the upper Fraser River in British Columbia. Its most easterly range is now probably North Dakota. To the west it is found as far as the summit of the coast ranges of mountains, it being found on the Pacific slope of these mountains only south of San Francisco, California. It reaches its largest size and its finest antler development in the Rocky Mountains from Colorado to British Columbia.

It is difficult to state just what kind of country the mule deer prefers. I have found it in wooded river bottoms and high up around timberline. In the Dakotas it frequents the Bad Lands. In Southern California I have shot it in pine forests practically at sea level and on the sage brush sides of high mountains. In some parts of Mexico and Arizona it is found right out in the flats and chaparral. On the northern rim of the Grand Canyon it spends the winters down in the bottoms of the canyons and valleys, and the summers high up on the plateaus. On the west coast of Mexico Sheldon found this deer inhabiting the high mountains with habits similar to sheep. In some countries it has migratory habits, probably induced by snowfall or food conditions, that is to say, it has a summer and a winter ground, usually defined by altitude or snowfall only. Thus on the east side of the Coast Range in British Columbia the deer went back into the high mountains in the spring, where they were to be found almost everywhere from river bottom to timberline, except in the very deep and thick forest growth on the northern slopes of the mountains.   But in the fall, when the heavy snows came, these same deer migrated down into the valley of the Fraser River, and the tributaries of the Fraser.   In some places this migration covered a distance of a hundred miles, and the deer trails were as plainly marked in these mountains as the horse trails in a forest reserve.   It should be noted, however, that these mule deer, so far as known, always descend on the east slope of these mountains in winter, and never on the west slope towards the Pacific Ocean, this latter region being the range of the black-tailed deer.   This is probably not because of the presence of the latter deer, but because the western slopes and the lower valleys on the west side of the coast mountains are thickly, heavily, and densely wooded, and the mule deer is really an animal of lightly wooded, brushy, and chaparral country, and seems to prefer rough country to that which is level, smooth, or rounded.

The mule deer is the largest of our three species of deer, and it also carries the largest, longest and finest antlers.   In British Columbia, where I had my best chance to observe these deer, both sexes seemed to average quite a little heavier than any white-tailed deer, and the big bucks were most decidedly larger than the big bucks of the white-tails.   I have shot big bucks that I would estimate as weighing almost 325 pounds.   The summer coat is rusty yellow, the insides of the legs, the belly, and the buttocks being white.   There is a blackish patch on the forehead and a blackish bar on the chin.   These deer start to take on their winter coats usually in September, at which time also the fawns usually lose their spots.   This winter coat is brownish gray, the tips of the individual hairs being almost black.   This winter coat remains until about May.   The head, tail, legs, belly, and buttocks change little with the seasons.   The tail is all white except the bunch on the tip which is black all around, and by this tail it can be told from the other two species of deer.   In running the mule deer carries its tail drooped and swings it back and forth, while the white-tailed deer carries its tail stiffly erect.   The two deer are easily told apart when running.   With the white-tailed deer the most prominent part is the large, fan-shaped white tail, and it runs with long, graceful leaps.   With the mule deer the tail is not at all evident, although the white rump is.   The

Photo by K. D. Swan   Courtesy U. S. Forest Service

MULE DEER, TAKEN IN MONTANA

ears are very much larger than in the other two species of deer, and it is from these that the mule deer has obtained its name. These ears are very much in evidence when the deer is facing the observer. It may also be told by its peculiar method of bounding or jumping when going at good speed, this gait being a series of stiff-legged bounds in which all four feet seem to leave the ground at the same time, and land almost together at the same time and in almost the same spot. The mule deer runs or leaps in this way, not only on a level, but up and down steep hills and at great speed. The jumps are noticeably different from those of other deer, and in some localities have gained this species the appellation of "jumping deer."

The bucks shed their antlers about January, and the new ones start to grow almost immediately under their coating of velvet. The antlers attain their full growth usually some time in August, when the velvet dries, and the buck proceeds to rub it off against bushes and small trees. Antlers are usually free of velvet by the middle of September. The antlers average larger, longer, and heavier, and have greater spread than those of the white-tailed and black-tailed deer. In country where conditions as to food and climate are good many bucks grow heads which are superb trophies. A yearling buck will usually have a pair of spikes, but sometimes each of the spikes will be divided so as to make two tines. At two years a buck usually grows small antlers which possess four tines on each antler. The ordinary full-grown and well-developed buck has a head of five tines on each antler, four being the branches of the two main prongs and one a short tine an inch or two above the base of the antler. Sometimes extremely large antlers are developed, having a number of extra tines.

The rutting season starts in November and usually lasts for about a month, although sometimes bucks are found energetically rutting until late in December. The necks of the bucks swell to very large size, and they chase the does continually, and also battle with each other for the possession of a doe. Usually one sees merely a buck and one doe together, but quite often a big buck will collect several does together in a band, and these may also be accompanied by several yearlings. Roosevelt says: "During the period when the buck and the doe are together, the buck's attitude is merely that of a brutal, greedy, and selfish tyrant. He will unhesitatingly rob the doe of any choice bit of food, and though he will fight to keep her if another buck approaches, the moment that a dangerous foe appears his one thought is for his own preservation. He will not only desert the doe, but if he is an old and cunning buck, he will try his best to sacrifice her by diverting the attention of the pursuer to her and away from him."

One, two, or rarely three fawns are born late in May or June. The fawns are spotted, the coat being quite similar to that of white-tailed fawns. The mother hides the newly born fawn in some thicket and comes to suckle it a number of times during the day, and does not permit it to follow her until it is six weeks or two months old. The fawns usually remain with their mothers until about the following April.

I think that as a usual thing the mule deer does not whistle or snort nearly as much as the white-tailed deer. The fawns will often bleat to call their mother's attention. Roosevelt states that the bucks utter a barking challenge during the rutting season. With the white-tailed deer the usual noise which makes the hunter aware of the presence of the animal is the whistle or snort, but with the mule deer it is the thump, thump, thump of its four feet on hard ground.

Seton says that the mule deer is an adept at "freezing"—that is becoming as still as a frozen thing when it discovers anything strange. It has been my experience that if slightly alarmed it will usually take two or three jumps and then freeze. While standing still in this way it is watching with every sense alert to see what it was that disturbed it. Usually, if you jump a mule deer, you hear "thump, thump, thump," and then silence. If you do not see it at once you must be very careful for it is standing absolutely still somewhere trying its best to see or hear you. Look for all you are worth in the direction from which the sound of the feet came, but don't move at first. If you cannot see the deer, move slightly and slowly to one side, as some tree trunk may be obstructing your view. If then you still do not see the deer you should start towards where the thumping came from, provided the wind is favorable, going quietly but swiftly, and being ready to shoot at any instant. The deer will not stay frozen long. If it hears or sees you and is badly scared it will probably go off with high leaps and lots of thumping, and if you hear this thumping again the only thing to do is to run forward at once as rapidly as possible in the hope of getting a running shot. Or the deer may be only suspicious and may decide to sneak off quietly, in which case you will never know anything about it unless you see it sneaking off or follow its tracks to see what it did. Once in a great while, while standing still, it will give itself away by stamping or pawing the ground.

It is this habit of mule deer of usually stopping to look when slightly alarmed that makes them so much easier hunted and killed than white-tailed deer, and as a consequence mule deer will be exterminated long before the other species. Don't get the idea that these deer always stop in this way, however. Often they will go off just as quickly as do the white-tails.

I had a strange coincidence of experiences on mule deer which bring out some of these points. In the fall of 1901 in British Columbia I was hunting along the side of a mountain when I heard the thump, thump, thump above me, and looking up I saw a buck spring to a sudden stop in front of a thick bunch of small balsams. I was carrying a .40-72 black-powder rifle at the time, and the day was damp, almost foggy and it took a couple of seconds for the smoke of the rifle to clear away after I fired, during which time I distinctly heard the buck's feet thumping again. When the smoke had cleared off there stood the buck, almost in the same place, apparently having jumped only two or three steps. I was sort of nonplussed because I had called my shot exactly behind the shoulder, and the rifle was an extremely reliable one and the range only about 100 yards. However, I lost no time in firing again, and when the smoke cleared off the deer was running down straight towards me. Almost at once it ran into a little pine stub, broke it off and fell dead there. I went up and dressed this deer, which had only one bullet hole in him. Then I thought I would climb up to the thicket of balsams and see if I could see where my first bullet had gone. The thicket was very thick, and there was one queerly shaped little tree in front of which the deer had been standing when I first shot. When I got there I was surprised to find another buck, identical to the one I had just dressed, lying stone dead at the base of the little balsam, with a bullet hole behind its shoulder. Evidently when I fired at and instantly killed the first deer, the second one jumped up from its bed and froze, and I fired at the second thinking that it was the first.

The second experience happened several years later in the Santa

Lucia Mountains in California. A certain mountain near my camp was all tracked up by a bunch of deer, but in three days' hard hunting I failed to catch up with any of them. The fourth morning I was going along the side of a valley, about half way up the hillside. Below, the hill dropped off steeply so that the bottom of the valley was a miniature box canyon with almost vertical cliffs. The opposite side above these cliffs was steep and covered with sagebrush and here and there a pine tree or a live oak. Suddenly, across the valley and above the cliffs, I saw a buck jump up, take a couple of bounds, and stand looking at me. I was using the same old black-powder rifle, and lost no time in sitting down and letting him have a shot. The range was about 150 yards and I distinctly heard the bullet clap into him, but to my surprise, when the smoke cleared away, there he was still looking at me. I fired again, and this time I saw the buck fall down, and then apparently jump up again and start running up the hill through the sagebrush and pines. I got in one more shot before he was out of sight, but I felt certain that it had not connected. I cussed myself out for doing a lot of perfectly rotten shooting, and climbed down to and through the little canyon and up the other side to take up the trail of what I supposed was a badly wounded deer. When I got to where the deer had been when I fired the first two shots I stumbled right onto two bucks, lying one on top of the other in the sage brush. Evidently there had been three deer, and each time I shot another one had jumped up, and had frozen to look at me before running off.

Mule deer seem to band or herd together more than the Eastern deer. They are frequently seen in quite large bunches in localities where they are plentiful, but these are not necessarily herds. Perhaps it is more correct to say that in a given locality there may be many deer feeding in close proximity to each other. One snowy day in British Columbia I was walking through a little wooded creek bottom when a bunch of mule deer drifted past me about fifty yards off. They came in single file like phantoms through the snow, and I counted fourteen does and fawns, with a small buck bringing up the rear. This was in the middle of September. That same fall, coming back to camp one evening in the red glow of sunset, I suddenly ran right into a bunch of does and fawns lying down in a little pine thicket. As soon as I saw them I stopped at once, and then quietly sat down and watched them. I was not more than twenty feet from them. One doe evidently saw me make some move for she eyed me very suspiciously, and after several minutes she got up and walked around to where she could get my wind. As she took the first jump after smelling me, the others were on their feet instantly and away out of sight. There were seven in this bunch close by, and I think two or three more on the other side of a spruce tree. At other times I have frequently seen four or five mule deer together. But in the late fall there seems to be a real tendency for these deer to herd together in big bunches, particularly when about to start their migration from their summer to their winter grounds. Many observers have described the big band at this time of the year.

The mule deer is essentially a browsing animal. He prefers the leaves and twigs of small trees and brushes. They often eat willow and aspen leaves and small twigs, and are very fond of blueberries. In the winter they eat tree mosses and lichen, and paw under the snow for anything in the way of tree stuff and grass that they can get. In the spring they are very fond of grazing on the green grass when it first comes up, but at other times of the year scarcely do any grazing in country where the browsing is suitable.

The mule deer is not holding its own as well as the white-tail. In the country which it inhabits it is much more easily seen than the white-tails are in their country. It often has no chance to sneak away in thick cover, but goes bounding off with its peculiar high jumps, and the thump, thump of its four feet as they come down also give it away. Often when disturbed it gives two or three jumps and then stops to look back. All of these things make it much more easily hunted and killed than the other species of deer, and it is being rapidly thinned out over much of its range. It multiplies quite rapidly, however, if protected from hunters and predatory animals. Probably the only way of permanently preserving our mule deer is to create large game refuges in our forest reserves for them where hunting is not permitted and where mountain lions and coyotes are kept thinned out. Around the edges of these game refuges hunting the overflow should be permitted in season during years when the numbers of the deer justify it. Also if the deer in a game refuge become so plentiful as to cause an exhaustion of their food supply within the refuge, as has sometimes happened, a certain number of licenses might be issued to kill deer within the refuge. In other words, the game should be administered by a commission or officials rather than by game laws. As such refuges are usually possible only in our national forests it would seem most sensible to have the game therein administered by Federal officials, that is by the Forest Service or the Biological Survey.

CHAPTER V

THE COLUMBIAN BLACK-TAILED DEER

Odocoileus columbianus, Richardson

Type Locality.—Mouth of the Columbia River, Oregon.

The Columbian Black-tailed Deer inhabit the Coast Range Mountains of the Pacific from slightly north of San Francisco, California, northward to about Juneau, Alaska, and also the majority of the islands off the coasts of British Columbia and Alaska. On the mainland it is generally scarce or absent on the eastern slope of the Coast Range, although in California and Oregon it will be found also in the Cascade Range, particularly in the summer. Generally it is most abundant on the western slopes of the Coast Range. Probably this is because this deer is essentially an animal of dense forests, and the forests are much thicker on the west than on the east side of the Coast Ranges.

The black-tailed deer is usually slightly smaller in size than either of the white-tailed or mule deer. The average weight of large bucks is about 150 pounds, although individuals have been shot weighing up to about 225 pounds. Towards the north of its range it appears to be smaller in size, and in Alaska there is a smaller form known as the Sitka deer (*Odocoilieus columbianus silkensis*.—Merriam). Mr. Tom Brazil of Hardy Island, 60 miles north of Vancouver, says: "Frequently the deer of the islands north of me are smaller than those of the mainland. It is believed that in the past, when the deer were more abundant, they wandered and spread out as people do. The younger and weaker were driven out by the older and stronger, and swimming readily, they traveled from island to island. Later the numbers decreased and, with plenty of food and shelter, the deer remained within the boundaries of the islands. This led to inbreeding, perhaps accounting for the smaller size."

35

The summer coat of the Columbian deer is yellowish-red to dull reddish-brown above. The white area extends between the thighs, and on the back of them and the buttocks, to the tail. In the winter the upper coat changes to tawny gray. This deer can be told from the other two species by the tail which is round and a dull black on the upper surface and sides and white on the under surface.

The antlers are similar in formation (*dichotomous*) to those of the mule deer, but do not run so large in size, and are more slender. Abnormal antlers with large number of points are much rarer than is the case with our other species of deer. The time at which the bucks shed their antlers seems to vary a little each year, and in localities, sometimes coming as early as the fifteenth of December or as late as March. The new antlers start to grow under the velvet almost at once, and are full grown by the fifteenth of August, when the velvet is rubbed off. The rutting season begins about the first week in November and may run until January. Mr. Brazil says: "In the rutting season the bucks are sometimes troublesome (on a game preserve where they are protected and tame.—T.W.). One once forced me up into a tree but later seemed to be extremely sorry and apologized by coming down the hill every night when all was still and bleating to draw my attention. The bucks are fierce fighters. Sometimes they challenge each other to combat by snorting, bristling like a dog, and charging each other. Frequently they lock horns, and once I had to cut off a part of the horn to separate two combative bucks."

One or two fawns are born in the months of June or July. They are spotted at birth and these spots persist until the gray coat of winter is taken on. The fawns remain with their mother almost a year until she is getting ready to bring another fawn into the world.

Throughout part of its range at least, the Columbian deer appears to have migratory habits similar to the mule deer, traveling twice a year between summer and winter feeding grounds, but not all deer in a locality will thus migrate, large numbers remaining in what may be termed the winter grounds the entire year. Speaking of the Oregon and California deer, Van Dyke says: "Before the snow is deep, nearly all the deer leave the high mountains, and in the Cascades most of them start even before the falling of any snow that is to be permanent. They

COLUMBIAN BLACK-TAILED DEER ON HARDY ISLAND, BRITISH COLUMBIA

wander down into the lower and more bushy portions of the range, sometimes on well-defined trails, but quite as often without any. Here, too, there is plenty of snow in the higher hills, and most of the deer keep in the lower flats and bushy gorges, or go on to the Coast Range. Here they join a number of their fellows who did not go to the mountains, but remained all summer in the Coast Range. The principle on which only a portion of these deer travel so regularly to the high mountains every spring is not known. It is plainly not for want of food, or the necessities of breeding, to escape gnats, flies, or other such cause, because the number that remain are very great, and they fare as well and keep as fat as those that go away. In some places, as in southwestern Oregon, the number remaining is plainly greater than those that depart, and the hunting is better there than in the Cascades to which the others have gone."

Like our other deer, the black-tail is a browsing animal, and it almost never grazes except, perhaps, when the tender, young grass first appears in the spring. Throughout almost all of its range this deer finds its food most plentiful, and therefore in hunting it does not, as a rule, pay to frequent places where the food indications appear particularly favorable, for these indications are almost everywhere. Its food consist of the tender leaves and twigs of bushes and shrubs that are so plentiful. In the southern portion of its range, that is in the United States, it seems to be particularly fond of feeding on sal-lal and huckleberry bushes, and on acorns in the fall.

In habits which need to be taken into account in its hunting, the black-tailed deer seems to strike a pretty fair medium between its two cousins, the white-tailed and mule deer. It is more difficult to still-hunt than the mule deer, due to both its habits and its habitat, but not so evasive as the white-tail. Mr. A. Bryan Williams, formerly game commissioner of the Province of British Columbia, writes me: "I consider the white-tail the most tricky of them all, and in any sort of an open country they lose no time in making themselves scarce when they are jumped. Once in a while, if you have crept up to them so as not to make them certain of your presence, they may stand for a second or two before going. A mule deer will often stand for quite a time when he is roused, especially when the rutting season is over and they are thin. A Columbian deer is in some ways a bit like the white-tail, though it is nothing like so clever. Usually they make off as soon as you jump them, but frequently a shot or a shout will make them stop. If somebody else has disturbed them and they come your way on the run, any loud, sharp noise will stop them; perhaps they will then allow you to fire several shots at them, provided you miss them clean, before they go."

Van Dyke says: "The eyes of the black-tail seem fully as keen as those of the Virginia deer, but like the mule deer, he is not so easily startled by noise. This is not because his ears are at all inferior. He is simply taking chances instead of leaving chances well in the rear, as the Virginia deer generally does nowadays. Nor does it prove that quiet walking is not important. On account of the nature of much of the ground you must make considerable noise, or you cannot move fast enough. And you will find that many a deer must have heard you coming but does not run without waiting to see what you are. These deer hear you and are generally calculating on outwitting you by hiding. But they often change their minds when they find you are coming closer, and too often they cannot resist the temptation to stop a second to see if it is really worth while to run at all. After much hunting they learn to act on the presumption of danger; but even then you occasionally meet a very great fool of a deer which will persist in staring at the new rifle of the rawest tenderfoot that ever, with hob-nailed boots, smashed dead sticks it was more easy to step over. Meeting such a deer often makes the novice think he is a born hunter, but if he will keep on for a while he will recover from the delusion, and begin to wonder what has become of his keen eye and steady hand."*

A good time for hunting the black-tail is a bad, rainy day when the wet makes the brush and leaves noiseless, and when the deer are almost constantly on the move, often coming out into the open on the bare ridges because they cannot lie up in the thick, wet sal-lal and other bushes with any degree of comfort. Also on the Pacific Island beaches and on the coast of the mainland they may sometimes be shot by paddling quietly around the points of land, for they often come down to the beaches early in the morning or at sundown. At other times of the day they seem to love to lie in the thick bushes and in the slashings, and it is extremely difficult to see them in such cover.

---

* "*The Deer Family,*"—Roosevelt, Van Dyke, Elliot and Stone. The Macmillan Company, New York.

In the southern portion of its range in northern California this deer is found chiefly in the evergreen brush and chaparral, as it does not like the open country. This is too thick a country in which to hunt them with success, but in country like this in the California mountains there are many openings through which the hunter may stalk in quiet, and there are also many ridges with vantage points where one may sit and look over many a square mile of alternating brush and open country, and see deer as they pass through the less thickly covered places.

In one respect the black-tail is as difficult to circumvent as any of his family. He has a very keen sense of smell, and if he gets one whiff of man-scented air he is off in less time than it takes to tell, stopping to take no chances.

We therefore see that the black-tail must be hunted in the usual manner that the white-tail is still-hunted (see Chapters III and XV), but that often the hunter will find the pursuit of the black-tail easier than the white-tail for apparently the former often lingers a little before going off. Mr. Clive Phillipps-Welley describes the sport of hunting this deer exactly when he says: "If you do not love the game so much that you would be content to play it without ever winning a prize, don't waste your time upon it. Still-hunting is not the game for the pot-hunter or the man whose time is valuable. It is the game par excellence for the man who loves the woods and the wild things of them. In writing of our small deer, the true black-tail, I cannot help speaking of him with a certain amount of affection in spite if his many evil habits, because he is, in his way, a great and true friend of my native country. He is the real musketry instructor who teaches the youth of British Columbia to become marksmen valuable to the Empire; he is in no small degree the advertising agent who, by his presence, attracts the masculine adventurous element to settle in our lands, and he provides much of the meat which feeds our pioneer settlers, and for these reasons it is infamous that our Government is not more active than it is in suppressing the sale of hides, which alone seriously threatens his existence."*

We do not know as much of the habits and life history of the Columbian deer as we should. Information in this subject is very meager. For this reason sportsmen who hunt this deer should

---

* In "Big Game Shooting," *Country Life* Library of Sport.

take particular pains to observe it most carefully, reporting all their experiences and observations to the end that we may learn more of it, not only from a hunting standpoint, but for conservation purposes also. Due to the excellent cover and the sparsely settled condition of its range, it is probable that the black-tailed deer, together with the white-tailed deer, will be the last of our big game to survive. But only if we learn enough of its habits to give it adequate protection will this deer survive, and provide sport for many generations to come.

CHAPTER VI

THE WAPITI OR ELK

Cervus canadensis, ERXLEBEN.

TYPE LOCALITY.—Eastern Canada.

The Wapiti is the largest and grandest of the round-horned deer family, and the bull wapiti carries the finest antlers, which are marvels of symmetrical grandeur. An average full-grown bull wapiti will stand nearly five feet tall at the withers, and weighs about 700 pounds. Adult cows are slightly smaller and weigh about 500 pounds. The body of the bull wapiti in the fall is a brownish-gray, darker on the spine, changing to chestnut-brown on the neck, head, and legs, and to yellowish-white or straw-buff on the rump, and reddish-brown on the belly and breast. The hairs on the neck are long and form a shaggy mane. As the coat ages it fades so that in the spring many bulls are so bleached that at a distance they appear almost white. The summer coat is a little deeper and darker than the winter coat. The coat of the cows resembles that of the bulls in summer, but in fall and winter the color is less intense. The calf when born is a dull yellow with large spots of dull white on the body, neck, and thighs, the spots remaining until winter.

The young bull grows a pair of short, sharp spike antlers starting the latter part of his second winter. Each succeeding year the antlers increase in size up to the sixth or seventh pair, when they begin to go back, and are liable to become irregular. The second pair of antlers usually have five tines on each antler, and thereafter usually six. A greater number of tines are, however, frequently seen, as well as freak antlers. One freak head is known to have had as many as 28 points. One of the largest record heads has 21 points, the beams being 66½ and 64¼ inches long, and the spread 52 inches. This head was killed in Gallatin

43

County, Montana. A Wyoming wapiti head belonging to Schoverling, Daly, and Gales of New York has seven tines on each beam, the right beam having a length of 64 inches, left 60¼ inches, and the greatest spread 52¾ inches. In the old days in the Rocky Mountains, when the summer and winter ranges of the wapiti were unlimited, and there were no restrictions on their migration to regions of good food conditions, the bulls often grew antlers with far heavier bases and beams than any seen today. As a boy I remember seeing a number of antlers in the possession of Mr. D. M. Barringer which had beams far heavier and thicker than any I have seen which have been shot since about 1895. In 1912 I saw a pair of very old shed antlers at a cabin near Ovando, Montana, which were far heavier than one ever sees today.

The bull sheds his antlers each year about the middle of March. A few days later the new antlers start to grow under their covering of velvet, and in two weeks attain a height of several inches. The antlers are full grown under the velvet by August, and the velvet then dries, shrivels up, and hangs in long shreds, and is rubbed off by the bull on the trees and bushes. By September the antlers are free of velvet.

The Wapiti had originally the widest distribution of any of our larger hoofed game animals. It existed all over the United States and Southern Canada from the Allegheny Mountains and Quebec to the Pacific Coast. In the West it ranged from Arizona and New Mexico, north to about latitude 59° in Canada. In late years it has been largely killed off and its range restricted, so that today (1925), except for certain localities which have been restocked, it is found only in western Wyoming, western Montana, western Colorado, Idaho, northwestern Washington, (Olympic Mountains), Oregon, northwestern California, Arizona, New Mexico, in the Rocky Mountains of British Columbia and Alberta as far north as the upper Fraser and Athabasca Rivers, on Vancouver Island, and occasionally in Manitoba and Saskatchewan. It remains plentiful and is still seen in large herds only in and around Yellowstone Park.

The history of the wapiti has been quite similar to that of the buffalo—a persistent and ruthless slaughter by man. As the country became more thickly populated and the settlers pressed westward, the wapiti retreated before them, and were slaughtered

WAPITI IN MONTANA

in great numbers for food. About 1900 only a small number were left in the more inaccessible parts of the Rockies, and those wapiti now found in the United States are mostly the increases from these remnant bands resulting from the protection afforded by the game laws and public opinion. Even so, the future of the wapiti is uncertain, for while in many places they still have their summer ranges in the high mountains, their winter ranges in the foothills and on the plains have been almost wholly settled up and fenced off. Thus the animals are forced to remain in the high mountains all winter, and in years of heavy snows great numbers die of starvation. So much has this been the case in recent years in the country south of Yellowstone Park that the Biological Survey, assisted by organizations of sportsmen, has been obliged to resort to feeding hay to the animals in winter to prevent the almost complete annihilation of the herd by starvation. If our wapiti are to be preserved adequate winter feeding grounds adjacent to their summer ranges are just as important as adequate administration of good game laws.

In the Rocky Mountain regions wapiti are migratory to a certain extent. That is to say they migrate in bands between their summer feeding grounds, usually in the higher mountains, and their winter grounds, usually in the foothills, lower valleys, and plains. Prior to about 1890 these migrations took place in great herds, and in many places by regular, well established routes. The movement from the summer to the winter grounds begins usually in September, depending on the cold and snow in the high mountains. In some localities the bands apparently start the migration as soon as the first heavy snowfall of fall comes, while in others they remain in the mountains until actually driven out by the deep snows. Sometimes small bunches remain, prevented from crossing the high passes by deep snows, and these have a hard time pulling through the winter, many dying of starvation. George Bird Grinnell says: "In these modern days, we read of the elk as found only among the mountains and the timber, and some young people may think of it as a mountain animal—one that dwells in the forest. As a matter of fact the elk of old times was quite as much an animal of the open country, the plains, the high plateaus, and the naked, bald hills. If alarmed it plunged into timber or thickets, but it loved the open. * * * In my youth the whole of the western plains was a resort for elk, which lived in part also in the timber and willows along the river bottoms. In the Yellowstone Park today elk are found in the open, which is where they live and feed; but if frightened they run into the timber or the brush, where their enemies lose sight of them and they lose sight of their enemies. * * * While the elk in the Park spend their summers in an absolutely protected area, they must leave it when the heavy snows come. The Park is a rectangle straddling the Continental Divide, and surrounded by fenced ranches, beyond which the elk cannot pass. They are shut up in a territory where there is not enough food for them, and so in winters of heavy snowfall they must starve. I believe that the number of calves born each year after the animals have gone back to their summer range, exceeds the winter's loss, and that the elk herds are slowly increasing, but in the area they occupy their food is not increasing, but is growing less. The future of these elk is therefore uncertain."

After the spring migration to the higher summer feeding grounds the bulls and the cows separate, the cows going to the rich, upper valleys, but the bulls continue higher up to around timberline on the peaks. The calves are born some time in May or very early in June. A cow usually has one calf, but sometimes two, and rarely three. The first week or two the mother hides her youngster in the bushes, after the habits of our other deer. She feeds around in the neighborhood, and several times a day comes to the calf to suckle it. During this period the calf apparently has no scent, and hence is not easily found and destroyed by predatory animals. By the end of June or the first of July the cow elk are usually in bands, and the calves are running with their mothers. During the remainder of the summer the cows and calves stay in and around the high mountain valleys, devoting themselves to each other.

In the meantime the bulls are usually at a much higher elevation, up among the peaks and timberline, away from the heat and flies, and concentrating on growing their new antlers, which are very tender until the velvet dries up in August. September sees the bull well fed, strong in body, proud of his now hard and bare antlers, and ready for battle. It is then that the bulls begin to bugle. Seton says: "Filled with courage and desire, proud of his horns and conscious of his strength, this greatest bull of the valley gets up on some commanding ridge, fills his lungs,

Photo by F. M. Dilly

BULL WAPITI

Courtesy U. S. Biological Survey

and raising his muzzle, he pours forth a tremendous guttural roaring that rises in pitch to trumpet tones, higher and higher, till it breaks into a shrill, screaming whistle, then fades and drops again to the guttural, concluding with a few savage grunts. * * * The deep bugle notes are characteristic of the prime bull. Younger bulls are often called 'squealers,' and, being more numerous, they are responsible for the bugling being sometimes called 'whistling.' "

The bugling is apparently a challenge to fight. The mating season in the Rockies usually begins about September 15, and sometimes continues until the middle of November, but the bulls may bugle before and after these dates. During this period the strong and successful bulls, by much energy, chasing, and herding, gather together a bunch of cows which they jealously guard against all comers, driving off the young bulls, and battling fiercely with the older ones. My friend, Mr. Steven Camp, who has spent a lifetime among the wapiti, writes me: "I have read in books that a bull elk is often found at the head of a bunch of 'admiring cows,' but this I have never found to be the case. If there was any admiring it was probably due to the imagination of the observer, as some wise old cow leads the herd, and the bull brings up the rear where he can keep watch that none of the cows stray far from the herd, as it is up to him to keep the herd he has and see that no other bull steals part of his cows. Even when two bulls are engaged in a fight the cows seldom appear to be even mildly interested, and at the termination of the fight the victorious bull is generally kept busy seeing that none of the cows stray away, and this I have found to be characteristic of all the cervidæ."

Towards the end of the rut the weather has begun to get cold, and the deepening snows make it difficult for the animals to reach their food. Then they band together and start their migration to the lower winter feeding ground. Generally a few bulls will gather in a small bunch, and the cows in larger bands. Camp says: "I found their habits differ somewhat in different sections. In the Clearwater country of Idaho they would move to the lower country when the first snows fell in the fall, while in the Big Horn Mountains of Wyoming, the Flat Tops of northwestern Colorado, and here in Montana, they stay in the higher mountains until driven out by the deep snows." They wander down to their winter grounds usually by well-established routes along certain valleys, and through certain passes. As they concentrate in the lower country the small bands mingle and increase into large herds. In olden days these herds sometimes numbered into the thousands, and very large herds may still be seen in winter south of Yellowstone Park. Roosevelt says that: "Nowadays these Yellowstone elk are, with the exception of the Arctic caribou, the only American game which at times travels in immense droves like the buffalo of the old days." Here in the lower country the wapiti remain all winter, striving their best to obtain a meager living from the scant and partly snow-covered feed.

The Wapiti is both a browsing and grazing animal. Regarding the wapiti of Montana, Steven Camp writes me: "During the spring the elk nibble at tender buds, as well as graze on various varieties of grasses, and during the summer and fall they feed on bunch grass, and they also browse, but not to the same extent that they do later in the season. In the winter they browse exclusively, as the grass is generally under several feet of snow. In the winter the tip branches of willow, service berry, huckleberry, and the moss found on pine trees forms an acceptable diet." Roosevelt, in describing the wapiti seen in Yellowstone Park in April, 1903, states: "During the winter the elk had evidently done much browsing, but at this time they were grazing almost exclusively, and seemed by preference to seek out the patches of old grass which were last left bare by the retreating snow. * * * They fed at irregular hours throughout the day, just like cattle; one band might be lying down while another was feeding."

There is no mistaking a wapiti range, and the locality that these animals are frequenting in the mountains is easily found. It will be much tracked up. Many bushes will be scraped or broken where the bulls have been rubbing the velvet off their horns, or later hooking at the bushes in sheer bravado. Here and there may perhaps be found wallows in damp places and in springs, or even in dry earth, where the wapiti likes to wallow and stand around similarly to the moose or the hog. There will be plain trails leading to these places. The tracks of the wapiti are quite similar in shape to those of deer, but much larger of course. A large bull's track will be about five inches long, and

Photo by S. N. Leek

A PORTION OF THE YELLOWSTONE WAPITI HERD IN JACKSON HOLE

Courtesy U. S. Biological Survey

that of a large cow about four inches. The adult's sex can usually be told from the size of the track alone.

One fall I was hunting for several weeks on White River, a tributary of the South Fork of the Flathead in Montana. The valley was originally covered with jack-pine, but a fire had swept through and killed all the trees, and then a heavy wind storm had blown them down jackstraw fashion. Between the fallen logs a fine growth of bunch grass had sprung up. In this valley were several fair-sized bands of wapiti, and the ground was all tracked up. My three companions each got a fine bull while I hobbled around camp with a badly sprained ankle, the result of trying to negotiate a steep, grassy, snow-covered hillside in moccasins. On the mountainside, about a mile above camp, in one of the few bunches of green timber remaining, there was an elk lick, a flat, damp place, fed by a spring, a large muddy puddle with trails leading to it from the surrounding hillside. One morning I hobbled up there and surprised a bunch of cows in the wallow. There were three cows standing in it, and others around through the timber. I circled around them trying to see if there was a bull in the bunch, and they got my wind and stampeded down the mountainside. I have never heard such a racket made by any bunch of wild animals as these made going through the fallen jackpines. They seemed to hit their shins a resounding whack against every fallen tree they come to. It was a continuous crash, crack, slam as they raced down until they reached the river. Then apparently they ascended the opposite side of the valley more cautiously, as the sound ceased. But one would have thought that every leg in that bunch of cows would have broken the way they knocked them against the fallen pines.

The wapiti is not a particularly difficult animal to hunt successfully. The character of the country which he frequents usually makes it necessary to circumvent him by a combination of still-hunting and stalking. It is very necessary to hunt upwind and to keep out of sight. The legal open season usually coincides with the rutting season, and the bugle or whistle of the bull contributes in no small way to the locating of one's quarry. Very often the animal is unsuspicious to the point of stupidity. It has not such a highly strung nervous temperament as the deer, and when it is startled it is much given to hesitating before running away. It is, however, the hardest of the deer family to kill, and rather heavy rifles are necessary. There have been many failures on wapiti with rifles like the .30-30, .32 Special, and .33 W.C.F., which do not seem to drive their bullets through to the vitals.

The foregoing notes pertain more particularly to the wapiti of the northern Rocky Mountain region, that is to Wyoming, Montana, and Idaho. In other regions these animals may have quite different habits due to environment, food, climate, etc. Thus the northern half of Vancouver Island is covered for the most part with a high, dense forest of spruce and pine, and the wapiti there are essentially forest animals. Of these Charles Sheldon says: "The wapiti, *Cervus occidentalis,* occurs everywhere in the forests of Vancouver Island, decreasing in numbers southward to within thirty miles of Victoria, in which area but few range. They keep well back from settled districts, and are quite scarce near the east coast and the adjacent woods. They are most abundant in the north end of the island, particularly in the northwestern section and the vicinity of Kuyuquot Sound. Living in the dense forest they feed on some of the weeds and grasses and browse on the leaves of the salmon-berry, *Rubus spectabilis,* and those of the huckleberry, *Vaccinium.* I saw but few signs high up on the mountains or near the tops of the higher ridges; they seemed to wander on the lower slopes, in the marshes, along the rivers or near the lakes, and sometimes near the beaches."

CHAPTER VII

THE MOOSE

Alces americana, CLINTON

TYPE LOCALITY.—"Country north of Whitestown," (probably in the western Adirondack region), New York.

The American Moose is the largest of the deer family, living or extinct. A large bull will stand 6 to 7 feet high at the withers, be from 8½ to 9½ feet long, and will weigh from 1,200 to 1,400 pounds. The cows are about three-quarters the size of the bulls. The general color is from blackish-brown to black with pale brownish-gray on the lower belly and lower legs. There is a varying amount of gray on the muzzle and face. The summer pelage is somewhat lighter. The calves are reddish-brown, unspotted.

In the United States moose are found in Maine, Minnesota, western Montana, northwestern Wyoming, and Idaho. In all of these States they are rather scarce except in northern Minnesota and within or close to the Yellowstone National Park. Stray moose are sometimes seen in New Hampshire and in northeastern North Dakota. A few other localities have been restocked with moose in recent years.

Canada is really the home of the moose. Moose are found distributed all over Canada where the local conditions are suitable. They are absent from Ungava, the plains country, and the barren grounds, although sometimes found in the thinly wooded strips of country extending in many places into the plains and barren grounds. They are plentiful in parts of Nova Scotia, New Brunswick, Quebec, Ontario, Manitoba, and Saskatchewan, and in western and northern Alberta except south of the line of the Canadian Pacific Railway. In British Columbia they are quite plentiful in almost all parts of the northern half of the province,

but scarce or absent in the southern portions. Generally they do
not seem to range very close to the Pacific Ocean. They are
found in almost all the wooded portions of northern Canada to
the delta of the Mackenzie River, on the Horton and Dease rivers
and McTavish Bay in the Great Bear Lake region, on the Arkil-
inik River, and at York Factory on Hudson Bay. Yukon Territory contains moose very generally distributed north to the limit
of trees—almost, it might be said, to the limit of willows. In
Alaska they are found almost wherever there are trees, and extend
out on the Alaska Peninsula as far as a point due north of Kodiak
Island, to the mouth of the Yukon, and in the valley of the
Porcupine.

There are three species of moose, closely related and hardly
to be distinguished by the sportsman. The common moose,
Alces americana americana, was first described by Clinton as
Cervus americanus, in 1822, the type of locality being "Country
north of Whitestown," (probably the western Adirondack region),
New York, and afterwards in 1835 by Jardine as *Alces americanus.*
The moose of Wyoming have been described by Nelson as *Alces
americana shirasi,* the type locality being Snake River, Lincoln
County, Wyoming. On the Kenai Peninsula, Alaska, moose un-
doubtedly reach their greatest size and largest development of
antlers, and these moose have been described by Miller as *Alces
gigas,* the type locality being North side of Tustumena Lake,
Kenai Peninsula, Alaska.

Many sportsmen consider that the head of a large moose makes
the finest trophy of any antlered or horned animal. The young
bull grows his first antlers in his second summer. These are
mere spikes. The next year he grows prongs on his antlers, and
then he is commonly known as a "boot-jack." The third pair
have a beginning of palmation. Thereafter each succeeding pair
is usually more palmated, larger, heavier, and wider of spread,
the full development being attained in the seventh or eighth year.
This development of antler is then usually maintained for three
or four years provided that food and other conditions are favorable, after which there is a general decline. Antlers are shed
annually between December 1 and February 1, the young bulls
carrying theirs longer than the old bulls. The new pair start
growing under the velvet a week or two after the old ones have
been dropped, and when full grown, by about the end of August,

Courtesy Mr. A. O. Seymour, Canadian Pacific Ry.

MOOSE IN MOUNTAINS OF ALBERTA

the bull proceeds to scrape off the velvet by rubbing the antlers against small trees. Antlers just out of the velvet are a light, yellowish color, in some lights appearing almost white, but they are later stained dark brown by constant rubbing and scraping against bushes and tree-trunks.

So far as known the record moose was killed in Alaska. These antlers when fresh probably had a spread of about 84 inches. As they now hang in the Field Columbian Museum in Chicago they measure 77½ inches. The dry skull with antlers attached weighed 91 pounds. The record eastern moose is probably that killed by Dr. W. L. Munroe of Providence, R. I., on the Nepisiguit River, New Brunswick, October 12, 1907, and has a spread of 68¼ inches. No moose having a spread of antlers of less than about 45 inches should be shot.

Moose are browsing animals. Their food consists of the foliage and twigs of shrubs and trees, and aquatic plants, more particularly the twigs and bark of willows and small bushes, and pond lilies. Mr. Charles L. Barker, of Riley Brook, New Brunswick, who has spent his whole life among the moose of his province, writes me relative to their food: "In the spring and summer moose feed on the grasses and weeds that grow in the waters of lakes and streams, usually in much deeper water than deer feed in. Frequently they feed in water so deep that they have to dive. A moose can remain under water nearly a minute. Since the spruce-bud worm killed so much of the New Brunswick forests, moose have about forsaken the lakes and streams for the abundant food that has sprung up in the killed and blown-down areas; so much so, that if one were to hunt around the water altogether in September, as we used to do, he would feel sure that there were no moose in the country, whereas if he goes back from the water along some hillside where everything is blown down, and full of whitewood, moosewood, and the shoots of the other hardwoods that are springing up, he will probably find moose in plenty. They also feed on grass as do the deer. They yard in much the same place as they spend their summers, feeding on the twigs of all the young hardwoods, the needles of the fir (Canada balsam), and also on the bark of the mountain ash, the larger dogwoods and whitewoods, and sometimes the bark of spruce and fir." In the summer and fall in northwestern Alberta the moose were feeding almost exclusively on the bark and twigs of the small willows that lined the streams and draws on the mountainsides, and the damp places, and they were occasionally cropping the leaves of aspen.

The calves are born about the last of May or the first of June, and are suckled by their mothers until about the middle of August, not later than the last of August. The calves usually remain with their mothers during the first winter, leaving them in the spring when the new calves come.

In the winter moose congregate together in "yards" in the forest. An exception to this is in the mountain sections of the Northwest where they can often find a winter feeding ground in some big, low valley which is practically free from deep snow. This yard may be many acres in extent, the snow being tramped down in paths so that the animals can get at their food—bushes, twigs, and even bark. The whole area will not usually be tramped, but there will scarcely be a spot 25 yards square which does not contain a path. The moose is almost helpless in very deep snow, and it breaks trail with difficulty. Barker says: "Unlike the white-tailed deer in yarding, the bull moose keep to themselves, and perhaps half a mile away there will be a bunch of cows and calves. I have known seven bulls all in one yard, but generally only one cow and her calf will yard together, that is, there will be several cows and calves yarded in one section, but each cow and calf will keep by themselves."

When the snow melts in the spring moose leave their yards and start to roam for better green feed. The bulls go off by themselves and remain solitary all summer while they nurse their growing and tender antlers. The cows go off with their calves, and then as the new calves are about to be born they drive the old calf away. During the summer all moose usually frequent the shores of lakes, ponds, and the still-waters of rivers and creeks where they feed much on aquatic plants and grasses.

The rutting season starts about September 15, and the active part of it lasts about a month, although the bulls frequently continue their excitement and their doing of foolish things for about a month more. In most hunting countries the legal shooting season for moose occurs when the bulls are still more or less under excitement from the rut, and therefore we are somewhat concerned with the habits and peculiarities of moose during this season. While the moose is usually a most cautious animal, with

Photo by A. H. Cobart

BULL MOOSE FEEDING ON BOTTOM OF STEWART RIVER, MINNESOTA

Courtesy U. S. Forest Service

highly developed senses of scent and hearing, all caution seems
to leave the bulls during the rutting season. They then run wild
and no one can foretell what they will do or will not do. During
this season the bull seems to think that everything that he hears
and almost everything that he sees is a cow. This is much more
pronounced in remote regions where they have little contact with
human beings. In eastern Canada long contact with civilization
has taught them some sense which persists to a certain extent
even during this season. But the only sense of the bull that

Photo by Charles L. Barker
MOOSE IN WINTER YARD, NEW BRUNSWICK

seems to be always reliable during the rutting season, and often
for a month afterwards, is that of smell. While a deer will at
once become suspicious and decidedly alert at any sound in the
woods, if that sound is at all natural, and not most decidedly a
man-sound, a bull moose on the rut will either ignore it, or will
often come to it. So also as regards a moving object in the woods
—they have frequently been known to trot right up to a hunter.
But if the hunter stands motionless the moose cannot tell him
from a stump. I have had both bulls and cows walk all around
me, sometimes within a dozen feet, while I stood without moving.

One fall in New Brunswick, just after the end of the rutting season, and during the first snow of the winter, I was hunting and happened on a nice buck. I shot it, and it ran a hundred yards before falling. Dressing it, I then cut a couple of poles with my hand-axe, hung it up, blazed a few trees, and then went on my way. Within 200 yards I ran into a bunch of four bull moose and a cow. They had been within full hearing of my killing of the deer, had heard my shot, had heard the chopping afterwards, but their tracks in the snow showed that they had not been in the least alarmed, had not moved in fact, nor apparently had they even become alert. I monkeyed around those moose for at least half an hour trying to get a good view of the heads of each bull. They saw me and heard me a number of times, for towards the end I got careless and made a lot of noise. They often looked at me in curiosity, but they stood a whole lot before they began to get nervous and moved off at a slow walk, and without a sound. There was no wind blowing at the time.

I have never seen a place so cut up with moose sign as was a certain little river bottom and hillside deep in the Canadian Rockies, the river being one of the tributaries of the Peace. There were moose trails all over the bottom and the hillsides, some of them extending for miles, worn a foot deep in the soil. Along these trails were many wallows or licks, big puddles of mud where the moose love to wallow and stand. Coming down a mountainside late one afternoon with a companion, we surprised a four-year-old bull moose in one of these wallows. He saw us coming and he waded out of the wallow and advanced to meet us up the trail. We stood fairly but not absolutely still. There was no cover but small willows and little jack-pines. This moose came up the trail to within about thirty feet of us, then started to circle us to the left, grunting all the while. He went almost completely around us, and at no time was he over 40 feet from us. Finally he got directly above us where he could certainly smell us. Then he seemed to get disgusted, not alarmed, and he slowly climbed the trail that we had just descended. We watched him go up the mountain until he was out of sight, at no time was he alarmed nor did he hurry, notwithstanding that he was walking directly in the trail which we had just come down, which must have been redolent with our scent.

A BULL MOOSE HEAD WITH SCALP MAKES A HEAVY AND AWKWARD
LOAD OF FROM 125 TO 175 POUNDS

The next day I was hunting on the opposite side of this same valley, and I disturbed another fair-sized bull moose. Instead of running off he stood watching me and grunting. I came up to within 25 yards of him in the low bush, and stood there for quite a time trying to take a photograph of him. Finally, when I endeavored to get nearer he jumped off about 50 yards, and again stopped to look back. I monkeyed with that bull for almost an hour but could not get closer, although at no time did it seem to be really alarmed.

But the climax of all my game experiences occurred in this same region several weeks later. I had been hunting sheep, and late one afternoon was descending from the main range of mountains. All day I had been without water, so when I came to the first little creek at the base of the mountain I lay down for a good drink. Just as I got down I heard a whack, whack, whack, just as if someone was hitting a big tree very rapidly with an axe. Then I heard the hoofs of some animal coming in a hurry, and up ran a big bull moose. He ran right up to me and stood right over me. Another step and his feet would have struck my feet as I lay at the edge of the little creek. I rolled over and pointed my rifle at him so as to be ready to shoot in case he attempted to stamp on me. We continued thus for probably ten seconds. There was no doubt but that the moose could smell me—I could certainly smell him. By this time I must confess I was getting rather nervous, and I asked him in the vernacular of the West what he was doing there. He almost fell over backwards, and in about three jumps he was fifty feet away. There he stood, horning some bushes and grunting continuously. I grunted too, and we played with each other for fully five minutes until I got tired, took my drink, and went on, leaving him there still grunting and horning the bushes.

Again in New Brunswick my friend Charlie Barker, hunting with a sportsman, had a bull run right up to them in the woods. He hit it with the side of his axe to make it get to a safe distance. Speaking of unusual experiences with moose, Charlie writes me: "The actions of an old cow moose this past December puts all the fool things that I ever knew a bull to do in the shade. One of my guides, Harry Harris, an old woodsman, ran across this cow just as he turned aside to reset a trap that was perhaps a half mile from the main line. He noticed that the old lady did not seem to be unduly alarmed when he passed her. Instead she walked down towards him and followed along in his tracks until he came to the trap, all the time keeping rather close for comfort. While he was cleaning the snow from the trap she was an interested onlooker. Then when he turned to go back she refused to turn out of the path, so rather than dispute the point he went around her, whereupon she kicked up her heels and followed him back to the main trail, and thence to camp about two miles. He stated that a number of times he could have put his hands upon her, she came so close. Needless to say he was alarmed. I saw the tracks the next day when I went over the trail. She stood around the camp for some time before she at last wandered off. Harris states that she was perfectly normal and in good condition. The only thing that I could think of was that she had been tamed some time, but I never heard of a tame moose in this section, and cannot think this was the case."

Now all these cases happened during or soon after the rut. I do not believe that they will happen at other times, but it is interesting for the sportsman to note what darn fools moose can be during the rutting season. A tyro could easily mistake many of these actions for a vicious charge of the moose. But personally I do not believe a moose ever charges unless he is cornered or wounded and cannot get away. My friend Colonel Honeycutt and I were hunting moose one fall in New Brunswick. Honeycutt wounded a bull and it ran down hill, and he after it in such a way as to cut it off. He came to it around a fallen tree where he had the moose backed up against the tree. This moose charged viciously, stamping and gnashing its teeth, its mane all bristled up, and Honeycutt killed it with a well-directed shot at 8 feet. This was a big bull in its prime, and at least a month after the close of the rutting season.

During the rutting season and for perhaps a month thereafter the bull moose calls or grunts. This is sometimes for the purpose of enticing the cow, but more often as a challenge to another bull. It is a hoarse, nasal grunt, sounding like "Wough," "Wough-ah," or "Wough-hugh." I have often seen bulls wandering through the valleys in the northern Rockies grunting every five or ten steps. I cannot find words to express to my readers what a wonderful sight this is, to see this magnificent wild animal, the largest in America, wandering unalarmed in such a

Photo by Author

MOOSE TRACKS ON SHORE OF FROZEN LAKE

glorious setting. It is well worth journeying across the continent to see. Once with a companion, Stanley Clark, I had been hunting sheep. We had each gotten our ram, and the stalk and subsequent butchering had kept us up on the mountain top until dark, and we had to come back through a burnt-over country with lots of willows and muskeg meadows. There were lots of moose in this burnt country for we could hear them grunting at us every few minutes, most likely at the noise we were making, undoubtedly thinking that we were cows or other bulls. The cow also has a call, longer and not so nasal as the bull, and with more of the "Moo" of the domestic cow in it, something like "Moo-wough-yuh."

In eastern Canada one of the favorite ways of hunting moose in the early rutting season is by calling. The guide imitates the call of the cow moose, using a birch bark horn to amplify it. Calling is usually done on a moonlight night near water, and is quite often successful in enticing a bull to show himself nearby. I do not like this time of hunting, however, chiefly because there is so much chance of merely wounding the bull in the poor light, or of shooting an immature bull or even a cow. It is better, I think, to call in daylight, either very early in the morning or an hour or two before dusk. Then if you get an answer you have located your bull, and if he does not come at once you can proceed to stalk him and kill him by still-hunting. To again quote my friend Charlie Barker, who knows the moose more intimately than anyone I know: "As to calling moose, early morning and late evening are the best times because there is usually a breeze blowing during the day with the attendant noises of the forest, and it is the habit of the moose to lie down during the day, and feed during the evening and night. More than once I have called on a still afternoon at a pond where I knew a bunch of moose were hanging out, and at last after several hours and near sun-down I would hear them get up only a short distance away, and the bull would answer my call although he might not come out in sight. However, during the rut a lone bull is apt to be roaming around at any time in the day or night, and he is liable to answer a call at any time or place, as he is looking for a cow and don't care whether she is in a pond or on top of a mountain. But again in the daytime when there is usually more or less wind, an old bull will nearly always try to circle so that he can get the scent from the supposed cow. Some of those old bulls are foxy. The old Indian way was to get out on a pond on a still moonlight night and call until an answer was heard or until daylight, but this was very unsatisfactory. I remember once, years ago, I was calling on a pond with a hunter from Virginia. We had gotten answers from several different moose, and had paddled the canoe alongside of an old pine tree that had been uprooted and lay out in the pond at just the right height to sit on with our feet still in the canoe. We had occupied this position for a few minutes when a bull moose came wading out alongside the canoe and stopped directly in front of us. He looked as big as an elephant, and the sportsman jammed his rifle barrel into his ribs and let go. I assure you there was hell to pay for a few minutes, and when we got straightened up we were in the lake on the other side of the old tree, the canoe was upset and sunk, and the moose was gone. We found him the next morning and he was only a boot-jack, something we would not have killed if we could have seen him. We have given up calling after dark or at night altogether. It is more satisfactory calling in the morning and evening and any place that looks promising as you hunt through the woods during the day."

Calling moose is seldom attempted in the West, and many suppose that the western moose will not come to a call, but this is not so. It has been demonstrated many times that western moose will answer a call just a readily or as often as eastern moose will. Indeed the moose is much the same in its habits all over America, subject to the slight differences that the country he inhabits makes. For example, in parts of the Canadian Rockies the moose do not yard up in the winter, merely because there are plenty of low valleys where their food is good, and where there will not be over six inches of snow the winter through. In the West, while many moose are killed along the rivers, one of the best methods of hunting them is to watch for them from the sides or tops of mountains where the country below is to their liking. Choose a mountain that overlooks a rolling or flat, low country with willow-clad streams, and little lakes or ponds, and small muskeg meadows. Such country is more or less open, and frequently moose can be seen feeding, walking, or standing at any time during the day. The heads can be readily examined during the daytime with field glasses, and then if desired the animal can be gone after, the hunt being partly in the nature of a stalk, and partly a still-hunt, depending upon local conditions and circumstances.

A moose is often not much disturbed by a rifle shot, and sometimes not much frightened when a bullet strikes him and wounds him severely. I think that this is because they often inflict such dreadful wounds on each other, and because in fighting they come together with such a terrific crash. You shoot and hit a bull moose and sometimes he thinks that he has simply been struck by another bull. Then again a rifle shot may sound like a clap of thunder to a bull, or like the explosive crack of young ice that constantly sounds through the north country when the lakes are freezing over in the fall. In no other ways can I explain the fact that many bulls, when wounded, do not seem to be at all alarmed, but walk away slowly. I do not want to create the impression that this is by any means the general rule. The rule is that when you hit and wound a bull he goes off like lightning, and he does not usually care how much noise he makes either. He will often crash through the forest, knocking down small trees with his antlers, and making a swath through the woods that can be seen for months afterwards. But some of

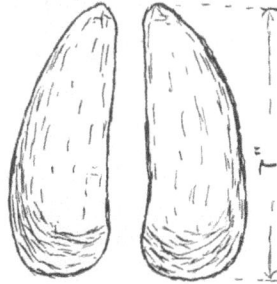

MOOSE TRACK. THE TRACK OF A LARGE BULL MOOSE IS ABOUT 7 INCHES LONG. A BIG COW WILL OFTEN LEAVE A TRACK ALMOST AS LARGE. IN SNOW OR MUD, THE DEW C L A W S WILL SOMETIMES SHOW

them do act as though they had simply got something that was perfectly natural when they are wounded.

The track of a moose is shaped very similar to that of a deer, only very much larger. A big bull moose will leave a print quite seven inches long, but even if the hunter sees a track as large as this he cannot be sure from the track alone that it is a bull for some cows have awfully big hoofs. The only sure way to tell the tracks of a bull from that of a cow is to follow them some distance and look for other signs. These other signs of sex in a moose trail are much more numerous than with others of the deer family because the moose as a rule inhabits thickly wooded or bushy country, and because the antlers of a big bull spread very much wider than his body. As a consequence a big bull cannot go far through thick woods or brush, before his antlers will rub the snow or bark off of some bush or tree close to the trail. And conversely, a cow cannot go far before she will pass between two trees close together without leaving a mark, and where a big bull could not possibly get through.

I had one experience with moose which most aptly illustrates some of these things which we have been discussing. I was hunting in rather thick woods, a gently sloping hillside, with much moosewood and small bushes. There was about five inches of freshly fallen snow on the ground. About eleven o'clock I came across fresh moose tracks, and following them for about three hundred yards I caught up with a bunch of moose. At first all that I could see ahead was four or five black spots, with now or then a slight motion or movement to them which would catch the eye. I stood perfectly still and looked. Then I moved about ten feet to one side and looked again. Finally I caught just a glimpse of a big antler above one of the black spots, and this told me all that I wanted to know—that it was a bull with a head that I wanted. Working a little to one side very carefully I got a vista between some bushes and trees so that I could see a big patch of that particular black spot, so I raised my rifle and when the ivory bead front sight showed up squarely in the center of the black I carefully squeezed off the trigger. At the shot there was a good deal of commotion and milling around of the black spots, but seemingly no particular hurry on the part of any to get away. The bull stood still for perhaps ten seconds and then moved off slowly. As nearly as I could see the others followed him. Nothing was very plain, just a lot of black spots moving slowly through the thick woods about a hundred yards off. When they had all gone I went up to where the bull had been standing, and sure enough there was a great big track and lots of blood in the snow. I cut some balsam boughs, made myself a seat on a fallen log, and had a good comfortable rest and smoke for an hour. At the end of the time I started to follow the trail of the wounded bull. He was going slowly at a walk, and there was lots of blood dropping off the right side of the body. After a few paces it apparently stopped dropping off and instead ran down the right hind leg, appearing only in the track. I followed slowly, keeping a good look ahead and ready

to shoot if the bull should jump up out of a bed. Pretty soon I
began to get suspicious for I had passed many bushes and trees
close to the tracks, but not one of them had any snow brushed
off where it ought to have been by the antlers of a big bull passing
along, nor had the bushes lower down and close to the trail where
the body of the animal had brushed against them, any sign of
blood on them. But the track with the blood in it kept on until
finally it went between two trees barely two feet apart. There
I stopped because I knew that something was wrong. I felt
sure that I had wounded a bull and not a cow, but no bull could
possibly have gone between those two trees. I could not imagine
what had happened unless the bullet had passed clear through
the bull and also wounded a cow, so I decided to go back and look
the trail over from the start again. I was more careful this time,
and I finally came to a place where another trail crossed that of
the wounded bull. A cow had stepped in the bloody track of the
bull, and had walked off carrying blood on her hoof, and it was
this trail that I had followed. Here the bull had turned to the
left around a small spruce, and I had not noticed his trail. I then
took up this right trail and followed it for about a quarter of a
mile, finally seeing the black spot ahead for which I had been
straining my eyes. Very carefully I crept forward so as not to
make a sound, not wanting to shoot a cow or another bull.
Finally I made out big antlers and I let him have it again. At
the shot I saw all four feet of that bull high above the bushes,
looking as though they were ten feet in the air. I crept up
slowly but all was still. Then I came on him, stone dead, lying
on his back, the points of both antlers buried deep in the ground
where he had fallen over on his back. My first shot had struck
him in the right hip, and had ranged forward into the abdominal
cavity. He had bled a lot, most of it flowing down the right hind
leg. The last shot had struck him in the point of the chest as
he was facing me, cutting the aorta and blowing the heart to
pieces. It was a great satisfaction to get him and save him the
agony of a lingering death. He was a magnificent bull, carrying
a really good head of 48 inches, the blackest and glossiest moose
I have ever seen.

From what I have heard from guides and sportsmen, and from
my own experience, I imagine that the greatest difficulty that
the novice will have in hunting moose will be in seeing them in

thick woods. They are not easy to see. They look like black spots as I have already indicated. But lots of other things look like black spots, too—stumps and tree trunks in the deep shade, for example. And after the tyro has looked at a lot of stumps and trees, each time getting up much enthusiasm in the belief that he has discovered a moose, only to find out his mistake, he gets careless, and pretty soon he passes up a black stump that is alive, and he gets so near to it that the first thing he knows it runs off before he can collect himself and fire. It takes quite a time before a city man can quickly tell a moose from other black things in the woods. I think that when one gets so that he can do it he finds that he does it with his sub-conscious mind. The sub-conscious sees more than the conscious mind anyhow. It sees all black spots whether we are aware of it or not. After a time it gets trained, and it can tell the black spot that has hair on it, and that has those almost undiscernible movements that mean it is alive, and at once it calls our conscious mind's attention to it.

Before we close with our talk on the moose let me caution you again about the wind. Read Mr. Barringer's experience in the chapter on Still-Hunting. The moose has a most keen nose, and it is extremely important not to let him get your scent even for an instant. If you have the wind wrong all the fool stunts that bull moose play in the rutting season won't avail you a bit. An occasional stick cracked, a leaf rustled, or a branch brushed against won't alarm moose much, will seldom send them off, but breath of man-tainted air, and they are away and will travel for miles.

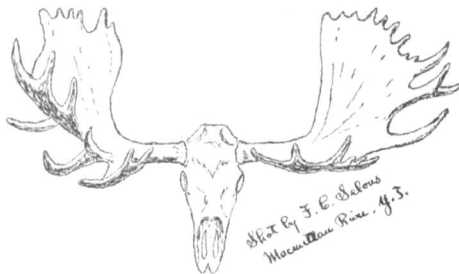

CHAPTER VIII

THE CARIBOU

Up to the present time it has not been possible to define accurately the exact relation and demarcation between the types and species of American Caribou. No other large animal of the North is so difficult to observe, and it will require many years to accurately determine the species of caribou and their distribution. While some naturalists have divided the caribou into sixteen or more species, generally speaking it may be said that there are four general and well-defined groups as follows:

Rangifer caribou (Gmelin). Type Locality.—Eastern Canada. The Woodland Caribou of eastern, and southern central Canada.

Rangifer monanus (Seton-Thompson). Type Locality.—Illecillewaet watershed, near Revelstoke, British Columbia. The Mountain Caribou of British Columbia. In this group might also be contained *Rangifer fortidens* (Smoky River, Alberta) and perhaps *Rangifer osborni* (Cassier Mountains and Yukon Territory).

Rangifer terraenovae (Bangs). Type Locality.—Codrey, Newfoundland. The Caribou of Newfoundland.

Rangifer arcticus (Richardson). Type Locality.—Fort Enterprise, Mackenzie. The Barren Ground Caribou of northern Canada, northern Alaska, northern Labrador, and the arctic islands north of Canada. This group might include *Rangifer pearyi* (Ellesmere Land), *Rangifer excelsifrons* (Pt. Barrows, Alaska), and *Rangifer granti* (Alaska Peninsula).

Besides the skull differences, each of the species has certain typical characteristics which generally are present in a majority of the individuals of that species. But frequently in a species one may come across characteristics which rather tend towards those of one of the other species. The average size, the antlers, and the color of the pelage vary considerably in the different

79

species. The mountain caribou, particularly the Osborn caribou, are supposed to be the largest species, sometimes attaining a height of 55 inches. Also they seem to carry the heaviest and longest antlers. The woodland caribou and the Newfoundland caribou come next in size, adult males reaching a length of from 72 to 78 inches, a height of 42 to 48 inches, and weighing from 300 to 400 pounds. The barren ground caribou are somewhat smaller than the other species on an average. Generally speaking, the summer pelage of the greater part of the animal is brown to grayish brown, with the under parts and the extremities of the legs whitish. The under portion of the tail is white, and the tail is elevated when danger is sensed. In winter the body changes to a very light hue, almost white, often stained. The mountain caribou appears to be the darkest, and the barren ground animals the lightest in color.

No two pair of caribou antlers are ever found exactly alike. Between the very long, few pointed, and scarcely palmated antlers of the Greenland caribou, and the short, many pointed and widely palmated antlers of the mountain caribou, every conceivable form may be found. The Osborn caribou of British Columbia and Yukon seem to grow the finest antlers of any of the species. These are usually longer, have more points, and are more symmetrical than the others. The woodland caribou probably have the smallest antlers as a rule, the Newfoundland caribou the heaviest, and the barren-ground species the slenderest. The female caribou usually carry antlers which are lighter and generally shorter than those of the male. An Osborn caribou has been shot with antlers having 57 points. Rowland Ward states that the record head has a length of 62 inches along the outside curves of the beam, 37 points, and a spread of 49¼ inches.

The caribou has a pelt which is designed to most wonderfully protect it from the rigors of an arctic climate. Next to the skin is a coat of oily wool, and growing through and extending beyond this is a dense growth of straight hair, each hair being hollow and containing air and thus making an excellent non-conductor for conserving the heat of the body. Among the Eskimo the skin of the caribou is preferred to any other for winter clothing. Skins of animals killed in the late summer after the bot-fly holes have healed up are used, skins of the young animals or calves being used for underwear and inside socks, and those of the older animals for outer garments and boots. The skin with the hair on also makes the warmest sleeping bag known, and with the hair removed and made into rawhide makes the best lacings there are for snow-shoes. The meat of the caribou too is delicious. Indeed this animal furnishes food and clothing supply for three quarters of Canada's great area at the present day.

The hoofs of the caribou spread greatly when they walk on soft ground or snow, and when they trot or run. The tracks of a large bull will be about 4 inches wide by 7 inches long, including the pasterns which almost always show in the track. On very soft ground such a hoof will spread an inch wider and several inches longer than this. It is this ability of the caribou to spread his hoofs that enables him to negotiate muskegs and soft and deep s n o w s with such ease. The track of a caribou on snow is a line of single hoof-prints running one directly behind the other, w i t h an average span of 25 inches between t r a c k s when walking.

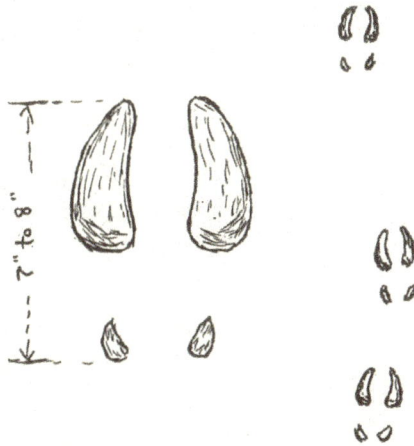

CARIBOU TRACK. THE SOFTER THE GROUND THE WIDER DOES THE HOOF SPREAD. THE LENGTH IS THE AVERAGE FOR LARGE BULLS IN ALBERTA AND B R I T I S H COLUMBIA. BARREN GROUND CARIBOU WILL AVERAGE SLIGHTLY SMALLER

Caribou are much given to following in Indian-file, and a bunch will tread down a thin, narrow path in the snow. In running the hoofs of these animals make an audible click which can be heard up to about 100 yards in still weather. This is caused by the cracking of the knuckle-joint as it bends.

In the southern portion of its range the caribou is partly a forest and partly an open-country animal. As a rule it is not found much in deep forests unless driven there to avoid man. It seems to prefer those localities where spruce and pine forests alternate with open muskegs, meadows, bog swamps, moss-cov-

ered plateaus, lakes, and ponds.   Indeed, in some localities it is
called the swamp deer.   In eastern Canada it will often be found
on mountain tops, and on the high plateaus, probably both on
account of the food conditions, and to avoid the plague of mosquitoes in the low-lands, but in winter it often comes down into
lower country.   In the mountains of northwestern Canada it
ranges well up to timberline and above in the spring, summer,
and fall, and is then found mostly in the park-like country just
below timberline, and in the basins at the head of creeks where
the melting snows above make little rivulets and favor the growth
of moss and tender green grass.   It prefers mountains of the
subdued type with dome-like summits, and not too much rock
or erosion.

The chief characteristic of the caribou is restlessness.   It is
constantly on the move, never satisfied with one place, it is here
today and gone tomorrow, and is the greatest roamer and
traveler among our animals.   One hundred or two hundred miles
is nothing of a journey to a caribou.   Probably much of this
restlessness comes from ages of travel to avoid the plague of
mosquitoes which are almost always extremely bad in caribou
country in the summer.

To a certain extent the southern species of caribou are migratory in their habits.   Thus the Newfoundland caribou migrate
to the southern portion of the island in winter and to the north
in summer.   In other localities they may have summer and winter
feeding grounds between which they journey in spring and fall.
But generally the caribou is not obliged to change its range on
account of heavy snow fall as most other large animals are, for it
can travel well over soft and deep snow, and is able to forage
fairly well under quite deep drifts.   The Barren Ground caribou,
however, are very much more migratory than the other species.
In fall and spring on the arctic prairies the migrating herds
sometimes number into tens of thousands, being comparable to
nothing but the buffalo in the old days on our western plains.
Many travelers who have had the good fortune to see these
wonderful herds have stated that the land for miles as far as the
eye could reach was black with a dense mass of caribou, and
that the movement in such density sometimes continued for
several days.   It is often stated and believed that the caribou
migrate north in summer and south in winter.   In some localities

Photo by E. Mallinckrodt, Jr.

ALASKAN CARIBOU, SHOWING TYPICAL NORTHWEST CARIBOU COUNTRY

this is true, but it should not be implied that they do so to avoid cold. It is more accurate to state that caribou migrate or travel over routes that have been long and well established as leading to country which particularly favors it at certain seasons of the year. Cold and shelter probably have nothing to do with the migration of caribou, for next to the polar oxen (musk-ox) it is better endowed to stand extreme cold than any other of our large animals. It is believed that its migrations are induced by two things only—food and mosquitoes. Incidentally deep snow has its influence, but only because it may hinder the animals from getting at their food so readily. On the southern edge of the barren grounds caribou usually do travel south into the wooded country in winter, but it is probably because these southern herds have found the food there at that time of the year better to their liking or easier to obtain, and they go north again to the open country in summer because the winds there give them some slight relief from the mosquitoes.

In their migrations caribou usually appear to travel up wind. To gain distance in a certain direction they must travel longer hours when the wind comes from that direction. Apparently this is more generally true of the Barren Ground caribou than of the other species. Most observers of the Barren Ground caribou make mention of it.* It is natural that it should be so for by traveling up-wind the animal will scent danger quicker, in summer it will better avoid mosquitoes, and in winter it keeps warmer as the wind will flatten down the hair instead of blowing in under it. But when not migrating caribou do not pay so much attention to traveling up-wind. Rather, in a country with which they are familiar, they have certain well-established routes, and they travel along these when they are undisturbed. All of the caribou of a given area do not always migrate. Often small bands or individuals seem to be content with the same general locality the entire year, and their restless wanderings may extend for only 50 or 100 miles, these bands or individuals not joining in the general migration. When big migrating herds reach timbered country they usually break up into smaller herds, and the movement then becomes more in the nature of an infiltration of small bands of restless animals appearing up-wind at certain seasons. Mr. Charles Sheldon, describing the habits of the

* Handbury, Seton, Stefansson, Buchanon.

Alaska and Yukon caribou, says: "The caribou in the Ogilvie Rockies is the true Barren Ground type. It is smaller in body and skull than the woodland type, its horns are less diverging and lighter in beam, although many of the horns of both types have characters so identical that the resemblance is complete. The only difference in the habits of the two types consists in the Barren Ground Caribou's tendency to wander more restlessly over a wider area, and especially in its banding together in the fall and migrating. In Yukon Territory its habits are similar to those of its neighbor in the Barren Ground of Canada, except in so far as the habits vary to suit the mountainous country in which the Yukon animal roams. Scattered bands, always restless, traveling among mountains, always feeding and resting above timber-line, are found all summer throughout its range. In the fall large bands assemble far in the north and begin to migrate southward, passing through the Ogilvies in November and December. The main band, numbering between fifteen and twenty thousand—perhaps more—has provided the greater part of the winter supply of game meat for Dawson and the mining camps of the Klondike. After the winter hunters had disturbed this band for a few years, the caribou changed their route of migration farther to the east along the Peel River water-shed. In March the majority return northward. Numerous other small bands keep wandering about the Ogilvies during the fall and winter. Formerly, during the migrations, large bands of caribou crossed the Yukon River in the vicinity of Eagle, but at present this habit of crossing seems to have ceased. I have been unable to determine the limits of the southern range of these caribou. Probably it does not pass from the Ogilvies to the Selwyn Rockies. The Barren Ground caribou range well to the south on the Mackenzie side of the divide, and Mr. Keele advises me that he has seen them near the head of the Pelly River. A few may cross the divide in that latitude. But none are found elsewhere in the Selwyns, unless very near the Ogilvies."

"The woodland caribou, *Rangifer osborni*, exists throughout the Cassiars and the Selwyn Rockies. It does not occur in the Pelly Mountains or the Glenlyons. It is abundant in the mountain groups between the Pelly and the MacMillan and in the mountains near the South Fork of the MacMillan. It prefers mountains of subdued type with smooth, dome-like summits free

ONE OF THE ENORMOUS MIGRATIONS OF BARREN GROUND CARIBOU, PHOTOGRAPHED NEAR GREAT BEAR LAKE BY MR. JOHN HORNBY

from too much erosion. Its favorite ranges are quite locally distributed in the regions it inhabits. It keeps within a definite habitat and, though restless and roaming in its habits, it does not gather in large bands and migrate. During the winter, however, scattered bands often gather to the number of two or three hundred and range in a well-defined route of travel over a limited area, usually less than a hundred miles."*

The yearly life of the caribou is quite similar to that of our other cervidæ. In the early spring the old males usually go off by themselves in small bands, and remain apart from the calves and cows until fall. The calf is born early in June, and has a reddish-brown coat, varied with white, but not spotted like the deer. Usually a cow will have but one calf, occasionally twins. The bull's antlers are free from the velvet by September, and the rutting season starts early in October, the bulls bellowing, snorting, and stamping much as do the wapiti. But unlike the wapiti, the caribou bulls do not seem to gather to themselves such large herds of cows—usually there are only two or three cows with a bull, often only one. Then when the cold and the deep snows of winter start, the small bunches of Barren Ground caribou unite into larger herds and begin their migrations towards their winter grounds. The Newfoundland caribou also start their migration to the south of the Island, and the other species wander farther and more restlessly in search of good feeding grounds. At this time the bulls and cows are frequently seen in mixed herds, and may remain together all winter. The old bulls begin to shed their antlers by the middle of December, and most have dropped by February. The young bulls and cows retain theirs until much later, usually until March, although in the far north the cows may carry theirs until May. Apparently the farther north the longer into the spring are the antlers carried. The cows can usually be distinguished from the young bulls by the relative slenderness of their antlers. By the middle of May the new antlers of the old bulls are almost a foot long.

The food of the caribou is mostly moss and lichens, but those caribou living where there are weeds usually include almost all green things in their diet, particularly marsh grass. In winter their method of feeding is to dig down to the ground surface with their remarkably sharp forefeet, and then to work forward in

---

* *"The Wilderness of the Upper Yukon."* Pages 322 to 324.

the channel they have made in the snow. When the snow is very deep caribou seem to prefer to feed in open muskeg valleys where the wind sweeps away part of the snow and makes it easier for them to reach the moss and grass.

Besides being restless, the caribou seems to be erratic and inquisitive. Ernest Harrison, a forest ranger in the Athabasca Reserve, told me that once when traveling down the valley of Sulphur River with his pack-train, a caribou bull ran up alongside, and then trotted parallel with the train for over two miles, stampeding most of the horses. Again, in the Ogilvie Rockies in 1904, Mr. Carl Rungius, the artist, shot two bulls from a herd of sixteen caribou. After he had fired the leader, followed by the whole band, came trotting up to him in curiosity. One day in 1922, while following a well-defined moose trail in the Rockies south of Peace River, I jumped a bull moose with its cow, but the two animals ran down over a cut-bank into a mass of willows before I had a good look at them, so I ran up to the edge of the bank to see what kind of a head the bull had. While I was looking down into the willows trying to see the moose I heard a lot of stamping above me, and made out a small herd of caribou in the trees a hundred yards up the mountainside. The leader of the herd, a most magnificent bull, snorted and stamped, and finally trotted down to the edge of the cut-bank about 50 yards from me, and proceeded to look over as I was to see what the commotion below was all about. He paid the penalty for his inquisitiveness with his life, and his head is now one of the finest trophies of my collection.

Caribou are usually found in more or less open country—in the north almost entirely in the open. Their hunting, therefore, partakes more of stalking than of still-hunting. In the northern mountain ranges where sheep also are present, it is sometimes difficult to distinguish them at very long range from sheep. The experienced hunter identifies them by their characteristic attitudes, and the tyro would do well to study the outline and positions of caribou in all the game photographs he can find. When lying down caribou and sheep look very much alike at long range, and they are also liable to lie down in very much the same kind of country. But when walking or standing there is a decided difference. Caribou at rest usually hold the head downward. Apparently they doze in this position like horses, sometimes main-

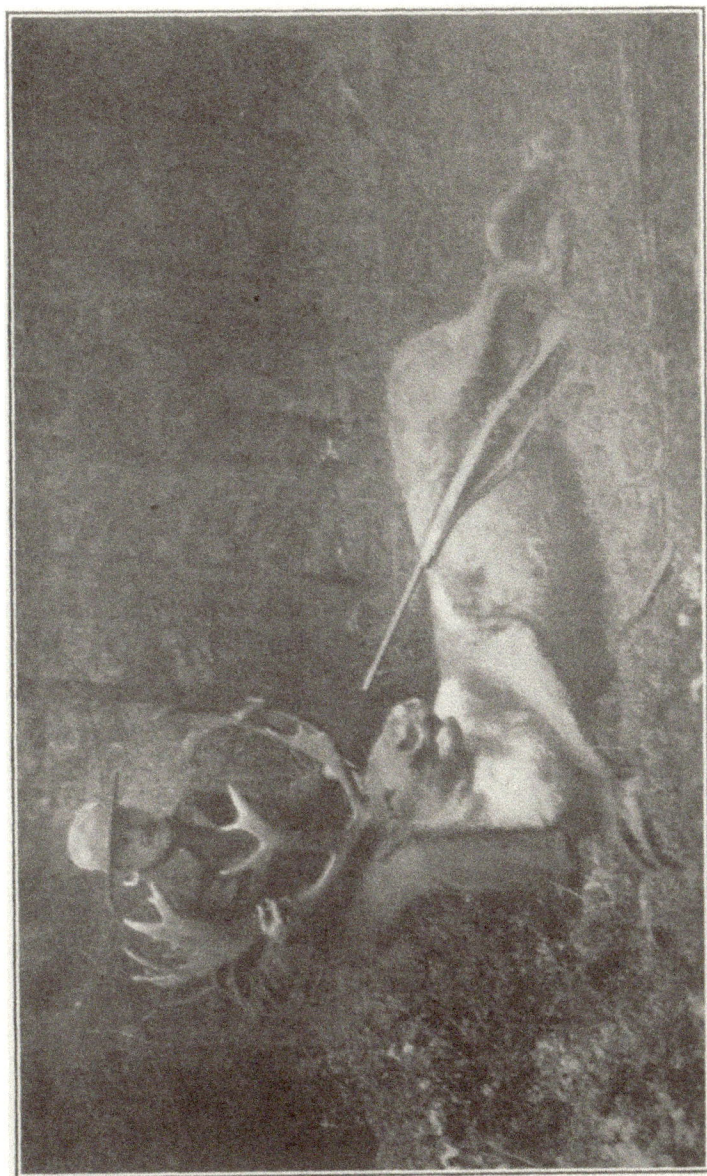

RANGIFER FORTIDENS, SHOT BY AUTHOR, ALBERTA, 1922

taining it for several hours. The head, too, when the animal is
not alert, has some resemblance to the head of the domestic cow.

Caribou have a keen sense of smell and good ears. Their
near vision is good, but their distance vision does not seem to be
very keen. The stalker can usually disregard cover until within
about 400 to 500 yards of a herd. Handbury says: "I have
invariably found that the caribou are more easily frightened by
sound than the sight of a strange object." Caribou seem to relax their watchfulness in a blizzard, but increase it in foggy
weather. They also seem to be subject to constant false alarms.
From the top of a high mountain I one day made out a fine bull,
a cow, and a half-grown calf close to timberline in a valley below
me. I climbed down the mountainside towards them in full view
of them, but about 1,000 yards distant, and they took no notice
of me. At about 500 yards I started the stalk, creeping forward
while keeping small bunches of alpine firs between myself and
the animals. I am certain that they had not seen nor scented me,
but when about 400 yards from them, suddenly without warning
all three animals jumped up and started off at full speed. I first
thought that a wolf perhaps had alarmed them, for I knew that
there was not another human being within 200 miles. I was just
about to risk a running shot at the bull at this very long range,
when suddenly I remembered reading somewhere that caribou
were subject to false alarms like this, so I decided to wait, and
sure enough, after running several hundred yards at full speed,
those three animals circled around, trotted back, and started to
feed within a hundred yards of where they had been in the first
place.

Hunters and explorers in the far north depend largely on the
caribou for food and clothing, as do also the Eskimo. In the
interior, away from the coast and the sea, the Eskimo live entirely
from the caribou herds. The works of Vilhajalmur Stefansson
are a perfect mine of information on the hunting of Barren
Ground caribou, and also on every other detail connected with
hunting, camping, traveling, and maintaining oneself in plenty
and comfort in the Arctic. From one of his descriptions of
caribou hunting I take the liberty of quoting the following:

"It must not be supposed that killing twenty-three caribou in
twenty-seven shots is remarkable. This will appear when you see
how it was done. To begin with, my powerful field-glasses sighted the

band at seven or eight miles. I advanced to within about a mile of them, climbed a hill much higher than the rest of the country, and used half an hour memorizing the topography. There were various small hills and hollows and creek-beds here and there, with branches in varied directions. All this could be studied from the elevation. The main difficulty was to remember the important details after you had descended into the lower country, where everything on closer view looked different. The wind was fairly steady and I made the approach from leeward. But I found that when I got within half a mile of the deer that they had moved to the top of a ridge and were feeding along the top about sidewise to the wind. There was no cover by which they could be directly approached, so I went to the ridge about half a mile from them and lay down to wait. They grazed in my direction very slowly for half an hour or so, and then lay down and rested for an hour and a half more. Meantime I had nothing to do but wait. If, when they got through resting, they decided either to descend from the ridge or reverse their course and graze back to where they came from, I should have to make another detour and start the hunt over again. But they grazed towards me, and in another hour every one of the twenty-three was within two hundred yards, and some of them within fifty yards. Caribou and other wild animals commonly fail to recognize danger in anything that is motionless, so long as they are not able to smell it. They saw me plainly, of course, just as they saw all the rest of the scenery, but their intelligence was not equal to realizing that I was something quite different.

"About this season, when the lakes are freezing all around, the lake ice and even the ground itself keeps cracking with a loud, explosive noise, so caribou frequently seem to take rifle-shots for the cracking of ice and are not disturbed. I took pains to see that my first shots especially should be of the right kind. What you must guard against especially is a wound through or near the heart, for an animal shot that way will startle the herd by making a sprint of fifty to two hundred yards at top speed and then dropping, turning a somersault in falling. But he will always run in the direction he is facing when shot, so that you can control his movements by waiting to shoot until he is facing in a suitable direction. When an animal is frightened he will run toward the middle of the band, and if he is already there he will probably not run at all, at least for the moment. But caribou shot through the body back of the diaphragm will usually stand still where they are, or, after running half a dozen yards, lie down as if naturally. I therefore now did the thing that may seem cruel, but which is necessary in our work; I shot two or three animals through the body and they lay down quietly. The shots had attracted the attention of the herd but, sounding like ice cracking, had not frightened them. Furthermore, the sight of an animal lying down is conclusive with caribou and allays their fear from almost any source. I then moved my rifle so slowly that the movement was unnoticed, and brought it to bear on the next one, holding it near to the ground so that the working of the bolt in reloading was equally not noticed. After the first animals had lain down I shot two or three that were near instantly dead with neck shots, and then began to aim for the hearts of those farthest away, so that any, if they ran, would run toward me. The calves were left until the last.

"The very deliberation with which this sort of hunting is done, while it makes conspicuous the element of apparent cruelty, makes it the least cruel method possible in point of the pain caused the animals. A number of hunters, greatly excited and blazing away in the manner of those inexperienced or afflicted with "buck fever," will mean all sorts of painful wounds that are not fatal and that may be borne for days or weeks by animals that escape. The most cruel of wounds to caribou is a broken leg, for there is no hope of recovery, and yet they can escape for the time being. I have on two or three occasions had a chance to study these animals afterwards. They appear to realize that their speed, now that they have only three legs to run on, is inferior to the rest of the herd, and they are in evident and continual dread of the wolves that are sure to drag them down unless a hunter's bullet mercifully intervenes. In a properly conducted hunt by such a method as ours a wounded animal hardly ever escapes, and with our powerful rifles even a shot through the abdominal cavity will insure death in five minutes to half an hour.

"The reason for killing entire bands of caribou is conservation and convenience. If you kill them in scattered places the freighting problem becomes serious, and especially the matter of protecting the meat from wolves. But with a big kill you can camp by the meat and see that none of it gets lost. Furthermore, in an island like Banks Island, caribou are so scarce that in the ordinary fall hunts in order to get enough meat we have to kill 75 per cent or more of all animals seen. In the fall of 1914 we had only two or three weeks of reasonably good daylight in which to get meat for all winter. For when the daylight comes again in the spring we are not only busy with exploratory work, but also the meat is lean and neither as nutritious nor half as palatable as if fall-killed." *

One would hardly call the killing of twenty-three caribou sport, and I do not think that Mr. Stefansson ever so regarded it. It was a necessary piece of business akin to going to market, and it had to be done to further geographic knowledge and scientific investigation. But the finding, the stalking, and the outwitting of the caribou was sport. There can be nothing but regret at having to kill so many fine animals. But I think that a real man can take a pride and get a big thrill out of killing his first caribou, provided that it is a big bull, and also provided that he kills it as a gentleman should, that is by fair stalking, and by

---

* *"The Friendly Arctic."* Pages 281 to 283.

nail-driving marksmanship which causes no suffering. Also this hunt of Mr. Stefansson's brings up another point in connection with the hunting of caribou which I may be pardoned if I dwell on for a moment. I refer to the matter of rifles, and marksmanship. Mr. Stefansson used a powerful rifle, and one which was extremely accurate at long range, and he himself was a good shot. To my mind it is decidedly unsportsmanlike to use a small rifle which only too often wounds instead of killing outright. The hunter, also, should not take on a shot unless he knows that he is close enough so that he can place his bullet where he wishes. Caribou are often sighted, and often alarmed at long range, and there is decidedly too much tendency to "shoot into the brown" with all the suffering that it entails.

CHAPTER IX

THE MOUNTAIN SHEEP

"To my mind nothing compares with the hunting of wild sheep, a sport which calls forth the highest efforts of skill as well as of endurance, the whole craft of hunting in the most magnificent and terrible places on God's earth. I would rather have hanging on my wall the head of an old markhor than that of the best lion I have ever seen, and all the more because I know the time has now gone by when I could stand the work necessary to win this prize."—Sir Alfred Pease, in "The Book of the Lion."

"No systematic comparative study of North American wild sheep has been completed. Since all museums together do not contain sufficient numbers of specimens of sheep from localities which they inhabit, it has not been possible accurately to determine the local races and their distribution on this continent. The sheep have been accurately separated into two well-marked groups, one existing south of the latitude of Peace River, about 56 degrees; the other north of that latitude.

"The former group includes *Ovis canadensis canadensis*, Shaw, type locality Bow River, Alberta, the Rocky Mountain sheep and its local races. There are two sub-groups of the Rocky Mountain sheep which are well differentiated from each other; the northern one inhabiting forested mountains, mostly above timberline, in Alberta, British Columbia, and all the Western States north of New Mexico, Arizona, and Southern California, except parts of Nevada and Utah, and the Dakotas, where, though formerly abundant, it is now probably extinct. The following local races of typical *Ovis canadensis canadensis* have been described: *Ovis canadensis similkameensis*, Millais, type locality Similkameen Mountains, British Columbia. *Ovis canadensis californiana*, Douglas, type locality Mount Adams, North Yakima County, Washington. *Ovis canadensis sierrae*, Grinnel, type locality East Slope of Mt. Baxter, Sierra Nevada, California. *Ovis canadensis auduboni*, Merriam, type locality Bad Lands of South Dakota, probably extinct. The other group includes the sheep of the desert mountains of the Southwest, including the States of Chihuahua, Senora, and Lower California in northern Mexico. The following local races have been described: *Ovis mexicanus*, Merriam, type locality about Lake Santa Maria, Chihuahua, Mexico. *Ovis canadensis gaillardi*, Mearns, type locality Tinajas Altas, Gila Range, Arizona and Sonora. *Ovis canaden-*

97

sis texiana, Baily, type locality Guadalupe Mountain, El Paso, Texas. *Ovis nelsoni,* Merriam, type locality Grapevine Mountains, boundary between California and Nevada. *Ovis canadensis cremnobates,* Elliot, type locality San Pedro Martir Mountains, Lower California. *Ovis sheldonia,* Merriam, type locality El Rosario Mountain, extreme northwestern Sonora, confined to this one isolated mountain."

"The sheep of the group north of latitude 56 degrees are smaller than these of the southern group, and include two well-marked species: *Ovis dalli,* Nelson, Dall's sheep, wholly white in color, type locality the Tanana Hills between the Yukon and Tanana Rivers, Alaska. It does not inhabit the western slopes of the Pacific coast ranges, but is found elsewhere in most of the higher mountain ranges throughout Alaska, through the mountains near the Arctic coast, and in Eastern Yukon Territory north of the Ogilvies and south along the Mackenzie Rockies as far as the head of the Nahanni River, also in the mountains in the southwestern part of the Territory as far as Lake Bennet.

"*Ovis stonei,* Allan, Stones Sheep, the darkest of American sheep, type locality headwaters of the Stikine River, British Columbia. It ranges in the high mountains inside of the coast ranges of British Columbia north of latitude 56 degrees, as far east as Laurier Pass. It occurs very locally toward the south, and has probably been exterminated south of the Skeena River. The following local races have been described, but have since proved to be errors: *Ovis dalli kenaiensis,* Allen, type locality Kenai Peninsula, Alaska, identical with *Ovis dalli. Ovis cowani,* Rothschild, type locality Mt. Logan, British Columbia, identical with *Ovis stonei. Ovis canadensis niger,* Millais, type locality head of Skeena River, British Columbia, identical with *Ovis stonei. Ovis faninni,* Hornaday, type locality Ogilvie Rockies. Yukon Territory, an intergrade or interbreed between *Ovis stonei* and *Ovis dalli.*

"The sheep inhabiting British Columbia, Yukon Territory, and Alaska east of longitude 136 degrees, and between latitudes 58 and 65 degrees west of the divide between the Yukon and Mackenzie Rivers, are not uniform in color, but vary between dark and white, dark predominating towards the south, white towards the north. These are either intergrades or interbreeds." *

The typical pelage of the Rocky Mountain Sheep is grayish-brown, with often a reddish or bluish tinge, the coats being often much stained by rocks and earth. The back of the tail is slightly darker. The rump, under portions, and parts of the legs are white or creamy white. The old rams are uniformly much darker than the ewes as a rule. I have seen a number of old ewes which were almost white all over, or stained bluish-white, except for the tail. There is considerable variation in the pelage, however, particularly among the southern and desert species of these sheep.

---

* Statement of Mr. Charles Sheldon, given by him to the author, March, 1923.

Dalls sheep are almost entirely whitish, but the hairs are sometimes a little rusty at the tip. They are never absolutely pure white, for a few dark hairs will always be found on the dorsal line, the tail, and sometimes on the back. Also, except perhaps during the month of November, the coat of the white sheep is usually badly stained so that it takes on more or less of the color of the rocks.

The typical color of *Ovis stonei* is blackish-brown or gray. A broad, blackish stripe usually extends from the occiput, along the dorsal region, to the tail. The face and sides of the neck are paler. The front of the neck, chest, and sides are almost as black as the dorsal stripe. The rump, the back of the thighs, the under parts of the center of the chest and abdomen, and the back of the legs are white. The tail is black with some white hairs.

Between the typical *Ovis dalli* and *Ovis stonei* there are many variations or gradings in color indicating that these two species intergrade, interbreed, or else are descended from some common ancestor which was probably dark in color.*

The coat of all mountain sheep consists of very thick, coarse, stiff hair, quite brittle, somewhat like the hair of wapiti.

Both the rams and ewes have horns, but those of the rams are very much larger, massive, and more curling. Of the various species the horns of *Ovis canadensis* reach much the larger size, and the largest rams are probably found in the Rocky Mountains from Colorado to Central British Columbia and Alberta. The record head is somewhat in doubt as to both circumference at the base and length on the curve. Owen Wister records a basic circumference of 17½ inches in one head, and a length of curve of 35½ inches on another head. Hornaday gives one length of curve of 40½ inches. These are all dry measurements. Horns shrink considerably in drying, so that it is probable that a horn having a measurement of 16 inches at the base when dry, measured almost 17 inches when killed. I have heard tell of horns 20 inches at the base, but have never seen such a head, and there is no authentic record of such. When a sportsman gets a head which measures 17 inches and afterwards shrinks to 16

* For a discussion of the coloration of the northern sheep see *"The Wilderness of the Upper Yukon,"* by Charles Sheldon.

inches he may rest assured that he has a prize. The horns of the northern sheep, *Ovis dalli* and *Ovis stonei,* do not run as large as this, and in these species a basal measurement of 15 inches is exceedingly large, although some of them have almost as long a curve measurement as do *Ovis canadensis.* There may be said to be two types of horns; the diverging or spreading type, curving outward, with considerable distance between points, and the narrow type with tips much closer together. No species seems to have a monopoly on one type more than the other, but in some localities one type of horn is much more common than the other.

The horns of all the sheep are a dark, mahogany-brown in color, almost black, and are more or less ringed around their circumference from base to tip. Some of these rings are deeper and more in evidence than others, and they are not spaced with absolute regularity. It is thought that the age of the ram can be told from these rings. The constitution of a ram is probably more or less undermined by the rutting season, and the horns probably grow very slowly or cease to grow for some time thereafter. Then when the ram can get the nourishing green vegetation in the following spring the growth is resumed, and this is supposed to be the cause of the rings, or at least of the larger of the rings. The age of a ram can be told by its incisor teeth up to five years, a yearling having two, and there being two more each year up to four years, when the ram gets his full set of eight.

Mountain sheep, as their name indicates, are essentially inhabitants of the highest mountain ranges. They are not found in the lower country or in lower mountains, particularly lower rounded mountains which are smooth, if higher mountains are available anywhere near, except that they may come down to cross from one mountain to another, or perhaps for the purpose of visiting some alkaline lick or spring. Our first pioneers, however, found them on the lower buttes which in places formed the foothills of the Rocky Mountains, and also in the Bad Lands of the Dakotas, but they have long since been exterminated in such places. They are most abundant where the mountains are continuous and connected, rather than on small or short ranges, or on isolated peaks. But the sheep are by no means evenly distributed along such continuous ranges, as a rule. Rather they are found in spots, a group or band of sheep, or several bands

A NICE BUNCH OF RAMS (CANADENSIS), TAKEN 35 MILES WEST OF CALGARY, ALBERTA

occupying a particular range, a "sheep range," which is often very limited in extent, sometimes to a few miles, these sheep passing their whole lives on this same range. They will cling so close to their own range that they will usually be exterminated before they are driven off. Thus on a continuous, long range of mountains there may be many localities where there are no sheep, apparently never have been any, although seemingly all the conditions are ideal for sheep. A hunter visiting a long, continuous range might hunt for weeks and finally decide that there were no sheep on the mountains, whereas, if he went a little farther he might run into a sheep range and find them very plentiful. Sometimes, however, in days gone by, sheep have increased to such an extent on a range as to endanger the food supply, and then a gradual overflow to other ranges has taken place, thus causing an irregular migration. In the northern part of their range, where the higher mountains go up above timberline, and where there is usually some snow all of the year, the favorite haunts of mountain sheep are the fresh alpine meadows lying close to timberline and fenced in by tall peaks; or the rounded, grassy slopes which extend from timberline to the regions of perpetual snow. They are not rock animals in the same sense as the Rocky Mountain goat is. They prefer grassy meadows and grassy hillsides rather than those extremely rocky places that goats seem to delight in. And when they are alarmed they prefer to put great distances between themselves and their pursuers rather than to take refuge in cliffs and crags. However, they seem equally at home on the cliffs and crags as does the goat. Indeed in such places they seem to have superior jumping or leaping ability to goats. I have often seen them negotiate places by leaping that I think would stump a goat to climb sedately over.

In the southern portion of their range, that is, in Arizona, California, Lower California, and Mexico, they do not, as a rule, find mountains which go up to timberline. Nevertheless they will be found inhabiting the very tops of the highest mountain ranges, up among the jagged pinnacles that form the crests, where the rocks are interspersed with a little grass, perhaps some cactus, and little shrubs. They usually stick pretty close to the tops of the mountains, not coming far down on the sides. On these mountains water is often very scarce or totally absent, and the southern sheep seem to be able to get along almost indefinitely without water, seemingly obtaining the necessary moisture from such of the vegetation as contains it. The southern sheep are usually much lighter in weight and carry less fat than the northern ones of the species. A mountain sheep ram of Montana or Alberta will weigh almost 300 pounds, sometimes more, and in the fall, before the rutting season, is very fat. *Ovis dalli* and *Ovis stonei* are somewhat smaller and lighter. The ewes are all smaller and lighter than the rams. They are all shorter, chunkier, more compact, and more heavily muscled than deer.

Sheep are grazing animals. Their food is the grass that they find high up on the mountain pastures, or between the rock pinnacles and near the summits of the southern mountains. In the south they undoubtedly eat certain varieties of cactus, probably for the moisture which it contains. Sheep also undoubtedly do some browsing, particularly in winter when the deep snows sometimes make it difficult for them to get at grass, or the grass is too dry and cured for their tastes. But usually in high mountains sheep can always find grassy slopes or plateaus where the wind has kept them free from snow so that the grass is available for them. Speaking of sheep, on his visit to Yellowstone Park in April, 1903, Roosevelt says: "One of the rams rose on his hind legs, leaning his fore-hoofs against a little pine tree, and browsed the ends of the budding branches. * * * Although mountain sheep often browse in winter, I saw but few traces of browsing here; probably on the sheer cliffside they always get some grazing."

The rutting season occurs in November, and the lambs are born in May or June. During the summer and early fall the old rams are always off by themselves, never with a bunch of ewes and lambs. Usually, at these times of the year the rams are to be found higher up in the mountains than the favorite grazing pastures of the ewes and lambs. In hunting one usually sees many bunches of ewes and has much difficulty in locating the rams. An old ram may go off entirely by himself, or at this season they may congregate in bands of any number up to about twenty or thirty. So, too, one may come across single ewes, or bunches of two or three, with a lamb or so, but usually the ewes and lambs are in very much larger bunches than rams, sometimes many hundreds of them together. Occasionally one may see a bunch of rams close to a bunch of ewes in summer or fall, but this is only an incident of the two bunches happening to be grazing on the same pasture.

Having found a mountain range where there are fresh sheep signs, and then having located a bunch of ewes and lambs, the hunter can make up his mind that there are rams somewhere within at least ten or fifteen miles, sometimes very much closer, but they may be awfully hard to find, frequently taking many days of hard climbing and scouting to locate them. As a rule rams have a habit of grazing early in the morning and late in the afternoon, and of climbing up to the crest of some range, perhaps to a patch of snow, and taking a noon-day nap. Ewes, on the other hand, seem to take their naps at intervals, and on or close to the meadows where they happen to be grazing. Besides the big curling horns, rams of the Rocky Mountain species can often be told from ewes at a distance by their darker color, and with all species, if the bunch is comparatively small, and if there are no very small animals in it (lambs), the indications are that they are rams. Sheep are often discovered at a great distance in the mountains and it is important to determine if a bunch consists of rams or ewes as soon as possible to avoid much tiresome traveling and needless stalking. For this reason the sheep hunter should be equipped with a pair of binoculars of excellent definition or resolving power. Resolving power depends upon magnifying power, perfection of lenses, and particularly on the diameter of the object lens. A high-power glass does not necessarily give the best definition or ability to make things clear at a long range.

One must look, not only for the sheep themselves, but for indications of them in the shape of tracks and trails. It is easy for an experienced hunter to tell an inhabited sheep range after a little reconnoissance. Sheep in any number will leave their trails, and these can frequently be seen with binoculars from high points of vantage if one knows where to look for them. The shale hillsides and the slide rock will often be streaked with the thin trails. Where the small ravines running down the north hillsides make shaded places there is often a long streak of snow which persists throughout the summer, and this will often contain sheep tracks if any are present in the range. Or if there is no snow there may be muddy shale which will hold tracks a long time. There is little use in looking over grassy hillsides for sheep trails, as on such ground sheep scatter to graze, and do not follow the leader so as to make trails that can be seen at a long distance. Rocky Mountain goats often inhabit the same kind of country as sheep, but a goat's trail will almost always be on top or nearly on top of the ridge. Where you see an outcropping of rock near the summit of a ridge, and a well-marked trail descending down from the ridge, circling just under the outcropping, and again ascending to the crest of the ridge beyond the outcropping, if there are any goats in the country the chances are that this is a goat trail. But where there is a long, wide slope of shale or slide rock, particularly between grassy hillsides or near the head of basins, and a careful examination with glasses shows this slope to be criss-crossed and cob-webbed with faint trails, almost invisible lines that can just be made out, the chances are that these have been made by sheep. A close investigation of the grassy hillsides near these track-crossed slopes will show fresh or fairly recent sheep tracks to the experienced hunter if the range is still inhabited. Once the range is found to be inhabited, the next problem is to find the sheep, and particularly a bunch of rams. This is done usually by ascending in turn all the mountains that promise extended views over likely country, and carefully examining all the country in view with binoculars from the best vantage points. Once a bunch of rams has been located, the hunter should proceed as indicated in the chapter dealing with Stalking.

A typical sheep hunt is perhaps fairly well illustrated by an experience of my own in the Rocky Mountains of Northwestern Alberta. Stanley Clark and I ascended a creek valley into a range of high mountains on the hunch that there might be sheep there. We camped in a most beautiful little basin near the source of the creek, and the next day hunted and searched the mountain sides in view without seeing any signs of sheep. But the following day we crossed a high saddle between two peaks, and came into the basin at the head of another valley, where we had a good view of an entirely different lot of mountainsides. Almost at once we made out the tell-tale criss-crossed trails on the slides and shale hillsides, and knew that we were in a sheep country. Two hours later we located a bunch of fifty-four ewes and lambs, and I lay peeping over a crest for some hours watching them through my glasses. There were three ewes that were

Photo by M. P. Skinner

WYOMING RAMS (CANADENSIS)

Courtesy U. S. Biological Survey

almost perfectly white except for their tails. Their coats were stained slightly bluish from the rocks. I could not notice any lambs with them, so apparently they were very old and barren females. In the afternoon, as the sun went down, and the shadows of the peaks across the valley began to lengthen and creep up to the mountainside towards the sheep pasture, the ewes and lambs fed up the mountainside keeping in the sun, always just ahead of the shadow. In fact at no time were they more than twenty feet out of the shadow. We watched them until it was time to go if we were going to get back to our little bivouac before dark.

We hunted all the mountain slopes and tops of that valley for four days without finding a sign of rams, and our grub getting low, we had to pull out and go back to our main camp some twenty miles below where we had left our pack-train all alone with no one to watch after the horses. Two weeks later we were back again in about the same country, but we approached so as to take the range on the south side of our ewe valley on its southern side. We made our main camp deep down in the valley of a large creek, and the following morning we went scouting, Stanley into the mountains to the south of the valley, and I into those to the north, or towards our ewe valley. As I advanced over the foothills towards the range I saw a big billy goat sunning himself up on the highest ridge, and I thought that I might as well climb to that point, and perhaps I would be able to get a photograph of the goat as well as look the country over for sheep. I took a ridge that led up to the main crest near where the goat was, keeping on the side of it away from the goat, and an hour later I had gained the crest. Little peeps over the ridge on the way up had informed me that there were three goats on the ridge instead of only the one I had seen at first, but when I gained the high crest I thought that I had better look over and see what was on the other side before I started along it towards the goats. I got down on my hands and knees and crept along to where I could look over. On the north side there was a snow cornice, and just below that the mountain fell away with a sheer precipice of about five hundred feet into the head of a basin below. There in the little, almost-level meadow at the head of the basin where the stream started, were eight billy goats, and on the opposite slope were a bunch of nannies and kids. I had certainly gotten into a goat paradise. I got out my binoculars and watched them for some time, although they were not over three hundred yards from me, and I could almost have thrown a rock on top of them. Some of them were lying down and others standing. One stood knee deep in the little stream. All were contentedly resting, evidently having just finished feeding on the long stems of alpine flowers which were growing among the short grass. Then I started to search the mountainsides of the little valley below the basin, and soon I made out a bunch of four sheep grazing half way up a mountain. I made a little rest eight inches high, of rock for my binoculars, and perched them on it, resting my chin on my doubled up fists placed on the ground so as to get an absolutely steady rest, and watched these sheep. In a few minutes the highest one worked up to a small patch of snow, and as soon as it became silhouetted against it I saw the big curling horns of a ram. Rams at last, after over three weeks of climbing and the hardest kind of work and exposure over the sheep mountains! I watched these rams for some time and then turned the binoculars to other hillsides and made out another bunch of three rams, and then much farther down two sheep, the sex of which I could not determine because of the distance. All of these rams were too far off to undertake a stalk that day, so I decided to leave them and come back with Stanley the following day so that we could each of us try for a ram.

I crept back from the crest so that there would be no danger of the game in the valley seeing me, and just below the sky line I started along to see if I could get a close-up picture of the three billy goats. There were lots of big outcroppings of rock on the crest, and I crept forward under cover of these, using one as a mask until I reached it, and then selecting another to cover my approach. I came to one of these outcroppings that extended down hill some distance, and had to climb over it, and as I did so I looked square into the eyes of a goat that was lying on the other side not ten feet off. This goat took me entirely unawares. It jumped up and started off as fast as a billy can go. I jerked out my camera, but the goat was a long distance away before I could get it in the finder and snap the shutter, and the photograph proved worthless. This billy ran along the ridge, and alarmed the other three goats, and all four

OVIS STONEI, BRITISH COLUMBIA

of them climbed up on a little pinnacle, and stood all humped up looking at me, a most perfect goat picture if I could only have gotten close enough to have recorded it. But the goats were alarmed, and there was no use in going farther after them, so I started down the mountain to our main camp. It was on this afternoon on the way back to camp that I had the adventure with the bull moose, when I lay down to drink at the first little stream, that I have already described in the chapter on moose. That was certainly a grand game country, for I had also seen a bunch of caribou and two cow moose that same day, in addition to the game I have already mentioned.

That evening when Stanley got back to camp he stated that he had found a bunch of ewes, and as he watched them an old ram appeared on the crest above them and looked down at them, and then went back out of sight again. We decided to try to stalk the sheep I had seen on the following day.

We started an hour before sunrise, and instead of climbing up to where I had viewed the sheep the day before we made a circle to the east so as to enter the valley the sheep were in and come up to them from below, for I feared that we could not get down the steep bluffs below my observation point without revealing ourselves to the rams. When we got to where we could look up the valley we discovered the eight billy goats still in the little meadow at the head of the basin, and a bunch of seven rams on the hillside at the head just above the goats. Evidently this bunch of rams was the consolidation of the bunches of four and three that I had seen the day before. One old billy was feeding up towards the sheep, and evidently the rams did not like its intrusion for they kept looking down at it and edging farther up the side of the mountain. Finally they stopped feeding and walked up to the crest at the very head of the basin and lay down in a patch of snow between two pinnacles of rock looking exactly like the painting by Carl Rungius which is shown facing page 206 of Charles Sheldon's "Wilderness of the Upper Yukon." We decided that they had probably gone up there for their noon-day siesta, and the stalk was on. It was ten o'clock when we started, and we were obliged to first climb the mountain on the north side of the valley keeping behind an ascending spur which hid us from the view of the rams, and then having gained the crest of the range, to keep along just behind the crest until we came to the head of the basin where our rams were. It was a very long, hard, tedious climb, but we were constantly encouraged by being able to creep to the crest and see the rams still lying there and getting closer and closer. At three-thirty we were creeping along the crest within a few hundred yards of where our rams were lying when Stanley whispered to me to look down to the right, and there away below us was the very valley where we had found the bunch of fifty-four ewes three weeks before. At last we had found the pasture of the rams that belonged with that bunch of ewes and lambs! Three weeks of the very hardest kind of mountain climbing, scouting, and traveling that a man can do.

As we came closer to the rams we had to be very careful of noise. The wind was blowing almost a gale straight across the crest, so we had no fear of that. At every little high place on the crest we crept up, took off our hats, and looked over. Finally at one of these Stanley made out the big curling horns of a ram about two hundred yards ahead and moving. As we watched we saw the rams getting up, and then coming along towards us on the slide rock just below the crest to our left, and on such a course that they would evidently pass us about a hundred and fifty yards down hill, offering a perfect shot. They came so slowly that we had plenty of time. Where we were was a most perfect location. There was a little flat patch of snow on which we lay. Just in front of us was a little wall of rock about a foot high which hid us from the rams, and in it were two or three notches through which we could look with our field glasses, and through which we could fire at the right time—a most perfect and ideal ambush. We got our rifles ready, looked to our sights, got our slings on our arms, assumed the standard prone firing position, even pounded little holes in the snow for our elbows. I even took off my hat and placed a stone on it so it would not blow away in the wind. Then we watched the rams come on through our binoculars. Very slowly and sedately they came, a few steps at a time and then a pause to look over hundreds of square miles of snow-capped peaks and glaciers above a field of deep-green, forested mountains below, with creeks showing like curved bands of silver. It was a sight that comes to a hunter very seldom in a lifetime, the grandest of all American wild game in the most beautiful setting imaginable. We had such

OVIS DALLI, ALASKA

Photo by W. J. Morden

a good view of the rams as they came on that we could choose
the best and largest heads. The first ram had a wonderful head,
very symmetrical and perfect, and with a very long curve and
large spread with perfect points, but the two rams following
appeared to have much more massive heads with larger circumference at the base, and we decided to take these two. We could
see no choice between them, although their points were not as
perfect as those of the leading ram. In this I was influenced by
the remarks of a sportsman whom I had met on the train coming
out West, and who was willing to bet any amount of money that
there was not a ram with a sixteen-inch head in the mountains
into which I was going to hunt. I wanted to show him that he

was dead wrong. I have always been rather
sorry that I did not take the leading ram, or
else wait for the last one, which we did not
get a good view of before we shot, but
which we saw afterwards, and which seemed
to have a much larger head than any of the
others. When our two rams got directly
below us on the slide rock very slowly we
raised our rifles until the gold beads of the
front sights steadied down right behind their

SHEEP TRACK

shoulders as they only can steady when one has a perfect prone
position and is using his gunsling in the correct manner. Very
carefully we started the trigger squeeze. At the reports of our
rifles absolutely nothing happened. All seven rams stood as
though frozen, including the two we had fired at. They stood
thus for apparently about five seconds. We could not believe
our eyes, and were just about to fire again when very slowly our
two rams started to topple over, not like one would expect
badly wounded animals to do, but rather like wooden toy sheep
that one was slowly pressing his finger against in such a way
as to make them very slowly fall over sideways. Their perfect
standing attitudes were absolutely maintained. There was not
the slightest collapse. Over they went slowly sideways, heads
and horns erect and legs stiff, and slowly they started to roll
down the slide rock, gradually gaining momentum, until they
had rolled down out of sight. Up we jumped and started down
after them, and then a very strange thing happened. The remaining five rams stood perfectly still, and Stanley and I ran right

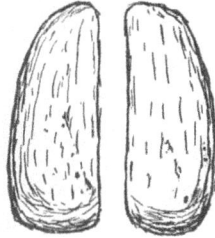

through them, and too late we saw that the last ram had a truly wonderful head of horns. I have never heard of rams standing like this before. Evidently these rams had never seen a human being before, and had no enemies, and they did not know what to make of it all. Way down below we found our two rams. Their long roll over the steep slide rock had not damaged their horns in the slightest as we had feared. The horns were very massive and heavy, and both rams were very old ones with many decayed teeth. One had a basal measurement of 16¾ inches, and the other 16¼ inches. We never knew which was which, but we each had a truly magnificent trophy, but after the sight of those wonderful animals coming along that slide rock so majestically amid such gorgeous scenery I could not help having pangs of regret at having shot them. It is the last time that I shall ever shoot rams of the *Ovis canadensis* species. If I am ever lucky enough to get another such chance I shall use the camera and not the rifle. We piled our two rams up together, and each of us posed for a photograph with them, then we dressed them and left them where they fell, and took our way towards camp a long, long way off and below, for it was beginning to get dark, the sun had just gone down, and we did not want to get caught up in that high, steep country after nightfall. We came back the next day, bringing pack horses as close as possible, and got out the heads and every bit of the meat.

This was a most remarkably lucky stalk, and lest the reader get the idea that sheep hunting is easy, I must state that it is very seldom indeed that a hunter ever gets the chance on mountain sheep that we had. Mountain sheep are the wariest of American game. They have the most wonderful eyesight of any animal, and their senses of smell and hearing are also remarkably acute. They are always on the alert, and it is very difficult to get close to them. Many hunters are forced to take their shots at three and four hundred yards, and only get running shots at that. And sheep hunting is the hardest work of all forms of hunting, requiring hour after hour of hard, steep mountain climbing, and long hours, almost days, of exposure high up on the roof of the world among steep, dangerous cliffs and dizzy heights, amid perpetual snow, and often in freezing cold winds. It is a game for young, strong men, or middle-aged hunters who have kept themselves in proper training only. Sheep ranges are no place for men soft from an office who have never kept in shape with strenuous athletics, or for those who have gotten fat and heavy at sedentary occupations. For such men sheep hunting is either impossible or dangerous for their hearts.

I have mentioned the keen eyesight of sheep. I had this very forcibly impressed on me once. With two friends, two guides, and an Indian cook I was hunting one fall in British Columbia. This particular day we had crossed a high range of mountains in a blizzard with our pack train, and had tumbled into a little valley just below timberline, half frozen, and made a quite comfortable camp. With everything arranged, the Indian cook climbed up on a little rise near the tents to take a look, the blizzard just clearing away above us. In a minute or two he came back and said that he saw rams on the mountainside above us. We went up a hundred yards with him, and none of us white men could see the sheep at all until we looked where the Indian pointed with our field glasses, and then we could make out a bunch of sheep about three miles away, but could not tell if they were rams or not. In camp I had a very powerful telescope, and I went back and got it, and with it I could see that they were rams and that they were looking directly at us. Since that day I have had a most wonderful regard for the eyesight of Indians and mountain sheep.

Mr. Charles Sheldon, who has probably had more experience among the sheep of America than any other hunter-naturalist, tells me that he considers that it is more important to keep out of sight of sheep, and avoid making noise than to try to avoid giving sheep your scent. He considers noise a very important thing in sheep hunting, and he takes unusual precautions not to make any noise when stalking close to sheep. If he should disturb a rock he stops and sits down, and waits a long time before going forward.

A few years ago sheep had almost become exterminated in the United States, and they are now protected indefinitely in almost all of the States. Under protection they are slowly getting more plentiful. There are now a number of quite large bunches of sheep in certain parts of Colorado where they have been longest under protection. There are quite a number of good-sized herds in Yellowstone Park where they will be protected for all time, and in northwestern Montana they are beginning to get a little more numerous. In the Canadian National Park at Banff they are getting really very plentiful, and lately it has been possible to capture and ship sheep from there to other localities. It is hoped that this protection will continue until the whole of the northern Rockies south of the Canadian National Railway becomes again the fine sheep range that it was seventy-five years ago. If sheep ever become plentiful enough to warrant an open season in any of our Western States I think that they should be placed on a little different basis than other big game. A fair-sized fee should be charged for a license to kill a ram, and it should be returnable in case the hunter is unsuccessful. The license should be issued only to men who certify that they have never killed mountain sheep of that species, and only one sheep should be allowed to a hunter. He should be required to kill it himself, and his guide should not be permitted to shoot. In these days a sportsman is entitled to just one ram head in a lifetime. If this is done when sheep become plentiful again our sons and grandsons will be able to enjoy and have the experience of this most magnificent and red-blooded hunting.

CHAPTER X

THE ROCKY MOUNTAIN GOAT OR WHITE GOAT

Oreamnos americanus americanus, HOLLISTER.
TYPE LOCALITY.—Cascade Range, near the Columbia River, in
Oregon or Washington.

Oreamnos americanus columbiæ, HOLLISTER.
TYPE LOCALITY.—Shesley Mountains, northern British Columbia,
Canada.

Oreamnos americanus missoulæ, ALLEN.
TYPE LOCALITY.—Missoula, Missoula County, Montana.

Oreamnos Kennedyi, ELLIOTT.
TYPE LOCALITY.—Mountains at mouth of Copper River,
opposite Kayak Island, Alaska.

The Rocky Mountain Goat is a large, "chunky" animal, usually
very fat, and of a brilliant white color. Its coat is usually im-
maculately clean. In comparison with the color of newly fallen
snow the coat has just a little tint of cream. The wool and hair
of the goat is the warmest, longest, and softest on any big game
animal that inhabits the United States. It is well calculated to
keep it warm and comfortable in a January blizzard on the top
of a sub-arctic mountain. The goat's sides are covered with a
fine, soft wool through and over which grows the rain-coat of
long white hairs. The goat is very solidly and stockily built,
and is usually very fat and in the best condition. Its body and
conformation remind one more of a small bison than of a goat,
although its attitude, walk, expression, and the way it uses its
beard are most decidedly goat-like. The resemblance in contour
to the bison is accentuated by the way it carries its head low, by
the humps over its back and hind-quarters, and by its short,
stocky legs and big hoofs. The hair is long and coarse on the

121

beard, on the rounded crests of shoulder and hind-quarters, and on the upper legs. The long hair on the upper legs, like knee-breeches, contributes to the heavy, short-legged appearance of the animal, dropping down so low that when the goat walks away from one its appearance reminds one of an old man whose pants are falling off! A large billy stands about 38 inches high at the shoulder, has a total length of about 60 inches from nose to root of tail, and its girth both behind the foreleg and around the belly will run about 60 inches or more in a specimen in good condition. The weight of a fat billy will run between 250 and 300 pounds. The tail is very short, not much over 3 inches, and is not in evidence. The nose, the horns, the glands, behind the horns, and the hoofs are jet black. The iris of the eye is straw color.

The horns are round, ringed near the base, smooth for the remainder, and very sharp. The horns of the billy are heavier, more heavily ringed near the base, and usually longer than those of the nannie. The nannie's horns may, however, look longer at a distance than those of a billy by reason of being thinner. There are several records of horns 11½ inches long, with a circumference at the base of nearly six inches, but the average length of the horns of a big billy is about 9½ inches. The hoofs have an outer shell or hard horn which incases an interior mass like soft rubber, an ideal construction for the steep rock climbing this animal has to do.

The known range of the mountain goat extends from the Teton Mountains in Wyoming, the mountains bordering the Salmon River in Idaho, and northwestern Washington, to about latitude 63 degrees in the Rocky Mountains, and to the vicinity of Mt. Wrangell in the Coast Range. Its furthest western limit is the vicinity of Cook Inlet, Alaska. It is not now found east of the Rocky Mountains, but on the coast of British Columbia and Alaska, it ranges almost to tidewater. In its chosen localities where it has not been disturbed it is quite numerous. In the Rockies of northwestern Montana, for example, where it has been efficiently protected for a number of years, it has become very plentiful.

The country of the mountain goat is the upper portions, ridges, and tops of high, rocky mountains. It particularly frequents broken, rocky ridges, summits, mountain peaks, and the top of the divides above timberline. It is fond of broken cliffs which are in the neighborhood of grassy hillsides and little meadows at the head of the basins where the alpine creeks rise. Generally the goat inhabits the highest country he can find that is reasonably close to good feed. He will, of course, not be found on mountains composed entirely of rock, snow, and ice. The sportsman should seek him on mountains composed of broken rocks, precipices, shale, slide rock, interspersed with grassy slopes, and with here and there small patches of snow, and particularly such mountains as embrace grassy basins. Here he will be found very high up, usually standing or lying on the crests of ridges, on the sides of rocky bluffs, or feeding on the grassy hillsides close to the rocks, or in the little grassy basins. On a mountain that is inhabited by goats their trails can frequently be seen with the glasses, running along the ridges and summits. If there is an outcropping of rock on the crest of a ridge such as to prevent passage along the crest proper there will almost always be found a trail or evident path leading down below and around it and again gaining the ridge beyond the outcropping rock, and such a trail is almost sure evidence of the presence of goats. Trails further down the sides of the mountain, but above timberline, are more apt to be those of sheep than goats.

Goats seldom range far down into the timber, though they may descend for shelter in a bad storm, and they inhabit some mountains, particularly on the Pacific Coast, which do not rise above timberline. Also they sometimes descend in and around wooded cliffs and bluffs when disturbed to hide. They sometimes have been encountered almost at tidewater on the British Columbia and Alaska coasts, and sometimes cross low valleys between mountain ranges, or visit licks down in the timber. About 30 miles up the North Fork of Bridge River in the Lillooet District of British Columbia are a number of alkaline licks about 1,000 feet below timberline that are much used by mule deer, sheep, and goats. When I was hunting in this valley in 1901, and again in 1906, goat hair was very plentiful on the bushes around the licks. But these are quite the exception, and almost invariably the white goat will be found well above timberline, near the summit of high mountains, on the crests of ridges or on the side of broken cliffs.

Like the deer family, the goat is partly a grazing and partly a browsing animal, but prefers browsing. In the spring of the year it grazes much on the young grass, but in the summer and fall it seems to prefer to browse and crop from the larger weed-like plants which grow so abundantly around timberline. In September and October I have seen goats feeding many times, and they seemed to let the grass entirely alone, but cropped industriously at the many weeds which grew from a foot to two feet high on the hillsides and in the basins, eating the leaves, dead flowers, and small stalks indiscriminately. In the winter the goat subsists on whatever he can get on the ridges and slopes from which the snow has been swept clear by the wind. He has been known even to browse on the tips of coniferous trees around timberline. He does not seem to descend to lower altitudes in wintertime like other alpine animals, but prefers his high country the year around. Hornaday examined the contents of a goat's stomach, killed in the southern Canadian Rockies in September, and identified the following:*

Lace-leaved Anemone—*Pusatilla occidentalis*
Mountain Sorrel—*Otyria digyna.*
Wild Valerian—*Valeriana*
Yellow Willow—*Salix*
Squaw Weed—*Senecio triangularis*
"Goat-Weed" with flower like candytuft—*Unidentified*
Mountain Timothy—*Phleum alpinum*
"Wild Pea"—*Hedysarum*
Wild Strawberry—*Unidentifiable*

The hunter will usually catch his first glimpse of the Rocky Mounatin goat silhouetted on the crest-line of the highest ridge, either standing like a sentinel on some little pinnacle, head low and shoulders humped up, or else lying in a bed of shale on the crest where it can look down both slopes. It will also be seen on the sides of broken cliffs, and on rocky hillsides where there are lots of little cliffs. Due to its brilliant white color, and to its almost always being right out in the open, it is a very easy animal to locate. In any mountain country there will be lots of white spots about the size of goats, but these can be quickly examined with binoculars, and there is no trouble at all in identifying a goat through good binoculars at distances up to about

---

* "Camp-Fires in the Canadian Rockies."—W. T. Hornaday.

Photo by Stanley H. Clark
GOAT SURPRISED IN PATCH OF ALPINE FIR ABOVE TIMBERLINE

two miles, and making sure that it is not a white rock or a small patch of snow before one starts to stalk.

The goat is the most expert and daring rock climber in America. He will go where no other animal can follow. His gait is almost always a slow walk. Even when alarmed he goes off at a sedate walk, trotting very seldom, and almost never galloping, except on fairly level ground, and then only when very much alarmed. But in his country his steady walk over the roughest and steepest places will take him quickly beyond any possible chance of pursuit.

The goat has excellent eyesight, and will certainly see everything in sight within half a mile, but it will not always become alarmed at the mere sight of a man unless it is apparent that the man is coming straight towards it, in which event it will get up, walk around a little, and finally go off, at a walk, going up or over a ridge if possible, and stopping continually at the high points to look back, provided the man is below the goat. But if the man appears on the same level as the goat, and particularly if he appears above it, it gets much more alarmed and goes off at a much more rapid gait, usually a fast walk, but still pausing to look back once in a while. The scent of man will alarm it at once, but it is very seldom that it gets such scent because where it lives the wind either blows very strong, or eddies around so much that the scent is usually dissipated, and does not travel far. Unless the wind is blowing steadily straight from the hunter towards the goat not much notice need be taken of the wind in stalking. It is much more important to guard against noise because the goat is very susceptible to noise, and can apparently distinguish between stones and rocks liberated by a clumsy stalker and those which are almost always falling from time to time in its steep country. It is very difficult, sometimes, on rocky hillsides, in slide rock, and on bluffs, to avoid disturbing rocks and have them go rattling down the hillside.

Many hunters have asserted that in stalking goats the thing to do is to get above them. I do not think so, and this statement is made after a total of thirteen months of hunting in country where goats were very plentiful. If you get above a goat and he sees you he will be much more alarmed than had he discovered you below him, probably because he figures out that he can always beat anything else climbing upward. Moreover, it is usually twice as much work to approach a goat from above than below because you have to climb around and above him. You can often walk in plain view through a valley or basin with goats on the surrounding cliffs and ridges. The goats will see you, and they may get up and climb up to some pinnacle and watch you, but they won't be seriously alarmed unless you continue to walk straight towards them. But when you start to approach and stalk them the main thing is to keep out of sight and not make any noise until you get within shooting or photographing distance. Ability to climb and a cool head for heights is certainly most essential in a goat hunter. No man gets a goat or its photograph without a hard, tough, and sometimes dangerous climb of several hours. But given the ability to climb, and a little common sense in choosing the route of approach to keep out of sight, goat hunting is easy. After one has gotten his trophy there is not much sport in continuing to hunt goats—they are too easy. But there is one superb sport that can be had with these animals and that is photographing them. The use of the camera on goats beats shooting them all to pieces, and it usually promises wonderful rewards. Stalking close enough for a good picture is often possible, but it takes hard work, much patience and skill. The animal is out in the open, its color makes it show up excellently against any background except snow, and the light for photography is usually the best. A successful picture at close range not only shows the goat clearly, but also usually contains most beautiful mountain scenery and surroundings. A camera with a long-focus lens should be used, and the reflex or graflex cameras are much the best. The lens must be a rapid one, as a snap shot will be necessary. A lens working at f 4.5 is a great advantage as it enables one to use a panchromatic film and a light-ray filter, which give much better results in mountain photography than the ordinary film.

My first goat was obtained under circumstances that show how easy it is often possible to get them. I was traveling along the east side of the Taughten (pronounced Tyaxin) range in British Columbia, in the Coast Range about 30 miles west of the Fraser River. I had with me an old hunter named Bones Andrews and his squaw wife. We had taken our pack-train over a high divide and were descending the other side, when

GOATS CORNERED ON ROCKY CLIFF

on the face of a high cliff about half a mile to our right we made out a large solitary billy. I at once decided to try for it. Leaving Bones and the squaw to take the horses along and camp in the flat below, I quickly changed my heavy boots for buckskin moccasins, and started off, telling my companions that I would get the goat and find my way to their camp later in the afternoon. The cliff was steep but broken by several ledges running horizontally across its face. The goat was just above the center one of these ledges. From my starting point at the north end of the cliffs I climbed to the middle and began the traverse along this towards the billy. Above and below me were almost perpendicular cliffs of about a hundred feet, while the ledge or shelf along which I crept was from five to twenty feet wide with a strong downward slope. As I got nearer to where I had seen the goat I progressed slower and with greater caution so as not to disturb any of the loose rocks with which the ledge was plentifully covered. As I came nearer to where the goat had been I suddenly heard a falling of rocks and a scrambling directly above me, and looking up I saw him on the cliff face directly above me. So straight up was he that all I could see was his belly and legs. I lost no time in putting a bullet straight into him from below, and immediately he let go all holds and came straight down at me. I made a tremendous jump sideways thinking that he was going to fall directly on me, but he struck the ledge about ten feet to one side of where I jumped to. As he struck he gave a tremendous grunt, and I don't mind saying that my heart jumped up into my throat. It was probably just the air rushing out of his lungs from the blow of alighting, because after a quiver or two he lay still, and I finally realized that I had killed him instantly. He was a big billy, in fact the largest I have ever shot, and immensely fat. I started right in to skin him and cut out the head, and right there I had my troubles, as anyone knows who has skinned a goat. The combination of very thick hair, very thick skin, and the heavy underlying fat make it quite a task. The skinning knife dulls very quickly, and has to be constantly sharpened. Finally I got it done, made a pack of the head, skin, and a chunk of the abdominal fat, tied it on my shoulders with a little piece of rope that I always carried, and started down the cliff as best I could to intercept the tracks of the pack-train. Below the cliff was a steep hillside covered with grass, weeds, and clumps of alpine firs, and below that was a flat of jackpines. I knew that Bones and the pack-train had crossed the flat of jackpines. There was no trail and I had to depend upon picking up the horses tracks and following them to find the camp. It started to get dark just as soon as I struck the pines, but I was fortunate enough to strike the horse tracks just about the time that I thought that it was too dark to possibly see them. It was fortunate that I was wearing soft buck-skin moccasins because from here on the only way to follow these tracks was to feel them out with my feet. I progressed thus an enormous distance, it seemed almost for hours, across the flat and then down, down a very steep hillside towards the bottom of the valley, before I heard the welcome tinkle of the horse bells and finally saw the gleam of the camp fire below me. The next day I climbed back to the goat and brought down a big load of fat and some ribs. From the fat of that goat we tried out four gold-pans full of tallow which we used for frying for the next three months. The meat of some goats is excellent, and that of others is apt to be too muttony. The fat is very good except in the rutting season which is late in November or early in December.

On another occasion many years ago I was hunting with two friends, their two guides, and a cook, together with a pretty formidable array of saddle and pack horses. We were moving from one valley to another, and as we crossed the divide and descended towards our new valley we began to see goats on the cliffs on the opposite side. Stopping the horses, we got off and took a look with our glasses, and we made out forty-two goats in sight at one time. The next day my friends went out with their guides and got a goat apiece, and the following day there was not a goat in sight anywhere. Word had passed among them that there were strangers in their valley, and they had hid them-selves away in niches in the rocks and among the little pines which grow part way up among the rocks.

It is difficult to tell billies from nannies at a distance. The billies are larger, heavier, fatter, and chunkier as a rule, and their horns are thicker and more wrinkled at the base. If there are a few goats together, and all appear to answer this descrip-tion, and, moreover, if all appear to be about the same size, they are probably billies. The billies stay by themselves until the

rutting season which is very late in the fall. They may sometimes be on the same hillside or ridge with the nannies and kids,
but some little distance will usually separate them. On the
other hand, if a bunch contains animals of different sizes, and
if they do not seem particularly fat, they are probably nannies
and kids. A small kid can always be told by its size in comparison with a full grown nannie, and the presence of one or more

Courtesy Mr. A. O. Seymour, Canadian Pacific Ry.
GOAT SHOT ON TYPICAL FEEDING GROUND OF THE SPECIES

kids in a bunch is almost certain to indicate that there are no
large billies present until late in the fall. It is where one sees
only a solitary goat that it is most difficult to make the identification, but when one gets within shooting range the wrinkles
at the base of the horns can always be seen with a good pair of
binoculars, and the relative thickness of the horns can also be
made out, and there is very little excuse in shooting a nannie
in mistake for a billy.

Goats are difficult animals to kill, and they often require a lot of shooting. For this reason the sportsman should try to stalk as close as possible and kill humanely. They have a most phlegmatic temperament and do not seem to be nearly as susceptible to shock as other American animals. Then their fur and hide is very thick, with a heavy cushion of fat under it. The hide itself is almost half an inch thick and very tough. Bullets seem to upset badly on the hide and they do not penetrate as deeply as is usual on other animals. The goat seldom flinches at the shot, and apparently does not mind the wound, but continues to walk slowly away as if he had not been struck, and also apparently he is not much alarmed at the report of a rifle. I once shot a goat out of a big bunch. The first shot was not immediately fatal and I had to get nearer and take another. The remaining goats walked and stood around in all directions not knowing what had happened, and even after I had come up to dress the goat that I had killed the others were not over 200 yards off. At the first shot a small billy ran down the mountainside about 25 yards and hid his head in a little bunch of alpine fir. The day after I found the eight billies in the basin as related in the chapter dealing with sheep. I stalked a bunch of rams on the hillside immediately above them, shot one ram, had it roll down the hillside within 400 yards of the goats, and dressed it out and walked down to within 200 yards of these goats, and they did not seem to be at all alarmed, but then I do not think that this particular bunch had ever seen a man before, and there were apparently very few eagles and coyotes in that country, the only natural enemies that the goat has.

CHAPTER XI

THE BEARS OF NORTH AMERICA

Perhaps it will come as a surprise to many sportsmen to learn that there are about one hundred and three recognized species of bears in North America. It used to be thought that our bears were only some half-dozen in number, the Black, Cinnamon, Grizzly and Silver Tip, "Kodiak" bear, and Polar bear. We now know that such popular classifications of our bears was far from correct. Our present knowledge of the American bears is due largely to untiring work and long years of study and research on the part of Dr. C. Hart Merriam. While a very large amount of work has been done, yet our knowledge of American bears is not yet complete, and Dr. Merriam himself states that the present classification must be regarded as tentative and subject to revision, that there are still many gaps in the series, and that many years must pass before the last word on the subject will be written.

"Many hunters and some writers have advanced the view that the various species of bear freely interbreed. Let those so minded ask themselves the question: If promiscuous interbreeding were to take place, what would become of the species? From the nature of the case the stability of the species depends upon the rarity of crossing with other species, for, if interbreeding were to take place frequently, the species so interbreeding would cease to exist, having merged into a common hybrid. Hybrids now and then occur, particularly in zoological gardens, but among wild animals in their native haunts they are exceedingly rare."

The family *Ursidæ*, the bears of North America, are divided into three genera as follows:

1. Genus *Euarctos*, the Black bears. Color black, brown, or cinnamon, the last two being merely color phases of the black. The bears of wooded North America. Thirteen species are recognized.

2. Genus *Ursus*, the Grizzly and Big Brown bears. Western and northwestern bears, not nearly so much of a forest animal as the black bears. The differences formerly supposed to exist between the grizzlies and the big brown bears appear, in the light of material now available, to distinguish certain groups of species from certain other groups, rather then the grizzlies collectively from the big brown bears collectively. The typical brown bears differ from the typical grizzlies in peculiarities of color, claws, skull, and teeth, but these are average differences, not ones which hold true throughout the group. Eighty-six species are recognized.

3. Genus *Thalarctos*, the Polar bears. White bears ranging along the arctic coast of North America and adjacent islands, living largely on the ice flows, sometimes at considerable distance from land. Four species are recognized.

"What is most needed today to complete our scientific knowledge of the bear family is a series of adults, particularly of uninjured skulls, and if possible of pelts, collected by absolutely trustworthy persons and labeled on the spot for locality and sex. Many specimens in museums are not labeled for sex; others have the sex wrongly marked; and many either lack localities or the localities given are open to serious doubt. A specimen is of little value unless one can pin his faith on the label. Many bears now roaming the wilds will have to be killed and their skulls and skins sent to museums before their characters and variations will be fully understood and before it will be possible to construct accurate maps of their ranges. Persons having the means and ambition to hunt big game may be assured that bears are still common in many parts of British Columbia, Yukon Territory, and Alaska, and that much additional material is absolutely required to settle the questions still in doubt." *

* "Review of the Grizzly and Big Brown Bears of North America."—C. Hart Merriam. U. S. Dept. of Agriculture, Biological Survey. North American Fauna No. 41, 1918.

CHAPTER XII

THE BIG BROWN BEARS

The Big Brown Bears of Alaska are the largest carnivorous animals in the world. Specimens of these bears have been killed which actually weighed 1650 pounds,* and it is probable that some killed but not weighed would have nearly reached 2,000 pounds. Some of them stand almost five feet high at the shoulders, and skins have been obtained which measure more than 13 feet in length. Mr. James H. Kidder states that the largest bear of this kind which he shot measured 8 feet in a straight line from his nose to the end of the vertebræ, and stood 51½ inches in a straight line at the shoulders, not including between 6 and 7 inches of hair. They are huge in bulk, powerful of limb, and stand very high at the shoulders in comparison with their length. The hind-quarters are higher in proportion than those of our other bears, there not being so much slope to the rear in the profile. The head is normally carried very low, and is of large size, skulls with a basal length of 20 inches, and a width across the zygomatic arches of 12 inches being on record. The pelage varies from a very dark brown, sometimes almost black, to golden or a light cream color.

The range of the big brown bears is the coast mountains of Alaska, usually only the Pacific slope thereof, north and west to the western end of the Alaska Peninsula. They also occur on certain of the larger islands off the coast of Alaska, notably Admiralty, Kruzof, Barnof, Chichagof, Hinchinbrook, Montague, and Kodiak Islands. On Kodiak Island the majority of the bears were killed by the exceedingly deep fall of ash which resulted from the eruption of Mt. Katmai on the Alaskan Peninsula, July 6, 1912, but in recent years they have multiplied in considerable numbers so that they are now (1926) quite plentiful again. I have just recently had the pleasure of viewing a

---

* Dr. Will Chase.

most remarkable moving picture of the brown bears on Kodiak Island, taken by Mr. Arthur Young and a companion. Among the pictures is one of a mother bear and her cub fishing for salmon in a stream. It was very wonderful to see the mother strike the salmon out on to the bank as she waded up the stream, and also to see the little cub struggling with the strong current in the rapids, its anxiety to keep up with its mother and yet not get wet, and finally the frantic joy with which it pounced on a salmon which its mother had struck out on the bank for it. Brown bears are decidedly an animal of the Alaskan coast mountains and of the sea-coast, and in the very rare instances where they are found inland to any considerable distance it is probable that they have been driven there by the encroachment of civilization on the coast. They hibernate in the mountains during the winter months, and spend most of their lives there, but in the summer they come down to the lowlands, swamps, salmon rivers, and sea-coast to feed.

Brown bears usually go into winter quarters and hibernate late in October. The place chosen is often a hole under some projecting cliff or overhanging rock high up in the mountains, or in an old windfall, or even in one of the holes in an alder thicket which they dig in the summer. If there is no overhang to the place they will often simply lie down and let the snow drift over them. They, however, always seem to choose a place which is dry. Here they remain throughout the winter, although during the first month or so they may come forth once in a while and make short trips. Also, occasionally, one will be found roaming around in the dead of winter, probably because the den was unsuitable or uncomfortable, or because of some physical incapacity which made them restless. After the first month or so they apparently lie absolutely dormant and still in their winter sleep, so much so that often when they come out the hair will be worn or matted on some particular spot on which they have been lying. They come out of their dens about May 1 to June 1, the young bears appearing first, and the extremely large males and females with young last. When they first appear they are very fat, but this wears off quickly. Their feet are also tender at this time, and for the first few days they only make short journeys from their dens, perhaps returning to them at night, and lying around on the summits of the moun-

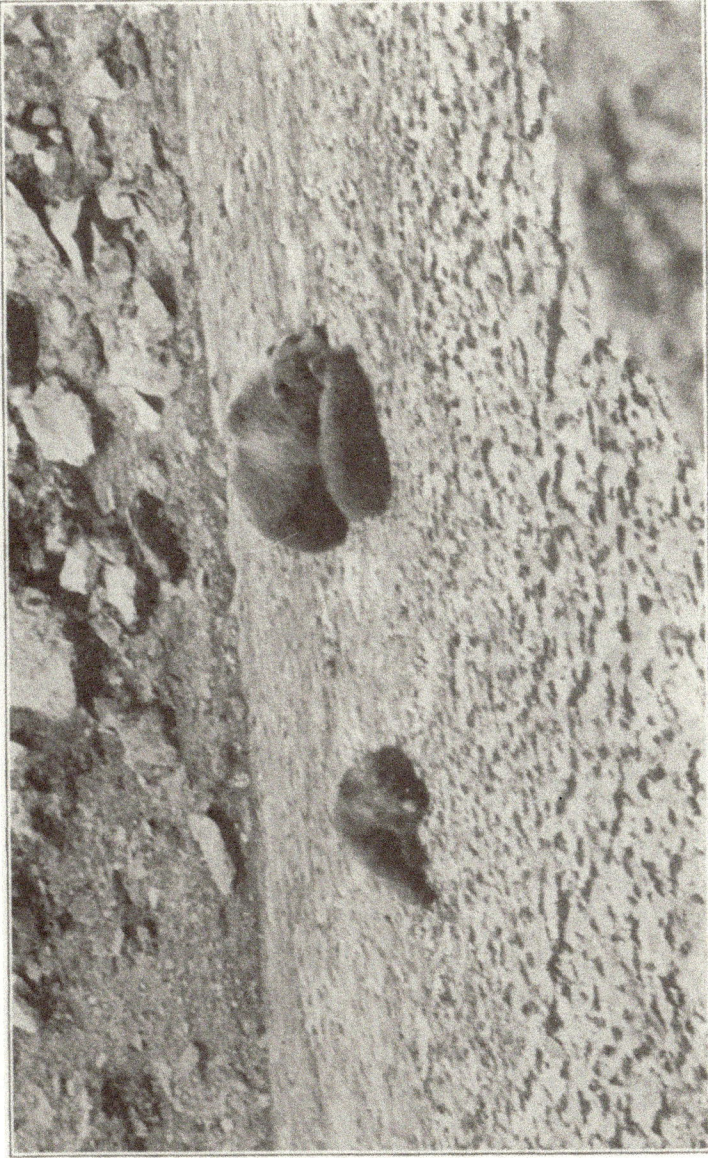

A BIG BROWN BEAR MOTHER AND CUBS WERE DISCOVERED ASLEEP BY MR. E. MALLINCKRODT, JR.

STONES WERE THROWN AT THEM TO AWAKEN THEM

THE MOTHER BEAR LOOKS BACK ANXIOUSLY AS SHE AND HER CUBS CLIMB TO SAFETY

tains in the sun in the daytime. During this period they are
feeding on ground squirrels which they dig up, and on bugs
which they find under the rocks, and a little later in early morning
and late afternoon they graze on the green grass which springs
up in the slides on the mountain sides. The male bears travel
almost continuously shortly after they come out in the spring,
and until about the first of July, this being the rutting season,
but otherwise the brown bears are abroad and feed generally
early in the morning and late in the afternoon, and in the middle
of the day they retire to some secluded place to sleep. At this
time of year in their habitat there is of course almost continual
daylight. As the spring progresses into summer they come down
from the high mountains into the lowlands, often to swampy
places, where they feed on marsh grass and on skunk cabbage
of which they are very fond. At this season they often lie in
wallows of mud and water to cool off and to rid themselves
of the gnats and mosquitoes. They are very much like hogs in
this respect and they will go out of their way to wallow in swamps
in the hot summer days, and at this time of year their fur is
scarcely ever dry. Then, when the salmon start to run up-stream,
the bears frequent the banks to feed on these. They wade or
stand in the stream and as the salmon swim by on their way up-
stream they strike them with their paw in such a manner as to
throw them out on the bank, and the bear then rushes out and
bites the salmon on the back of the neck, killing it. During the
summer they also feed on salmon berries and the roots of salmon
berry bushes, on wild strawberries, blueberries, birds' eggs, and
on mussels and shell-fish which they find on the beaches, so
that when fall comes, and it is time to retire to their winter dens,
they are hog-fat.

The female bear has one to three cubs every other year. They
are born during January in the winter den, and their mother
suckles them, although in a state of semi-torpor. They are
born hairless and with their eyes closed, and are exceedingly
small, being only about the size of a grey squirrel. The cubs
remain with their mother and follow her around all of their first
summer, and den up with her again that fall. They leave her,
or are driven off by her or by some male bear the following spring
or early summer, and thereafter they shift for themselves.

The best time to hunt brown bears is in the early spring,

during the months of May and early June. At that time their fur is in excellent condition, although not quite equal to the fall coat just before they hibernate. When they come out of their dens during May they wander around over the mountains in search of food, and the big males travel almost continuously in search of a mate. At these times they are very conspicuous against the white snow which still persists in the high mountains. The method of hunting is to climb to some high summit and examine and watch the mountainsides with field glasses. When a bear is seen it is stalked like any other mountain game, paying particular attention to the wind, for the bear's sense of smell is exceedingly acute. His hearing is good also, but his long-range vision is apparently rather poor. Hip rubber boots are often necessary in this early-spring shooting, on account of the wet, slushy character of the snow in the mountains. Later in the spring when the salmon begin to run and the skunk cabbage begins to get large and green, the bears come down from the high mountains, and then about the only practical way of getting them is to watch some likely spot on the bank of a salmon stream, or perhaps overlooking some marsh or alder thicket where tracks and paths indicate that the bears are present.

The localities in the mountains which these bears are inhabiting in the spring can often be told by seeing their tracks in the snow with field glasses. At this time of year the hunter can often tell a fresh trail from an old one at a considerable distance, for with the soft, wet, melting snow the crisp edges and definition of the foot-prints soon fade out and an old trail becomes little more than a shadow or line when viewed through binoculars. But when every foot-print is clear cut and distinct when viewed through binoculars, the trail is probably a very fresh one, and worth following, always, however, paying strict attention to the wind. The hind feet of a big male brown bear will sometimes reach a length of 18 inches and a width of 12 inches.

In the lowlands, if bears are about and plentiful, their tracks and paths will be very much in evidence along the streams and leading to and from the marshes and swamps where they have been feeding; also leading into the alder thickets where the bears have big holes which they dig and where they lie up during the heat of the middle of the day to keep cool and to avoid observation. In hunting in and around these lowland feeding grounds

the sportsman must be very careful where he goes and how he
tracks up the country, for the bear's sense of smell is exceedingly
acute, and he will smell a fresh man-track at a considerable
distance, or an old one for a long time after it has been made
if he should cross it, and one whiff of the tainted air and the
bear is off. Moreover, if the hunter tracks up the surrounding
country much the bears will soon clear out of that country completely. Where it is possible to do so it is best to travel to and
from the lookout points in a canoe or bidarka, and to pitch the
camp at a considerable distance from the lowland feeding grounds
of the bears.

In some sections the big brown bears have established quite
a reputation for ferocity, probably on account of one lone incident
which has been greatly magnified in the telling, and exaggerated
as time passes. So, with no more evidence, misguided and igno-
rant people have said that they should be exterminated, and efforts
in that direction have actually been started in some localities
from time to time. All this is entirely unwarranted. The big
brown bear left alone, is entirely harmless, and is naturally
extremely shy of man. It is true that if they are attacked and
wounded they will charge the hunter in a larger proportion of
cases than with our other bears, and when they do this, on
account of their bulk and strength they are most formidable
adversaries. But no animal should be condemned for defending
itself. The cases where big brown bears have attacked human
beings unprovoked are so extremely rare as to be almost unknown, although there are many unproved tales going around
in the North, where gossip flies as fast as it does anywhere else,
and where a good tale is never spoiled in the telling. But similar
incidents occur with every other animal—even dogs go mad,
but we do not advocate exterminating the dog for that reason.
Dr. Will Chase of Alaska has had perhaps as much if not more
experience with brown bears than any other man living, and has
written a most able series of articles on these bears in which he
says: "Owing to many unwarranted tales which have been cir-
culated, generally by people who have never even seen an Alaskan
brown bear in his native element, a fear born of prejudice has
developed against this most interesting and absolutely harmless
animal. The idea that Alaskan brown bears will deliberately
attack one without provocation is absolutely without foundation.

On the other hand, they are so timid and alert against the approach of man that many hunters come to Alaska each year to hunt them, and return after months of the hardest kind of work without ever having seen one. It is true that a man is occasionally hurt or killed by a bear, but this is the exception, and generally the man was hunting and had injured the bear before the attack. Or in some cases the man had suddenly run into one in a close place and the bear had knocked him down, and perhaps bitten him badly. * * * Innumerable cases are on record proving that domestic animals have attacked, bitten, and mauled people; but I cannot possibly conceive why the species should be condemned to extermination because of the act of an outlaw. Even humans sometimes go on a rampage and commit overt acts which call for censure. Let us all, as Americans, get together and preserve enough of our fast-disappearing wild life to at least perpetuate the species."

A rifle taking a fairly heavy cartridge should be used for the big brown bears. They are large, tough, heavy brutes, and it takes a fair amount of power to drive a bullet into the vitals, particularly at the long ranges at which many shots present themselves. Moreover, occasionally a bear will charge the hunter when wounded. The statement that no cartridge will kill unless it hits in a vital area is perhaps more true of the Alaskan brown bear than of any other American animal. The bear must be struck in a vital area to kill, and a medium-power modern rifle will do this just as well as the heaviest rifle made. The big-bore magnum rifles, when they do not strike in vital spots, will not kill any quicker or surer than other rifles or cartridges. It is an advantage to have a rifle of fine accuracy, flat trajectory, and with such light recoil that it can be shot rapidly with accuracy. Mr. Charles Sheldon used a .256 Mannlicher rifle for years on these bears with perfect success, and Mr. James H. Kidder used a .30-40 Winchester, both rifles of very medium power. It is my opinion that rifles of the .30-30 class are not powerful enough, particularly they do not give quite enough assurance of stopping a charge. On the other hand I should consider that the Springfield .30-06 cartridge, with one of its excellent, heavy, big-game loads was amply sufficient.

CHAPTER XIII

THE GRIZZLY BEARS

The Grizzly Bear occupies a unique position in the history of the animals of North America. It is inseparably connected with the early exploration and settling of our West. A large, powerful, and aggressive beast, and very difficult to kill with bow and arrow, it was practically never molested by the primitive Indian, and so our early explorers found it absolutely fearless of man. These first white men found it a tough customer to deal with for their small-bore, muzzle-loading rifles were almost as inadequate for the task as the arrows of the Indian had been. Such was the fearlessness and aggressiveness of the grizzly of a hundred years ago that he usually showed fight when wounded by these light weapons, and hence he gained a reputation as the embodiment of all that is ferocious and terrible among big game animals. This reputation still stands in public estimation, although the grizzly bear of today is usually a far different animal in character from those of a hundred years ago. He is now exceedingly shy as a rule and has the greatest dread of man. In the great majority of cases he will no longer attack or charge if wounded, even when he sees the hunter and seemingly appreciates that it is he who has caused the hurt. The reason for this great change in the heart of the former terror of the western mountains and plains is just one thing—modern rifles. The grizzly has been very quick to notice the difference in the weapons that are brought to bear on him. Our hunters and frontiersmen began to lose their dread of grizzly bears when Samuel Hawken of St. Louis started to make heavier muzzle-loading percussion rifles for the use of the hunters, trappers and adventurers starting into the Far West. These rifles carried a heavy ball and a large charge of powder, and they quickly took the place of the old

149

Kentucky small-bore, flintlock pea rifles. Then came the breech-loading Sharps rifle, taking a cartridge with still heavier charge of powder and lead, followed by the Winchester Centennial Model rifle, with its .45-75-350 cartridge, and in late years the modern high-power rifles. Today the very adequately armed sportsman finds that the shy and evasive grizzly is usually no longer to be dreaded, and that almost invariably it hunts the tall timber at the first sight or taint of the man animal.

The grizzly bear is deep brown in color, darker along the spine and on the limbs and ears. The hairs on the upper body have white tips which give it a grizzled or "silver tip" appearance. In some instances these hairs are white tipped to such an extent that at a distance the bear appears dirty white. On most grizzly bears there is so much of this white-tipped hair behind the shoulder that it appears as a white patch. The face is concave in outline, while that of the black bear is nearly straight and the polar bear concave in profile. There is a maned hump on its back over the shoulders, and the front claws are very large in size, but little curved, and about twice the length of the hind claws. The face, hump, and claws serve to distinguish it almost at a glance from the brown phase of the black bear, but it is not at present possible to distinguish it by external characters from some of the species of the big brown bears. Grizzlies are rather deceptive as to weight and size, and hunters almost always overestimate both these qualities in the bears they have seen or killed. The California grizzly probably grew to a greater size than any other of the species, but even so it is doubtful if it ever reached 1,000 pounds weight in its native wild. A very large male grizzly will stand about 3½ to 4 feet high at the shoulders, and will weigh from 600 to 700 pounds.

The original range of the grizzly bear was very wide. It extended from northwestern Mexico almost to the arctic coast, and from the Pacific coast all over the western portion of North America to western Texas, western Kansas, central Nebraska, the western Dakotas, Manitoba, and to the Mackenzie River in the north. Today the range has become very much restricted. It is generally extinct in the United States. There may still be an occasional grizzly roaming around in Arizona, Idaho, and northwestern Montana, and in Yellowstone Park they are of course protected and fairly plentiful, and have become quite tame. Wild grizzly bears are still to be found in northwestern Alberta, British Columbia, Yukon Territory, and Alaska, and in some remote localities are still fairly plentiful. One related species *(richardsoni)* is found a short distance inland from the arctic coast all the way from the delta of the Mackenzie River to about the head of Chesterfield Inlet on Hudson Bay.

Originally the grizzly was an animal of the plains as well as of the mountains, but he has long since been exterminated on the plains, except on the arctic prairies of the far north. The typical home of this bear is high, rolling uplands where open country alternates with rocky ridges and densely wooded thickets. Today the grizzly has been forced to its last stand in the mountains of our northwest and in these mountains it finds the conditions which are to its liking at and around timberline. So much so is this now the case that the grizzly of today may almost be said to be a timberline animal, and it seems to come lower down in the mountains only when the food conditions above are not to its liking, or perhaps when some salmon stream offers a special inducement, or berries or other fruit entice it down. In its preference for such country it differs greatly from the black bear which is essentially a forest animal.

The food of the grizzly is meat of all kinds, salmon and other fish when obtainable, berries, fruits, ants, grubs, and larvæ, and grass. They will eat almost any dead game that they come across, no matter how spoiled it may be, and in times past they have often been killed by using some dead animal, or specially killed animal for bait, and watching the carcass early in the mornings and late in the evenings. Grizzlies will often kill their own meat, and in days gone by in western United States they often played havoc among the sheep and cattle of the ranchers. A friend told me of seeing a grizzly bear chase a cow moose and her calf for over three miles until they went out of sight, and when last seen the grizzly was apparently gaining on the moose. But most of the meat that falls to the grizzly bears of today consists of ground squirrels and gophers which they dig out of their holes.

Grizzly bears are sometimes quite troublesome to trappers and other mountain dwellers, breaking into their cabins while they are absent to get any food which may be inside. In some mountain localities where these bears are numerous I have seen the cabins made with the frames of the windows and doors beveled down flush, and thick shutters provided for the windows so that the smooth surface does not offer the bear any chance hold with his claws when he attempts to break in.   There is one well authenticated story of a trapper returning to his cabin and meeting a grizzly emerging from the door with the little sheet-iron stove in its arms.   I once arrived at a cabin where there was considerable food cached, and on which we had planned to rely for several weeks, only to find that a bear had broken in and demolished almost everything.   There had been a sack of beans, and a pack rat had cached all these in the fire-box of the stove, and they were still in good condition, so we did not run entirely out of grub.

It will be noted that I stated at the beginning of this chapter that the grizzly of today is *usually* shy and has the greatest dread of man.   This is not invariably the case, there being an occasional exception where a certain bear has shown all the ferocity for which he has been famed.   There are any number of instances where these bears have attacked human beings unprovoked, and a still greater number where they have charged viciously when wounded. But I imagine that all these cases together have not been one per cent of the cases where the bear has shown nothing but dread or endeavor to get away.   I quote from a letter from Mr. F. W. Riggall, a very experienced guide of Twin Butte, Alberta, Canada, relative to the grizzlies of the eastern slope of the Rockies just north of the International Boundary, which sheds some very inter-esting light on this subject.

"You will note that I said that our bears are big, savage, and fear-less, and I want to tell you that there is an awful lot of difference in the disposition of the grizzlies in different sections, not far apart perhaps in miles.   For instance, in this particular section the griz-zlies are *all* cattle killers, and come right into the corrals and kill milk cows and calves close to the buildings, sometimes in broad day-light, but usually at night.   They run cattle for miles, like a hound, and several times have been seen to chase an animal across country and kill close to the home ranch.   They act here a good deal like lions in Africa, and at times my neighbors have set up all night with rifles and listened to the bears killing or chasing cattle 'round the houses and barns.

"Now, here is a strange thing.   Fifty to seventy-five miles north of here the grizzlies are *quite* different, and *never* or almost never kill cattle, although a thousand head of cattle are ranged in the mountains

Photo by F. K. Vreeland

WILD GRIZZLY IN NORTHWESTERN WYOMING

Courtesy U. S. Biological Survey

right up to, and sometimes stray over, the Continental Divide, with grizzly tracks and diggings all over, yet for years I have never known a grizzly to touch a cow! Here the bears come out of the mountains to the ranches to kill every fall regularly, and there the cows invade the grizzlies' own territory in summer and fall with perfect impunity.

"When Stewart Edward White wrote of 'Dangerous Game' in the *Saturday Evening Post,* he never mentioned 'Grizzlies and Small-pox,' but when you interpose the word 'Indians' between, it tells a whole lot that is not generally known about bears. Forty to sixty years ago the Indians here (Stonies) camped in small groups all through the mountains in the sheep, deer, goat, and bear country, and while so camped, in would ride a relative from a small-pox-infested camp, and in ten days half the camp would be dead or dying, and the survivors would leave all the tepees standing and ride off to spread the plague to other camps. Pretty soon the grizzlies here found that they could invade the tepees without fear and feed on the dead, and after a while on the dying, and from that it was only a step, soon taken, to hunting the unaffected Indians in after years, and they did so hunt them in certain sections, and taught their cubs to do so also; and some of those cubs are alive today, the Stonies declare, and I believe them! When I came here this was a wonderful hunting country, simply because the Stonies were too afraid of these grizzlies to venture into the game country, and up the best canyons no old Indian trails led through the timber at the mouths to the basins at the head. I had to cut these trails myself; and although each spring and fall the bands of Stonies passed, none would venture over my trails, and some of them at different times told me why, and warned me that the bears there were bad actors and would smell and stalk an Indian without hesitation, and myself also if I did not watch out! I had two *very* close calls from bears there the first year or two, and killed both bears within a few feet of me, and I believe that these bears were old timers who knew what human flesh tasted like, and were not at all averse to trying it again. I have since shot and killed grizzlies in many places as far north as the Big Smoky, and down in Montana on both sides of the divide, and I know that without question the bears here and just across in British Columbia and Montana are more savage and aggressive than in other sections. I am sure that this is not generally known or appreciated, so I have gone into some detail, as I think you will find it interesting and probably new.

"Another strange thing in this connection: Some years ago a few bunches of sheep were brought into the foothill country, but down there the coyotes were so bad in the brush that the sheep men beat a hasty retreat (and incidentally avoided serious trouble with the old-time cow-men). However, a few years ago—1915-1917—a bunch of 300 to 500 head were run on privately owned and fenced land 18 miles north of here by Ted Whipple of MacLeod, for the summer season, and during all that time not one sheep was known to be killed by the coyotes. The reason was that the coyotes there did not know what sheep were, or that they were good to eat. If they had ever started killing they would have killed half the herd in a month, but the sheep were not in there in the winter, and there were no deaths in the flock in the summer, so the coyotes never got a taste of mutton. Likewise I predict that if ever a cow-beast is killed by a grizzly in the section fifty to seventy-five miles north of here, the cattle men will have to kill all the bears off, or draw their cattle out of the mountain range, or lose a hundred head a year."

Grizzly bears hibernate in very much the same way as the Alaskan brown bears. They usually go into their winter dens some time in November, depending upon the depth of the snow, and emerge in May or June, the big males appearing first, and the females with young last. However, in the southern parts of the United States and Mexico there seemed to have been many grizzlies which did not hibernate at all. Apparently the controlling condition is the snowfall, and bears have developed the hibernating habit largely because they have been unable to get food on account of the depth of the snow.

The rutting season extends from June to August. One, two, and sometimes three cubs are born in the winter den of the female about January. The cubs at birth weigh about eight ounces, and are approximately the size of grey squirrels. The female breeds only every other, or every third year. Cubs remain with their mothers during their first summer, and usually den up with her again that fall. The following spring, when they come out of the den they leave her, or she drives them off, or they are driven off by some male grizzly.

Grizzlies are hunted today by packing into their country in the high mountains in May or early in June, and watching the mountainsides and slides with binoculars from some good lookout point. When a bear is seen it is stalked in a manner similar to other mountain game. Many grizzly bears are also seen and killed in the fall of the year when the sportsman is hunting sheep, goats, or caribou around timberline, and a few are killed when they are frequenting salmon streams in the summer.

My first adventure with a grizzly was not very successful, but it taught me a good lesson. Bill Andrews, an old time wilderness hunter and mountain man, and I were taking our pack-train up the north fork of Bridge River in the Lillooet

District, British Columbia. This morning I was riding in front and Bill behind driving the animals along over the route I was selecting. We were going along a bench about 40 feet above the river, which here was about twenty yards wide, when I saw a bear on the gravel flat on the opposite side of the stream. I jumped off my horse, dropped the reins over its head, jerked the rifle out of its scabbard, and sat down on the edge of the bench. The bear looked enormous to me. It was clawing at a fallen rotten log after ants. The distance was only about seventy-five yards, and as the bead settled down behind the bear's shoulders I squeezed off the trigger. At the shot the long hair on the bear's shoulders stood straight up. It whirled around and started off at a gallop, the hair rippling just exactly like a field of grain in the wind. I got in another shot before it disappeared in the willows. A few seconds later Bill came up and wanted to know what I was shooting at. We rounded up the horses, tied them to trees, and were about to cross the stream after the bear when I made a discovery. I had been shooting grouse loads! My rifle was a .30-30 Winchester, and for small game I had loaded a lot of cartridges with a 125-grain lead bullet designed by Horace Kephart and 10 grains of bulk du Pont smokeless powder. That morning, not expecting to see anything larger than grouse to shoot while traveling with the pack-train, I had loaded the rifle with these cartridges, There was, of course, no use of going after that bear. Ever since that day I have made it a rule to always carry my rifle, both barrel and magazine, loaded with full charged cartridges. I also carry ten rounds of full charged cartridges in my belt in a little cartridge box, but in my right hand trousers pocket I carry a few reduced loads for grouse and other small game. If I see any small game that I wish to shoot I take the full charged cartridge out of the barrel, and insert the reduced load, but I never go on again without changing back to the full load. I have used reduced loads in my big game rifle now for twenty-eight years, and they have proved most useful, and brought in a lot of very welcome camp meat, and this experience is the only time I have gotten caught with such loads in my rifle when big game was sighted.

One day I climbed a high mountain just to "look behind the ranges." When I got to the top the farther side fell off in an enormous cliff into a deep valley, on the opposite side of which rose another mountain with steep, wooded sides streaked by slides in which grew many small berry bushes and aspen trees. I sat down and got out the little brass ten-power telescope that I carried inside my shirt (in those days I did not have enough money to buy such expensive things as prism binoculars) and started to look the country over. On the ridge on the opposite mountain were three goats, and I watched them for some minutes. Then I started to examine the slides, and after a couple of minutes a female grizzly and two cubs came into the field of view of the telescope. I propped up the telescope with a few rocks and studied this family for over two hours. The mother was feeding on berries. She would walk up to a bush, rise up on her hind legs, reach out and sweep a bunch of branches in close with her fore-paws, and bite and lick the berries off, the two cubs the while played around near her. They would chase each other up and down and along the side of the mountain, never getting over about 50 yards from their mother. Then they would have great wrestling matches, and would clinch and roll over and over down the mountain, then separate, and stand up on their hind legs and look at each other, and then go at it again. Finally they appeared to get tired out, and they walked up near their mother, who paid not the slightest attention to them, and laid down and went to sleep, and so I left them in time to get back to my own camp before dark. It was one of the grandest sights I have seen in nature. I would not have disturbed that happy family for anything in the world. I think that female bears with cubs should be absolutely protected. Probably sentiment is the only way to do it. It is pardonable and often unavoidable to kill a female bear, for it is almost impossible to tell the two sexes apart, but at least a female with cubs should never be shot. She and her family should be game for the camera only.

As I have stated before I think that most grizzlies that are killed in the fall of the year are just happened on by luck when the sportsmen are looking for other mountain game. One evening early in October Stanley Clark and I pitched our tepee in a lovely little canyon deep in the heart of the northern Canadian Rockies. The country was entirely new to both of us, and we decided to spend the next day scouting around for game signs. Stanley chose to go west, and I east to investigate a high range of mountains to the east. I climbed all over that range all day long and saw nothing but old sheep sign, but I was repaid by a most delightful view of an enormous mountain mass far to the west where I could see a very high peak bearing a glacier on its side. That evening when Stanley got back to camp he had an exciting tale to tell. To the west he had found the valley of a large river, beyond which was a high range of snow-capped peaks. While examining this range with his binoculars he had seen an animal above timberline. Watching closely as possible at the distance of three or four miles he had seen that the animal would apparently spend quite a little time in one spot, and then move quickly to another spot and spend some minutes there. Only a bear digging up ground squirrels or gophers, or digging for roots will act in this way. Also it was extremely unlikely that a black bear would be so high above timberline out in the open as this one was, therefore it must be a grizzly. That evening we planned a campaign. The country to the west was far too rough for horses, so we decided to take light back packs over into the valley below the range on which the bear was, and hunt that range for three or four days.

We reached the river by noon the following day, quickly put up our light shelter cloth as a lean-to, and started up the range for a preliminary look around. It had been threatening rain all day, and when we got up to timberline, a climb of some four thousand feet, it was snowing hard and blowing a regular blizzard. It was difficult to see anything, although we did get glimpses of a large caribou and a bull moose. We were forced to descend again without really getting close to where Stanley had seen the bear. For four days it snowed and stormed, and the top of the range was continually shrouded in snow and clouds making it impossible to see anything. We spent the time making short hunts and trips from our little lean-to, and one morning I was successful in getting a very fine specimen of bull caribou with a splendid head. This also helped out on the food problem, for the grub that we had packed in was getting very low. Finally the fifth morning it looked as though the storm and the clouds were breaking away down the valley, so we decided to try our bear mountains again. When we arrived at timberline the clouds still hung low, and the side slopes were covered with a foot of very wet, slippery snow, but apparently there was a gleam of the sun through the clouds. We waited in hopes that the clouds would lift, making a fire with the dead roots of some small alpine firs, boiled a kettle of tea, and had a light lunch of caribou steak. After lunch, while monkeying around I discovered fresh bear tracks in the snow, apparently made only several hours ago. Following them up it was found

Photo by W. J. Bell   *Courtesy U. S. Forest Service*
GRIZZLY BEAR IN EARLY SPRING, JUST AFTER LEAVING WINTER DEN,
MONTANA

that the bear was digging up roots and just wandering aimlessly around the mountain. By this time it looked still more as though the clouds might lift any minute, but they were still so thick that we could not see more than fifty yards in any direction. We decided to go along the mountainside, Stanley keeping about a hundred yards below me so that we would get the maximum range of vision. After probably half a mile, the cloud began to blow down the mountain, we could see a hundred yards, and then two hundred yards, and then suddenly I made out the form of a bear looking like a ghost in the mist. My experience has been that a bear can get out of sight quicker than any animal that I know of, and when he moves he moves awfully sudden, so I lost no time in throwing a bullet into him, the range being about two hundred yards. At the shot the bear rolled over, started to bawl terribly, and bite at one of his feet. Before I could fire again he was on his feet, and running off. My second shot was fired before he had gone ten yards, and at the report he dropped his head, and curled up like a big ball of fur, rolled down the mountainside into the cloud and out of sight. We followed as quickly as possible and came on him a quarter of a mile below, stone dead. A bear is always a "he" until he is dead, but in this case, as often happens, the sex changed on close examination. It was a fair-sized female with a splendid coat of prime fur. The 180-grain open-point Lubaloy bullet from my old Springfield rifle had struck her just behind the shoulder, and had gone completely through, blowing the heart to pieces. The first shot had struck one fore-paw. While we were at the skinning the cloud descended and hung in the valley below us. Above its billowy sea of white we could see the snow-capped peaks of the range across the valley gleaming in the sunlight, a very fit setting for the killing of a grizzly.

The range of the individual grizzly is probably rather restricted. Seton states that a typical grizzly of today in ordinary mountain country will ramble over a home-region at least 25 miles across. This tendency to confine itself to one particular locality, and not to wander far is probably one of the reasons why there are so many species of grizzly bears, and why these species have not merged into a common hybrid. The old-time grizzly of the plains, however, was probably quite a wanderer, as he undoubtedly followed the buffalo herds, and the barrel-ground grizzly of today also probably wanders over a much larger area than the mountain grizzly.

In the south, in Mexico for example, the grizzly does not usually den up for the winter because the absence of deep snow enables it to obtain food the year around. The claws on the fore-feet of the grizzly are much longer and straighter than those of other bears, and this is the reason why grizzlies cannot climb trees. Also the long claws are clearly indicated in the track in favorable ground, and provide the means of distinguishing the track of a grizzly from that of other bears. The presence of grizzlies in a country can often be determined by their habit of biting trees high up, perhaps as high as six feet from the ground, tearing the bark open crosswise, or marking trees with their claws. These marked trees are probably their "sign posts," serving to assist them in locating other bears in that country.

A description of the grizzly bear from the standpoint of its hunting would not be complete without reference to Colonel William D. Pickett, probably the most experienced grizzly bear hunter. Colonel Pickett, a veteran of the War with Mexico, and a colonel in the Confederate Army during the Civil War, hunted these bears almost continuously in Montana and Wyoming from 1876 to 1883. Afterwards he settled on a ranch on the Grey Bull River in Wyoming where he continued his investigations. Since then he has twice represented Fremont County, Wyoming, in the State Legislature, and was State Senator from Big Horn County. He was a thorough sportsman, and a skilled rifleman, and his observations are accurate and truthful. He killed a very great many grizzlies with his old Sharps-Borchard rifle taking the .45-caliber long-range cartridge, and capable of using charges of black powder up to a maximum of 125 grains. His account of these experiences with grizzlies has been published in *"Hunting at High Altitudes,"* one of the works published by the Boone and Crockett Club, and makes most interesting and instructive reading.

CHAPTER XIV

THE BLACK BEARS

Thirteen species of the genus *Euarctos,* the Black Bears, have been recognized and described. This bear is essentially a forest animal, and was originally distributed over practically the whole of forested North America, from central Mexico and Florida, north to the limit of trees. It is still plentiful in most of forested Canada and Mexico back from the settlements, but naturally has become extinct in many parts of the United States. It is still found in Maine, and occasionally in New Hampshire, Vermont, and New York, and in some of the Southern States. It has become fairly plentiful in Pennsylvania. It is generally extinct in the Central States, but found in fair numbers in many of the Rocky Mountain and Pacific States.

In eastern North America the typical black bear is a deep, glossy black in color, except the muzzle which is brown, and sometimes there is a white spot on the breast. But as one goes west more and more of the bears are of a cinnamon or brown color, until in the Rocky Mountains fully one-fourth of the black bears are brown or cinnamon. A black mother may have cinnamon cubs, or vice-versa. Many female black bears have been seen with one black and one cinnamon cub, so that the variation between deep black and light cinnamon is only a color phase, and there is no such thing in America as a species of cinnamon bear. A fair-size, fat, black bear is about five feet long, a little over two feet high, and weighs about 300 pounds. Some species run larger, and some smaller. The Florida species, *floridanus,* for example, is seemingly quite a little larger than this average. Some very large males have been known to weigh slightly over 500 pounds, but these must be regarded as exceptions. The cinnamon or brown color phase of the black bear can be told from the grizzly and big brown bears by the profile of its nose, face, and forehead, which is almost straight or slightly

163

Roman nosed, and its short claws. The other bears have a facial profile which is slightly or decidedly concave.

The black bear is essentially a forest animal and a solitary animal. It is very seldom that two full-grown black bears are seen together except during the mating season, or perhaps when feeding on some dead animal, and they are seldom seen in open country. They are very timid and wary, and if the least alarmed they will make off with the greatest speed. They have a curious habit of scratching, tearing and biting trees. On birch, aspen, and poplar trees particularly the claw and teeth marks show up very distinctly, sometimes as high as six feet or more from the ground. This is probably the method taken by the bears of locating one another. A range in which black bears are plentiful can be told by these tree marks, and also by the trails that the bears make. A well-used bear trail can be told by its being made up most decidedly of tracks, for every bear seems to tread exactly where the bear preceding him trod. Also such a trail will go under many branches and logs, for a black bear stands only a little over two feet high, and they go under objects rather than over them, while the trail made by any of the cervidæ will usually avoid any obstacle which is about two and a half to four feet above the ground.

In their food habits, black bears are very omnivorous. They live on roots, grass, bark of young trees, berries, fruit of all kinds, insects (especially ants), honey, and even the bees themselves, fish, small animals, and carrion. About the only time that they are an annoyance to man is when they overcome their timidity and take to killing calves, sheep, pigs, and poultry.

The mating season of the black bear is in June, or occasionally as late as early in July. The female breeds normally only every other year, although if it should be so unfortunate as to lose its cubs during their first summer it will often breed again the following spring. One, two, or three cubs are born in January in the winter den of the mother. At birth they are about 8 inches long and weigh about 9 to 12 ounces. They are born hairless and with their eyes closed. Like our other bears, the cubs remain with their mother their first summer and den up with her the following winter, leaving her, or being driven off by her or some male, the following spring. The cubs are very playful little rascals, continually boxing and wrestling

Photo by Dr. Hopkins   Courtesy U. S. Forest Service

A FAMILY ROW. BLACK BEARS IN WASATCH NATIONAL FOREST, UTAH

BLACK BEAR MOTHER AND CUBS, TAKEN IN NORTHERN ALBERTA
ROCKIES BY H. S. CLARK

with each other, and practicing climbing various objects during all of their waking hours. Black bears are excellent tree climbers, and the speed with which one of them can climb a tree in their native wilds will astonish those who have seen these animals only in captivity.

In the north the black bear probably always hibernates in the middle of the winter, but it appears that in the United States they do not always do so, or at least only for very short periods. In fact throughout the southern portion of their range it may be said that they will only hibernate if they find it impossible to obtain food. Their winter dens may be in caves, holes in and under rocks, in hollow logs, or under logs and stumps, or under the roots of an uprooted tree, anywhere in fact where they can get some shelter.

The senses of sight, hearing, and smell of these bears is so acute that they are seldom come on by accident in the woods, and it is almost impossible to still-hunt them successfully, although one may occasionally come across one when still-hunting other game, or when paddling quietly along the bank of a river. The Canadian Indians obtain quite a few while traveling along the rivers, but most of the skins which they bring in are those of trapped bears. In the southern portion of their range about the only successful way of obtaining shots at black bear is to run them with hounds, when they tree very readily. But hunting bear with hounds, in these days when they are so scarce, should be regarded as hardly sportsmanlike, and in many States is fortunately being outlawed. In Pennsylvania, where quite a number are shot every year, they are often obtained by driving a certain piece of country with men, while the hunters take station at runways or points of vantage. If there happens to be a good tracking snow they can often be followed and obtained with its aid.

The black bear is a shy, inoffensive animal. Ernest Thompson Seton, who probably knows this animal as intimately as any field naturalist, says that a dangerous black bear is much less fre-quent than a dangerous dog or bull. It is one of the humorists of the animal world, the most human and understandable of our wild animals, easily tamed, tractable, playful in its disposi-tion, and clever at learning tricks. Its greatest misfortune is that it is a bear, and from their earliest days, starting with nursery tales, the children of the white race have been taught to regard every bear as a dangerous animal that carries off children and kills those caught out in the woods at night. Let one be seen and the whole countryside rises up in arms and hunts it to its death, and as it dies it will probably bawl like a little baby. Not so with the Indians. They always regarded the bear as their friend. Before the Whites came and set a price on its skin, it is doubtful if the Indians ever killed or disturbed bears. Even to this day the hunting Indians of Canada never shoot a bear without first begging its pardon, and afterwards its skull is always stuck up on a stick and adorned with ribbons as an act of propitiation. It is about time that we Americans woke up to what nature of animal our little black bear is, and our sportsmen should start a campaign for its protection and preservation.

CHAPTER XV

STILL-HUNTING OR WOODS HUNTING

Throughout the continent of North America big-game hunting, so far as its technique is concerned, may be generally divided into two classes, still-hunting or woods hunting, and stalking or mountain or plain hunting. The former pertains to more or less thick or forested country where the range of vision is short, and where everything tends to place one close to the animal before it is seen. The latter class deals with hunting in open country where the game is quite frequently seen and shot at a distance, and where long stretches can be *looked* over in searching for game.

The principal big-game animals of the wooded portion of North America are the deer, moose, and black bear, and occasionally the wapiti and caribou. I am here dealing with still-hunting alone, which is the only sportsmanlike way to hunt these animals. I would class calling for moose under still-hunting, because quite frequently the answer of a bull to the call merely indicates his location, and he then has to be still-hunted. Certainly the skill required to circumvent moose by calling places it in the category of legitimate sport.

For the pursuit of any animal a knowledge of its habits, of the locality, of woodcraft, and of the methods of hunting which these make necessary, are essential if one wishes to reap any great measure of success, and to have hunting remain an interesting sport for him. This chapter deals mainly in the methods of hunting for woods animals, the other matters being covered elsewhere. When game is very plentiful it is frequently encountered accidentally, but to maintain any consistent run of good luck, to obtain good heads, and, above all, to obtain game where it is scarce, knowledge and experience in all pertinent matters are necesary.

171

In any country big game will not be found evenly distributed all over it. Much of any country is unsuited to game, the feed being poor or the cover not right. In any country game will usually be found to occupy different localities at different times of the year, and also sometimes at different times of the day. A good guide knows where and when to look for animals in his own hunting country, and he saves the sporstman much time and contributes greatly to the chances for success. Put that same guide in another country and he may be all at sea for a time, but if he has hunted with his brains and used correct principles, it will take only a little scouting around for him to determine the game localities, when he will be almost as successful as in his own country. The most fascinating kind of a hunt, and one requiring the most skill and knowledge, and incidentally heaps of hard work, is where one enters a good game country that is entirely unknown to him. You start in all in the dark, but as you proceed you unravel the mystery which enshrouds the country, the animals, and their ranges. At first the creeks, lakes, hills, and other features are hidden by the forest. Little by little you discover the secrets of the silent places until you are able to map the whole country in your mind, and know just what game and fur-bearing animals it contains, where and on what they are feeding, and in what kind of a country they are laying up for the day. This is really a little intensive exploration, and to my mind it is one of the most interesting phases of hunting and wildcraft. Such a hunt may last for a day, a week, or may require much longer before one is able to obtain one of the animals he came in after. Perhaps I can do no better in the way of illustration than to describe a hunt of this kind that I took some years ago in the Canadian woods.

After a long day's hike of over 20 miles, under a heavy pack, I arrived at and camped alongside of a little lake in a big forest of which I knew next to nothing. The next morning I started around the lake and headed west, mostly on discovery bent. From the side of the lake opposite camp I saw a big mountain lying back of my camp from the lake. I fixed the appearance and contours of this mountain in my mind, and thereafter it proved a most perfect landmark which made it easy for me to find camp again. I continued on west, passing through a slightly

TYPICAL STILL-HUNTING COUNTRY OF DEER AND MOOSE, NEW BRUNSWICK. THE AUTHOR HUNTED IN THIS COUNTRY FOR SEVERAL YEARS

rolling country of pine thickets and small streams bordered with alder bushes. I made a big circle to the south, then east, then back to the camp again. I saw a few old tracks of deer on the move, but not a sign of any big animal other than this. It was not a deer country, and there was no game in it except rabbits along the creeks. The following day I climbed the mountain back of camp and spent all day on its sides. The woods were open, lots of low bushes, moosewood, whitewood, dogwood, willows in the draws. All bushes and willows had been nipped by moose, old moose tracks everyhere, but not a sign of deer. In other words, it was a moose country, but no moose were now in it. Nor were they liable to be in this country during the hunting season, for where moose frequent a country during the late summer and fall the bulls invariably leave their sign on the bushes and trees in the shape of skinned and worn bark where they rub the velvet off their horns and afterwards hook at the bushes. Also there will be lots of stamping places where the ground will be all torn up, and in damp and muddy spots there will be wallows, for moose in the early fall like to stamp around and wallow in the mud like domestic cattle. None of these signs were present in this country. I was sure seeing a lot of scenery, and I was gradually forming in my mind a beautiful topographical map of the region, but I was not finding deer. That little camp of mine was badly in need of meat, and I wanted a skin to lie on, for when one packs miles into a trackless forest he naturally has to go a little light on bedding.

The third day I headed north and ran into a different kind of country, beautiful shady woods and hills, just the right amount of bushes and underbrush in clumps rather than scattered, quite a little swampy or rather soggy land in the hollows, with green grass and a delicate little low plant that the local woodsman called "sorrel." The country had been lumbered a little many years ago, and there were places where there was lots of down timber and slashings where the sun had been let in, and raspberry bushes and little choke cherry trees had grown up. There were quite a few beech trees also on the ridges. The country was drained by many creeks, and almost every one was a continuous succession of beaver dams with their little swamps and meadows. Here and there was a knoll, almost open and meadow-like, with little clumps of balsam. I want you to remember this description carefully because it is a typical deer country of the north-east woods. Sure enough I began to see tracks of deer. I found them everywhere, fresh tracks, too, but the broad valleys where the ground was a little damp, and where the little green grass and sorrel were growing, were trampled up almost like a barn yard. A careful examination showed that the deer were browsing on the sorrel. I found acres of it with the tips all eaten off. At last I had arrived in the deer country.

Next day, the fourth, I went back there again. There was a long valley running east and west, full of deer tracks and sorrel, a fine feeding ground, but I got there after the feeding hours. On the north side of this valley was a long ridge with large trees, occasional fallen trees, little clumps of bushes, a typical place for deer to lie up in the daytime. I decided to hunt along it rather high up towards the top, because the bucks usually go a little higher than the does and fawns, and also because one's scent usually ascends, and does not descend, and by going along high up I would disturb less ground with my scent, and would have the lower hillside to hunt along if desirable on my way back. The light breeze was eddying around in all sorts of ways through the forest, and by watching the smoke of my pipe I came to the conclusion that I could walk just a little faster than that breeze was blowing, so that by stepping lively I could always beat my scent out. I was able to do this because there had been a three-days rain the week before, and the ground and leaves were still wet. Had the leaves been dry I would have had to go very slow indeed to keep from making noise that would have alarmed every deer within five hundred yards. The clouds were slowly moving from west to east so I decided to start in at the eastern end of the long ridge and hunt west. If I did not get anything in the morning I would probably work back east along the lower slopes of the ridge in the afternoon, unless the wind was decidedly unfavorable.

I had not gone very far before I jumped a deer. It was straight up the ridge from me and it had evidently gotten my rising scent. All I saw of it was a couple of flirts of its white tail as it bounded over some brush. I could not tell if it was a buck or doe, and there was no time to shoot. No use monkeying further with that deer. Nothing else did I see for an hour. Then I came to a sort of bench in the ridge. It was flat and there were clumps of trees alternating with more open places. In the clumps snow was still lying from the first fall of the season. I came to a place where it was rather open, and I could see off to my right for about 150 yards. Suddenly my subconscious mind seemed to catch something. Just what it was I cannot tell to this day, but it spelled caution. Often I have first discovered game in just this way. I stood perfectly still and waited. In about five minutes I caught a slight movement in the branch of a bush that did not seem altogether natural. By this time every sense was alert, and I watched carefully, ready for instant action. Then I saw something slowly rising where the bush had moved. Up rose the hindquarters of a deer, then with a jerk up came the forequarters and head. I looked hard as the deer stood there partly screened by the bushes. At first I could not see what I wanted, but in a few seconds there was a little more movement, and then I could make out the branching antlers. The buck had not seen me, but there was need for hurry. He had just risen from his bed, and even two steps might take him out of sight, and anyhow a standing deer is a darn sight easier to hit than a moving one. The bead front sight settled down steadily in the center of the gray-brown forequarters. Easily and carefully I pressed off the trigger. At the shot the buck took a great leap, and started off with a rush. I lowered the rifle and smiled, for as he ran I could see no white flag. I came to it fifty yards from where it had stood, a nice three-point buck shot through just behind the shoulder.

I had been hunting four days before success came, and considered myself fortunate, as I have often hunted from dawn to dark in a good game country for two weeks without getting a shot at a shootable animal. I had kept my eyes open and I had learned a lot. Some of what I learned I have tried to put down here. As you gain experience in hunting you will always be adding to your own sum total of knowledge of the game, the hunting, and nature. You will be able to read between the lines and piece out this book into volumes. You will have experiences in different places and totally different countries. Hunting deer in Texas is entirely different from hunting in Wisconsin at first, until suddenly you come to realize that the principles of woods hunting are the same everywhere, and that given a little knowledge of the habits of an animal, a man who is a good hunter in the Canadian woods can soon master the game in the tropical thickets of Mexico.

One can not tramp along, even through the best game range, as though he were out for an afternoon's exercise, and expect to see game except by the merest chance. He must *hunt*. With all large game, silence is a cardinal virtue. It often happens that very dry weather will make the carpet of leaves in a woods so noisy that there is no chance whatever of seeing big game. I have known sportsmen going into the North Woods for a hunt of two or three weeks to encounter this condition for their entire stay, and to be unsuccessful in a most excellent game country, and with the very best of guides. If one can do so, it is best to delay the fall hunt until the period when the first snows may be expected. A light fall of snow, a "tracking snow," is of enormous advantage in woods hunting, particularly when the sportsman hunts alone, although a first-class, experienced hunter will have almost as good a chance after a rain when the woods are wet, and the under-brush and leaves are noiseless.

In still-hunting, moccasins are a great advantage, as one can walk so quietly in them. I do not mean the soled moccasins, nor those with heavy, double-leather bottoms, but rather the soft, oil-tanned ones with soft, pliable soles. Smoke-tanned moosehide and buckskin moccasins are fine from the standpoint of noise, and do well in some of the dry mountains of the West, but they are not waterproof, and in damp woods or early snows they soak up water like a sponge, and one's feet are continually wet. With soft moccasins one can really walk noiselessly through the woods if he takes pains. His feet will feel every stick and twig which he might otherwise break. His feet will make no sound whatever if he strikes or slides on rock or stones. The only disadvantage is that in snow, if he be not born to the woods and that wonderful sense of balance of the woodsman, he will slip badly on every slope. For the sportsman, light lumberman's rubbers with well-corrugated sole and leather uppers are better than moccasins in snow.

One should not walk fast in still-hunting, unless he deliberately does so for a specific reason, as to keep ahead of a light, eddying wind. This is not a *tramp*, it is a *hunt*. A half a mile to a mile an hour is approximately the gait. As one proceeds he must be quiet, he must not brush against or disturb branches nor crack twigs, he must be constantly on the alert with every sense, he must see everything, and he must be ready to shoot at any instant. He pauses constantly to look and listen. Particularly at every rise in the ground where any view can be had ahead he stops and looks the woods over most minutely, front, flanks, and even rear, and listens. Nothing must escape his eyes and ears.

It is very difficult for the sportsman who spends eleven months of every year in a city to see game in the woods. The guide who spends all his time in the woods knows just what to look for, and he sees the game because it is perfectly apparent to him, standing out as totally different from any detail of the woods themselves. But even the city sportsman who hunts regularly every year, and may be said to have quite extensive experience in hunting big game, has trouble. So many red or gray spots might be deer to him, or black stumps a moose. He has a difficult time to eliminate the many things that might be game, and he spends valuable time looking hard at objects the guide would not even give a thought to. But to the tyro the matter is almost hopeless. Sometimes he cannot even see an animal as large as a moose, even when the guide points it out to him. First, his trouble is that his ideas are necessarily taken from pictures, or from stuffed animals, or tame ones in a zoo. In the woods one seldom sees half an animal, sometimes less, often only a part of the shoulder, or only an ear over a log or a leg under it, a bit of rump projecting from a bush, or a head and bit of neck reaching up for leaves. The novice does not even see these, and the chances are that at first he sees no game unless by luck an animal makes itself so very prominent by movement in the open at short range that a blind man could not miss it. The tyro must be made to realize this, and then he must have a long school of apprenticeship, having animals as they usually appear pointed out to him, before he acquires a half-way decent knack of seeing game in the woods.

Although I hunted every vacation I could obtain and although all my boyhood summers were spent hunting in the North Woods, I always had difficulty in seeing game. I was continually looking hard at every red and gray spot to see if it was a deer, and at every black spot or dark shadow expecting it might be a moose. This was wasted time, and, moreover, my eyes were often busy at this when they ought to have been used in hunting over the whole expanse in view for what *was* an animal. Then Birch came into my family. Birch is a Llewellen setter, the best companion I ever knew, and full of hunting instinct. He prefers quail or grouse, but when none are to be had, anything will substitute, squirrels, or even cats. I began to take long walks in the park two or three times a week with Birch, and I tried to see the things he saw or smelled—squirrels, rabbits, little birds, rats, even hop-toads. At the start he always saw them first, and I seldom saw them at all until they were scared away. Then gradually I began to see them more frequently, and finally I saw them as soon or as frequently as he did. Moreover, my distant vision improved greatly. About a year after Birch came, I had a chance to take a two-months big-game hunt, and on it I saw the game as quickly and as surely as the guide did. I had gotten the knack by practice, and that is the only way it can be obtained.

One of the last things the beginner thinks of is the extreme importance of seeing the game before it sees him. Given two creatures in the woods, each in search of the other, the great advantage is with the one that happens to be at rest when the other moves within range of its eyes. As it is next to impossible to see game when it is lying down in heavy cover, it should be sought when on foot. The best time for this is when it is feeding. The big game of the woods feeds and moves about very early in the morning, very late in the afternoon, and at night. Night usually is out of the question, as the sights of the rifle cannot be seen. The gray of dawn and the red glow of sunset are the best times for hunting. As the sun comes up one's chances fade enormously, so a few minutes' delay in starting may easily cost one a good shot. And there are many excuses for delay in a hunter's camp—not getting up early enough, delaying for a good breakfast or a shave, too dark to walk through the woods, etc. Let me suggest that a Baby Ben alarm clock is a good thing to have in camp, and that an acetylene lantern, an electric flashlight, or even a birch-bark torch, will show the way out or into camp in the dark. Van Dyke says: " 'Jumping a deer' is a highly attractive phrase, quite apt to make a tingling in the back hair of the tenderfoot who hears it for the first time. It is also intensely satisfactory to the chap who always has to shave before

wooing nature." You may, indeed, get a shot, usually a difficult one, in this way, and it is a grand sight to see a deer running
through a windfall, or a moose making a windfall all of his own
as he crashes through the woods. But jumping game in the woods
usually means out of sight and out of hearing, or both, or a flash
and it's gone with no time to throw the rifle to the shoulder.
There is no use in following an animal that has been "jumped."
It is like going in swimming after a hearty meal—you won't
find it there.

It is hardly ever possible to really track an animal on open
ground, that is ground free from snow. A good hunter can
sometimes follow an animal some little distance by painstaking
observation, but it takes lots of time, he progresses very slowly,
and sooner or later he loses the trail. A wounded animal can
more often be followed successfully because it usually is running,
and hence makes deeper and more evident tracks, because it
usually goes straight in one direction, and also because of the
tell-tale blood. This pertains generally to the thick woods of
the East and Northeast. I have seen open country in the West
where an animal's track could be followed as rapidly as one
could walk, and this for miles. Some few men are wonders at
tracking, and it is said that some South African natives are almost the equal of hounds in following a trail.

In still-hunting before the snow comes, tracks are of assistance
mainly in determining the recent presence of animals, their size
or sex, and the country they travel over and frequent at different times of the day. The age of the track is very important for
determining these things. It is difficult to describe in print how
to tell a fresh track from an old one. So many things have
to be taken into consideration—the character of the soil, grass,
and leaves, whether the sun has shown on the track, whether
the wind has blown on it, dew, rain, frost, falling leaves. The
good tracker is always studying tracks—not only game tracks,
but those of his own and his companions, and also it may be
said the droppings of the animals, which often tell a lot. He
notices how they look in all kinds of soil, leaves, pine needles,
etc., when freshly made; and he studies those same tracks an
hour, two hours, six hours, a day later. He notes the effects
of dew, frost, rain, sun, wind, a night's exposure on them. And
he keeps in his mind a clear memory of the past weather. He

can always tell you just what day and hour it began and stopped raining last, whether the ground got thoroughly soaked so as to be muddy, whether there was a frost night before last, when the sun was powerful enough to dry things up, etc. The good tracker has to be a keen observer and a close student.

What has been said so far pertains mostly to hunting on bare ground—damp ground if possible. On snow there is better chance because of the added quiet, and the ability to successfully follow a trail and come on or jump the animal close by, with the increased visibility of it against the white of the snow. A fresh trail can usually be easily told in snow, and readily followed. In following the tracks of an animal we must remember that they all instinctively watch their back trail, and that when they bed down they usually circle around so as to leave their trail up-wind from their bed in order that their noses may warn them of anything following. These habits and the tactics to be observed in circumventing them are best described in a story by that old and very experienced hunter, Mr. D. M. Barringer, told in one of the Boone and Crockett Club books, from which I take the liberty of quoting the following:

"I had started during the day eight different moose, each separately, without hearing or seeing a single one of them. This sort of thing lasted for twenty-two consecutive days, until I finally concluded that, as our Indian seemed to have no trouble in seeing moose, I would follow his tactics. Waiting, therefore, one morning until I was sure that the Indian had left camp, I changed my course so as to intersect his trail, following this for some distance, and watching carefully his footprints, so as to read the record of his hunt.

Pretty soon it became apparent that he had come across a moose trail. He tried it first with the toe of his moccasin, then with the butt of his gun, and satisfied himself that it was too old to follow. He went on until he came across another trail, and evidently had spent considerable time in making up his mind whether it was worth while to follow this trail or not. He then followed it for a few yards, and, to my surprise, suddenly left it and went off almost at right angles to the leeward. I supposed that he had given up the moose trail, but, nevertheless, I followed further on his track. Again to my surprise, I presently found him coming around in a circuitous fashion to the trail again until he finally reached it. He immediately retraced his steps, making another semi-circle, bearing generally, however, in the direction the moose had gone, and again came to the trail. This occurred four or five times, until finally the explanation of his conduct flashed upon me, for there lay his cartridge. I saw—as he afterwards described it to me—where he had shot at the moose, which had just risen out of its bed a short distance away, but, as usual, he had missed it. Now, I had noticed in my three weeks' experience, that I had come upon the moose either lying down or standing in some thicket, but that they had been able to wind me considerably before my arrival at the spot marked by their beds in the snow. Not until then had occurred to me what is well known to many who still-hunt moose, namely, that before lying down they generally make a long loop to the leeward, returning close to their trail, so that they can readily get the wind of anyone following upon it long before he reaches them, when, of course, they quietly get up and sneak away. In fact, they do not seem to have an atom of curiosity in their composition, and in this are different from most other wild animals that I have known. By making these long loops to the leeward the hunter reduces to a minimum the likelihood of being smelled or heard by the moose; and in these animals the senses of smell and hearing are very acute, although their eyesight seems to be bad.

"Having satisfied myself as to what it was necessary to do, I waited until the next day to put it into execution, because by the time I had made my discovery it was about half past 2 o'clock, and the sun was near the horizon. The following day I went out bright and early, and, after varying success in finding a good trail, I ran across a trail made by five bull moose. After satisfying myself that the trail had been made during the previous night, I began making the long loops to the leeward which I had found to be so necessary. I finally came to the place where the moose had laid down—a bed showing one of them to have unusually large horns—but they had gone on again, in a manner, however, that showed that they were merely feeding, and not alarmed. I redoubled my precautions, stepping as if on eggs, so as not to break the twigs underneath my feet. In a short time I heard the significant chatter of one of the little red pine squirrels so abundant in that region. I at once knew that the squirrel had seen something, but had not seen me. It did not take me long to make up my mind that the only other living thing in that vicinity which would be likely to cause him to chatter were these moose, and that they were probably startled, although I had not been conscious of making any noise. At any rate I ran quite rapidly toward the end of a small, narrow muskeg on my left, but some distance away, to which chance conclusion and prompt action I owe probably one of the most fortunate and exciting pieces of shooting that has occurred in my experience. I was shooting at the time a little double rifle (.450-120-375 solid bullet), which had been made for me by Holland and Holland, and which was fitted with one of my conical sights.

"Before I was within fifty yards of the end of the muskeg, I saw one of the moose dash across it, about 150 yards away. I fired quickly, and in much the same way that I would shoot at a jacksnipe which had been flushed in some thicket, but had the satisfaction of seeing the animal lurch heavily forward as he went out of sight into the timber. Almost immediately, and before I had time to reload, the second moose followed. I gave him the other barrel, but I did not know until afterwards that he was hit. In fact, it was hard to get a bullet through the timber. I reloaded quickly and ran forward to get to the opening, but before I reached it the third moose passed in immediately behind the others. I again shot quickly and felt that I had probably hit him. By running on rapidly I reached the edge of the opening in time to intercept the fourth moose. As he came into the opening I got a good shot at him, not over eighty yards distant, and felt very sure of this one at least. I then reloaded, when to my amazement the fifth, in a very deliberate manner, walked, not trotted, into the muskeg, which at the point where the moose crossed it was not over sixty or seventy feet wide. He looked up and down, as if undetermined what to do, and then, probably seeing one of the other moose on the ground, commenced walking up towards me. As luck would have it, I got a cartridge jammed in my rifle, and could not pull it out or knock it in, although I nearly ruined my fingers in my attempt to do so. Of course this was the biggest bull of all, and I had the supreme satisfaction of seeing him deliberately walk out of my sight into the woods, and he was lost to me forever. His horns were much larger than those which I got. Up to that time I had no idea that I had killed any except the last moose I shot at, but thought perhaps I had wounded one or two of the others, feeling that I would be very lucky if I should ever come up with them." *

Mr. Barringer got three of those moose, which would seem to be a large number, but this was over forty years ago, in the flat country west of Lake Winnepeg, and he had a large party, as well as ten sledge dogs to feed.

Drizzly or rainy days are the best time for still-hunting, except of course on a good, light, new snow. On such days one can walk with much less noise, and in addition the animals seem much slower to jump, and their senses of smell and hearing do not seem to be so keen. Windy days are good, too, for the forest is full of noise then which does much to deaden the noise you make, and there is then no doubt as to the direction of the wind. The early morning after a rain or heavy dew is also a good time. Keep your head up and your eyes skinned as you walk. Don't adopt the crouching attitude of the novice, for you cannot see nearly as much as if you walk erect, and in the erect position you can turn your head easier to see to one side or to the rear. Do not watch the ground at your feet either. Many men fail to see game because they are continually watching where they are stepping.

---

* "Dog Sledging in the North," by D. M. Barringer, in "*Hunting in Many Lands*," *Forest and Stream* Publishing Company, New York, 1895.

Take a quick survey of the ground thirty feet to the front, and then proceed for that distance without looking at it. Even on very rough ground this is easy after just a little practice, because the sub-conscious mind seems to keep watch of the ground and instinctively tell one where to place his feet.

During very dry weather, when the ground, the leaves, and the little sticks are so dry that it is impossible to walk without prohibitive noise, it is best for the man who must hunt under such conditions to take up his position on some point of vantage where he can overlook a lot of ground where game indications are numerous, and to sit down there and watch. The chances may be good for seeing an animal, particularly very early in the morning and late in the evening. There is no reason why one should not smoke while thus watching, for the smoke will go nowhere that one's scent will not go too, and a smoker finds much comfort from his pipe on such occasions. But don't relax your vigilance, keep your wits about you, and keep thinking game.

Horace Kephart, in *"Camping and Woodcraft,"* has some very excellent advice to give as to the procedure best to follow in learning woods hunting. He says: "Serve your apprenticeship under a guide. He can teach you more in a week than you could learn by yourself in a year. There are, however, two good books that every beginner ought to study before he goes to the woods: Van Dyke's *Still Hunter* and Brunner's *Tracks and Tracking*, both of them far and away ahead of anything else on their respective subjects. Don't try to memorize, but read and re-read until the lessons have soaked in. They will make it much easier for you to understand your guide's movements and directions (but don't quote your book-learning to him or to anyone else). After you have learned something of woodcraft by actual experience in company, make a practice of going alone and putting it to the proof. In still-hunting, two men working together make four times as much noise as one would by himself. They more than double the risk of alarming the game by their scent, as they are seldom right together. And each relies too much on the other. 'Tom may jump one to me,' is a thought that has spoiled many a hunt (and hunter). You don't want any Tom to think about: You want to think *deer*, if that is what you are after."

I have done almost all my hunting in the far wilderness, in

unspoiled country that I love, and in such places I have not been bothered by other hunters. Hence, safety precautions have never been brought very closely home to me, and probably I don't say as much of them as I should. But most of my readers will probably get their hunting in those little wildernesses and woods near home, where there will be numbers of hunters abroad and where it is very necessary to constantly keep a very important rule in one's mind: "Never fire at anything until you are absolutely *certain* that it is not a human being."

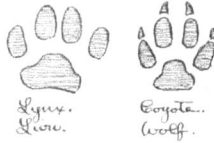

Lynx.   Coyote.
Lion.   Wolf.

CHAPTER XVI

STALKING, OR MOUNTAIN AND PLAINS HUNTING

This form of hunting differs from still-hunting, or woods, forest, and jungle hunting in that the game is usually discovered at a distance by sight in more or less open country, and it remains more or less in sight while it is being approached and until it is shot, the hunter, of course, taking advantage of whatever cover there is to screen himself from the animal. Stalking is the usual method of hunting sheep, goats, caribou, and grizzly bear in the open country of our western mountains and around timberline. On the plains of the United States hunting is almost a thing of the past, although occasionally the hunter may find that the pursuit of the mule deer savors more of stalking than of still-hunting. But on the arctic prairies the art of stalking must still be employed to bag caribou, polar oxen, and grizzly bears, and on the arctic ice polar bear and seal. Often the character of the country may be such that the hunter must combine stalking and still-hunting to obtain success.

A day's hunt in open country may, for convenience of description, be divided into two phases, first, the finding or locating of the game, and second, the stalk proper or approach to sure killing distance. The first phase may take hours or days. Game may be found so late in the day that there is no use in starting the stalk, and the hunter must return as early as possible the next morning. Or he may bivouac somewhere near so as to get as early a start as possible the following morning. In endeavoring to locate mountain game it is sometimes advisable to carry some kind of an emergency ration, enough for a day or two, for one never knows how long he may be out. On a still-hunt you usually return to your camp every evening, but in the Northwest you may first climb a mountain five or six miles from camp, and four or five thousand feet above it to reach a vantage point from which to examine a certain piece of country. What you see from there may entice you to go still farther, and the first thing you know it is late afternoon and your camp is ten miles away beyond two high ridges and with very rough ground lying between. You want very much to get a view of a certain piece of country where you think you may find game, and if you go back to camp it will take you nearly as long the next day to reach where you are now, so you decide to stay out all night, and drop down to the nearest good timber and water, and make yourself comfortable. All of this pertains more particularly to where the hunter is in a country that is new to him, and where he has to locate the game himself. Where the sportsman hunts with a guide, the guide probably knows to within very close limits of where the game sought will be found, and he can lead his sportsman straight there without any delay or preliminary scouting. Or perhaps the guide may leave his sportsman in camp and himself take several days scouting around, if need be, to find where the game is. Often he can then lead the sportsman on horseback close to the place, thus avoiding long and tiresome tramping and climbing to get to where the stalk proper must start. Under these conditions it is seldom necessary for the sportsman to remain out over night, and he can have the comforts of his main camp every evening. Nevertheless, I do not think that a sportsman ever realizes to the full the sport, pleasure, and fascination of mountain hunting until he has, by his own efforts, located his game in a country that is strange to him. Nor can he realize what downright hard and red-blooded work mountain hunting is, and how well deserved some trophies are, until he has experienced every phase of this form of hunting.

In finding your game your plan may be to proceed to a number of various high lookout points in turn and examine all the country in sight from each for the game you are seeking or for indications of it. As you proceed, even before you have reached one of your vantage points, different aspects of scenery are constantly being presented to you. A few steps may reveal a different mountainside or valley, and one of these may contain what you are looking for. So you must keep your eyes continually skinned and your senses acute. Your distance vision, particularly, should be good, and for best success you will need to supplement it by using your binoculars continually. So this brings us to the best methods of examining country, and of using binoculars.

First, let us look a minute or two at the qualities we should have in our binoculars. The most important quality is resolving power, usually called definition, the ability to distinguish between two objects close together, that is to see well at a distance. This quality depends upon a number of things—power, brightness, quality of the lenses, but more than anything else, upon the diameter of the object lens of the binoculars. Brightness or light gathering properties, and resolving power go hand in hand. To obtain brightness the exit pupil, that is the pencil of light which emerges from the eye-lens, must be large, usually at least 5 mm. in diameter. To obtain a 5-mm. exit pupil we must choose a glass the object lens of which is five times the power of the glass in diameter, expressed in millimeters. That is, with an eight-power binocular the object lens must be forty millimeters ($5 \times 8 = 40$) in diameter to obtain an exit pupil of 5 millimeters. Such a glass will be excellent for our purpose, provided that it is otherwise well made. But resolving power also depends on magnifying power, and in the matter of magnifying power we are limited practically by the size and power of our binoculars. The practical limit is reached in a ten-power glass, having an object lens 50 mm. in diameter and an exit pupil of 5 mm. Such a binocular, with its case, will weight over three pounds, and be rather larger and heavier than most men will wish to carry. A six-power glass with an object lens 30 mm. in diameter is rather low in magnifying power for mountain hunting. The above eight-power glass is a good compromise. It depends upon the hunter's viewpoint. If he arrives at a look-out point and away off in the distance makes out a bunch of sheep, but his glasses will not tell him if they are rams or ewes, and he has to spend hours of the hardest kind of climbing to get near enough for identification, he is liable to wish he had purchased and carried the most expensive and largest and heaviest glasses obtainable, with high magnifying power and large object lenses. The quality of the lenses, and the workmanship of the entire glass is also of great importance. I am sorry to say that in America we do not make binoculars which can compare for a moment with some of those made in Germany, where this instrument reaches it highest development. I have found the binoculars made by Zeiss, Hensoldt, Goerz, and Busch to be very superior instruments. The Hensoldt glasses in particular, while not being superior to the other makes optically, can be entirely dismounted and the lenses wiped off by anyone having a small screwdriver. For use in a wilderness this is a very great advantage; for example, if one should fall in fording a creek and get his binoculars thoroughly wet, if they cannot be properly dried and cleaned, inside and out, on the spot they must go to an instrument maker before they will be of any use at all. In very cold weather, do not take any optical instrument (or rifle for that matter) from the cold into the heat and damp of a cabin or house, for if you do it will condense as much moisture on it, both inside and out, as though it had been dropped in a lake.

The best results cannot be obtained from any binoculars unless they are properly focused. The best instruments have independent focusing arrangement for each eye so that if the eyes differ, and they often do, each telescope can be properly focused for the eye. Focus the left telescope first, keeping the right eye closed. Screw the eye-piece out beyond clear focus, then with the telescope directed at the object it is desired to observe, screw the eye-piece in until the image is perfectly clear, but not a bit farther. Then shut the left eye and do the same with the right eye and right telescope. Always start with the eye-piece screwed *out* to beyond focus, and bring them in to the exact focus, but no farther. Binoculars focused in this way will not cause eyestrain if used for a long time, while those adjusted on the short side of the focus may. There are several scientific ways of cleaning the lenses, but few of them are convenient for the sportsman. Probably the best he can do is to carry a clean, soft cotton or linen handkerchief for this purpose, and when the lenses become dirty or smudged dust them off, breathe on them, and then polish them clean and dry with the handkerchief, using a circular motion.

The searching of mountain country with binoculars for game, or for signs of it, is quite an art in itself. I know of nothing that so marks the difference between an experienced hunter and a novice as the way in which they use their binoculars. The novice stands up, sweeps the country in a jaunty manner with his glasses, and announces that there is no game in sight. Your

Photos by F. H. Riggall

MOUNTAIN HUNTING COUNTRY OF ALBERTA

UPPER—A SPRING BEAR HUNTER'S CAMP   LOWER—IN SHEEP COUNTRY

old timer exercises extreme precaution when he approaches the
top of a mountain or a ridge so that he shall not be seen by
any game that might be in sight, for almost all mountain game
has sharp eyes, particularly sheep.   When he has crawled up to
the place from whence he is going to look the country over he
gets out his glasses, produces a clean handkerchief, and leisurely
but thoroughly wipes the lenses absolutely clean.   He then lies
down, or sits down with his back to a log, tree, or stone so as to
get a solid rest for his elbows, either on the ground or on his
well-supported knees, so that he can hold the binoculars absolutely still and without fatigue for a long time if necessary.   If
he is going to observe at a very long range, he may build up a
little pile of stones or make some other arrangement for resting
the glasses on so that they can be held immovable.   Then he
focuses so as to obtain the clearest vision on objects at the average distance at which he is going to observe.   Having done this
he does not sweep all the country in view.   Instead, he levels his
glasses at one spot, and most carefully examines everything
within the apparent field of view of the lenses which might possibly be an animal.   Not until he has satisfied himself that there
is nothing within that field of view does he move his glasses
slightly so as to bring the adjacent circle into the field.   The
field of view of a pair of modern eight-power binoculars measures
about 110 feet in diameter at 1,000 yards, so it takes one some
time to search a piece of country thoroughly enough to find animals which are often hidden by their protective coloring.   It is
absolutely necessary to have the glasses practically still when
observing as critically as this, and thus it is not possible to use
them in the standing position with any degree of success, for
they tremble too much, and everything seen through them dances.
Everything possible of being an animal must be examined, and
this includes many things that at first glance look like rocks,
stumps, peculiar patches of grass, snow, etc.   It is often hard to
make out an animal, but once you have identified it there is
not the slightest doubt thereafter that it is an animal and not
a rock or stump.
  You not only look for the animals themselves, but for traces
of them.   Thus in sheep country, if there are any of the animals
around, there will almost always be the faint tell-tale tracks and
trails across the shale slopes and slide rock that forms the sides

of the mountain between grassy pastures. In goat country one will find trails along the crest of the ridges, and if there is a pinnacle of rock sticking up on a ridge, over which a goat cannot climb, there will be a trail climbing just below the rock and leading up to the crest again. Moose or caribou will often make tracks or even trails leading from below to the saddles and passes in the ranges. If the ground is at all soft, and if these trails or tracks are fairly fresh, that is, made after the last heavy rain, each footprint will usually stand out sharp and distinct, but if the trail is old it will show across soft ground as a hardly discernible line. On heavy slide rock, however, an animal trail is different. Footprints cannot be seen, and if you were on the slide rock itself you would never know that there was a trail. But from a distance an experienced hunter can often make out the succession of shadows in line where the rocks have been gradually pounded down into the semblance of a trail, discernible only because the same kind of shadows follow themselves across the slide. The fields of snow, and particularly the thin strips of snow which in far northern mountains often run down the north sides of the little gullies in the hillsides, will often contain tracks easily made out by steadily held and well-focused binoculars. Tracks in freshly fallen snow are, of course, the very best indication because you can tell how old they are within very close limits.

In looking for animals do not expect to always see them as they are usually pictured in books and magazines. Broadside, standing, is just one of the large number of attitudes in which you are liable to see the game. It may be facing towards you or away from you at any angle, and its silhouette may be very different from what you expected to see if you have in your mind only the animal standing broadside. If the game is standing it is usually moving, and hence is easily seen. But if it is lying down it may present many different profiles. It is a great help in finding and identifying animals to examine carefully the many excellent studies of these animals in all positions by our best animal artists. It is difficult to tell males from females at distances more than a mile or so. If it is before the rutting season of the animal, and there are small animals in the bunch the chances are that it is a bunch of females and young, and there is hardly any likelihood of there being a male with a sizable head among them. In Rocky Mountain Sheep (*Ovis canadensis*) the rams are usually much darker in color than the ewes, but you cannot always be sure of the color at a great distance, that is not sure enough to waste a whole day on a hard stalk on a bunch of ewes. Often the sex can be determined by watching the animals as they feed. An animal may cross a piece of light colored ground or a patch of snow which will silhouette his antlers or horns clearly, or he may rub his antlers against a bush or small tree. In other cases one has simply to get nearer to make a sure identification of sex and shootable heads.

Having found your game, the problem before you is the stalk, the getting within sure hitting distance. Mountain and plains animals have keen vision, particularly sheep, and it is absolutely necessary to keep out of sight of them. I should hate to say how far off they can make out a man. Probably sheep can see a moving man at over three miles. The stalk must be planned so as to keep you out of sight of the game, and when you get close it must also be conducted so as not to take you over ground from which the animals might get your scent. This often takes most careful preliminary examination of the ground so as to find the little gullies, folds in the ground, bushes, rocks, etc., that will give cover during the approach over a critical stretch, while over other parts very obvious hill-tops and crests will provide adequate cover. Through all this a route of approach must be selected, and sometimes it is best to sketch it out roughly on a page of the note-book before you start so as to be sure to remember all the various incidents of it. The hunter should also note all prominent landmarks near the animals so that when he gets close to where they are he can identify the exact place. Remember that a hillside almost always looks very different when you get on it from what it did when you viewed it from a distance, perhaps from a point far above it or away below it. Also remember that some things which do not look as though they were good cover, nevertheless do form a perfect screen under certain circumstances. Thus, if you are close behind a bush you may be able to see through it most perfectly, but the game at a distance will not be able to see you. The same thing pertains to the game. Do not think that because an animal goes behind a bush that it cannot see you through it, for it can if it is close to the bush. Often you will have to wait at a certain point for the animals to move into a more favorable place before you can get ahead without being seen. Sometimes these waits for the animals to move may take five minutes, and sometimes half a day.

It is often impossible to tell how the wind will be blowing over a certain piece of ground in the mountains. Wind sweeps up and down the valleys in various directions. Often it will change its direction with every change in the configuration of the ground. The general direction of the wind as indicated by the movement of the clouds is seldom a sure guide as to its direction at any place except on the most lofty summits where it is not influenced by any surrounding hills and valleys. Usually one has to trust more or less to luck that the wind will be right as he advances, making changes in direction of the stalk from time to time if he finds it unfavorable. Finally, towards the end of the stalk you must pay particular attention to the wind, for it is here that it is of the most importance. In the woods wind very seldom descends a hillside, that is, blows downward, but in open mountains it is liable to blow down a valley and down the adjacent hillsides, so one is not always but only usually sure of having the wind in his favor if he gets above his quarry.

Noise in mountain stalking is not of so much account as in woods hunting or still-hunting. Not that it does not alarm the game as quickly, but one does not come so close to animals in the open mountains. He probably first sees them at a long distance, and he may finally stalk to within 150 yards. But in the woods one may get within 50 yards of game before he knows of its presence, and a small sound which the animal might not hear at 150 yards may disturb it instantly at 50 yards. Thus hob-nailed shoes would be most impossible in still-hunting, but they are not much of a handicap because of the noise they make in mountain hunting, and in rough rock work they are an absolute necessity for sure footing, but still you must always take care that the hob-nails do not ring out from contact with rocks. Take care as you walk that you do not start little avalanches of rock sliding down the mountain, or that your rifle or field glasses do not strike a rock. Be as silent as you can.

Having gotten to where you must fire from, take your time if the game is not alarmed. Let your heart beats die down to normal. Estimate the range most carefully, and the wind velocity and direction too if it is blowing hard. Decide just exactly where you are going to aim on the animal, whether you have to hold over for long range, or to one side or the other to allow for the wind. Adjust your gunsling and take all advantage possible of this valuable adjunct to hard holding. Aim accurately for that one vital spot, and slowly and easily squeeze the trigger. Reload instantly and be ready for a second shot if it is necessary.

In the high northern Rockies, mountain hunting may take on some of the aspects of mountaineering or alpine climbing, the pursuit of game leading one into steep and perhaps dangerous country. Only experience will teach mountaineering, although something can be learned from any standard book on the subject. It does not pay in hunting to take any chances, or to venture into dangerous situations. I will always remember my first venture into high country. I was entirely alone, and attempted to cross a steep snow slope in moccasins, thinking I would easily stamp footholds in the snow. The snow was as hard as solid ice, and instantly I shot to the bottom, several hundred feet below. It was only due to the character of the slide rock below the snow that I lived to tell the tale, it being that fine kind down which one can run in great leaps, the rocks sliding about two feet every time one takes a step, thus slowing one's feet up gradually without jar. But some slide rock is exceedingly hard and tedious to negotiate, particularly that composed of very large rocks, and it often pays to detour such sections, even if it is a much longer way around. It also does not pay to shoot game when it is in such a steep place that it would fall and damage the head. Sheep can fall over small bluffs ten feet or so high, or roll long distances down slide rock, without injury to their horns, but goat horns are easily injured by falls or long rolls on rocky hillsides.

There is no hunting on earth that can compare for a minute with the stalking of mountain sheep, our wariest animal. It takes every sense and all the craft that the hunter possesses to outwit an old ram. The stalk takes place in the grand scenery of high mountains, snow-capped peaks, deep valleys, and glaciers. The air is keen, cold, and exhilarating. And above all, the quarry is almost constantly in sight. As you get nearer and nearer the excitement grows. Will they wait? Can I get near enough without being seen, heard, or smelled? Gradually you draw so close that you can see them distinctly. Now the big, curling horns come into view, and then you get close enough to make out the rings on the horns. Which ram has the largest head? Which has the longest curl and the greatest base measurement? Are the tips of the horns on that big bungler perfect? Oh! If we can only get one hundred yards nearer!

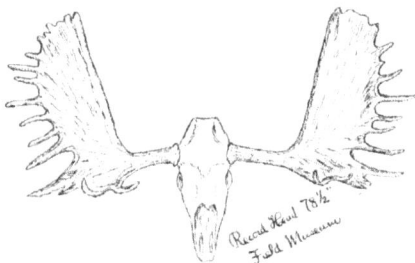

Record Head 78½
Field Museum

CHAPTER XVII

FINDING ONE'S WAY

It is seldom that one finds a hunter or outdoorsman who is so utterly lacking in powers of observation as to be unable to find his own way about the woods or mountains, or who is continually losing his camp when out alone. We may therefore infer that if one lacks these qualities he will also lack those tastes which will make the wilderness attractive to him, hence will not be one of our readers, and that in these hints and suggestions we have to deal only with those whose powers of observation and orientation are merely more less undeveloped, and not lacking to a serious extent.

Finding one's way through an uninhabited or unknown country, be it woods, jungle, plains, or mountains, is but a matter of common sense, observation, and education or practice. It is easily possible for a man to be excellent at it the very first time he tries it if he uses his brain. We may suppose that no man with common sense will try to enter a partly unknown country, or travel in one unaided by a guide unless he first procures the best map available, or obtains any other information. Even in partly unexplored country the large rivers, mountain ranges, and coasts will be shown more or less accurately on any map, and these may be of inestimable value particularly if one gets really lost. We may also infer that all have common sense enough to carry a compass in such a country, and can tell the points of the compass from the sun, moon, and North Star. That he knows if he goes north three miles, then west four miles, that by then traveling southeast about five miles he should be back in the vicinity of his starting point or camp. That if his camp is on a river or tote road, or in a valley running east and west, and he hunts to the north, a course to the south will always bring him back to the line east and west through his camp. We may also suppose that one is observant enough to note the prominent landmarks around his camp so that he can walk right to it when he once gets in that locality. That as he journeys he makes notes of the hills, valleys, creeks, and other incidents of the terrain that he passes, and those in sight to the right and left of his route.

If he does all these things he retains in his mind a map of the ground he covers, therefore he can always follow this mind map back to camp, or can take a short cut back, or return by another way because he always knows where he is. All this, first, provided his memory plays him no tricks—if it does he had better make a rough sketch map as he goes along. Sometimes in a very thick or monotonous country the making of such a map and keeping it continually up to date while traveling is essential to knowing where he is. And second, provided one does not get excited in the presence of game and forget to keep his mind map up to date. But more of these two exceptions later.

To illustrate these points, and show how common sense and observation will always keep one accurately located, let me take three cases based more or less on my own experience. First take mountainous country. I mean the mountains of the West which are more or less open, from which a view of the country can be had, and which have characteristic shapes of summit and ridges easily impressed on the mind. This is the easiest country of all to find one's way in, because every mountain and valley, every stream and cliff has its own characteristics and appearances, and one or more of them will be in sight from any considerable elevation. Northwest of camp about two miles is a mountain. It has certain peculiarities which, after you have looked at it for a minute or two, you feel sure you will remember. If there is any doubt about remembering these make a memorandum sketch in your notebook. Be sure to note the appearance of the right and left face of the mountain or other landmark, as well as the face towards you. Now this mountain or landmark will always locate camp for you, because you know your camp is so many miles in a certain compass direction from it. When you start out from camp you go towards another mountain or hill, and you note its peculiarities and its direction and distances from camp and from the first mountain, making a memorandum or sketch in your notebook if necessary. You reach this second mountain

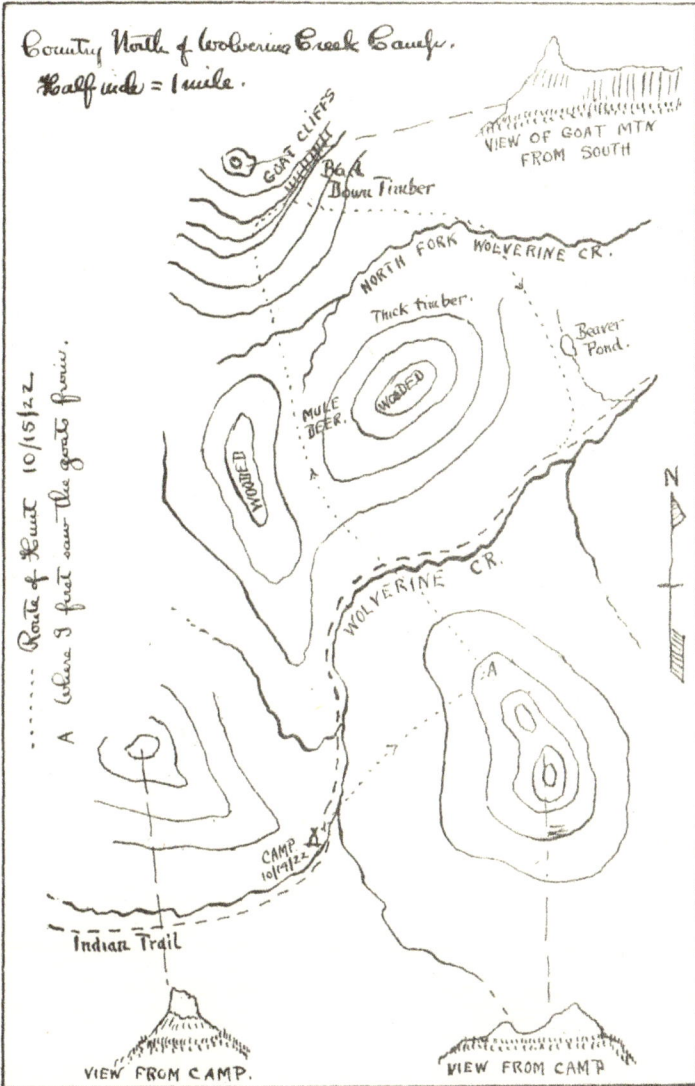

Country North of Wolverine Creek Camp.
Half inch = 1 mile.

GOAT CLIFFS

VIEW OF GOAT MTN FROM SOUTH

Bad
Down Timber

NORTH FORK WOLVERINE CR.

Thick timber

Beaver Pond.

MULE DEER.

WOODED

WOODED

N

WOLVERINE CR.

A

Route of Hunt 10/15/22
A where I first saw the goat from.

CAMP
10/14/22

Indian Trail

VIEW FROM CAMP.

VIEW FROM CAMP

and from it you go towards a third, and again you make notes, and so on. Always be sure to keep oriented with your compass or the sun so as to keep your directions straight. If you are experienced you will naturally observe all these landmarks, and you can trust your head to remember them, but if it is your first year of hunting or traveling alone you had much better use your notebook freely. The accompanying sketch shows how such notes might be kept on a leaf in your notebook. All this takes only a little pains and but a few minutes, but it keeps you straight. The very best woodsman always takes these precautions and these few minutes, and if you watch him you will see him continually turning around and pausing to do so, although he may hardly realize it himself. In my opinion there is no such thing as the "homing instinct" in man. Some men seem to find their way by instinct, and may tell you that it is instinct, but it is nothing but instinctive close observation that eventually comes

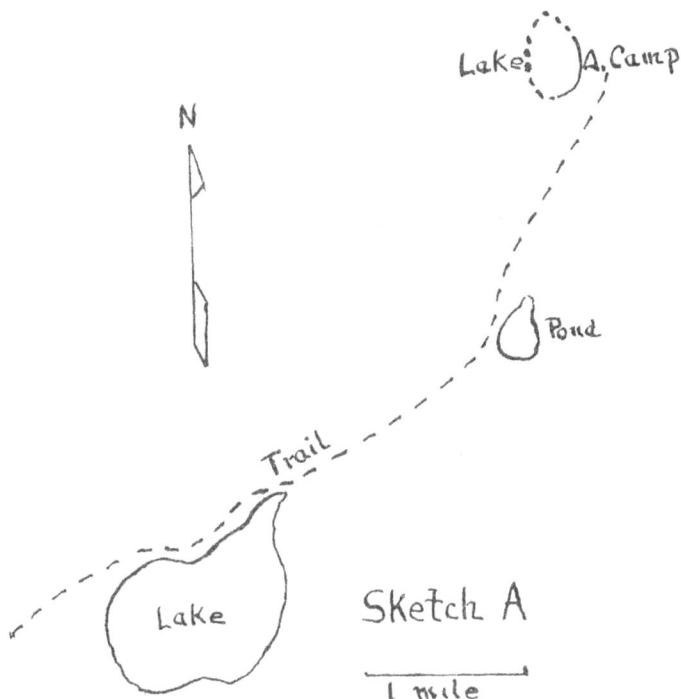

Sketch A

1 mile

to everyone with deep interest in their surroundings. A lover of beautiful scenery and unspoiled country will be much better at it than one who cares only for the killing of game.

Next, take the case of thick woods, such as the hunting country of eastern Canada, or the Allegheny Mountains. Eastern mountains are round topped and wooded to their summits, their appearances not differing greatly like western mountains. There

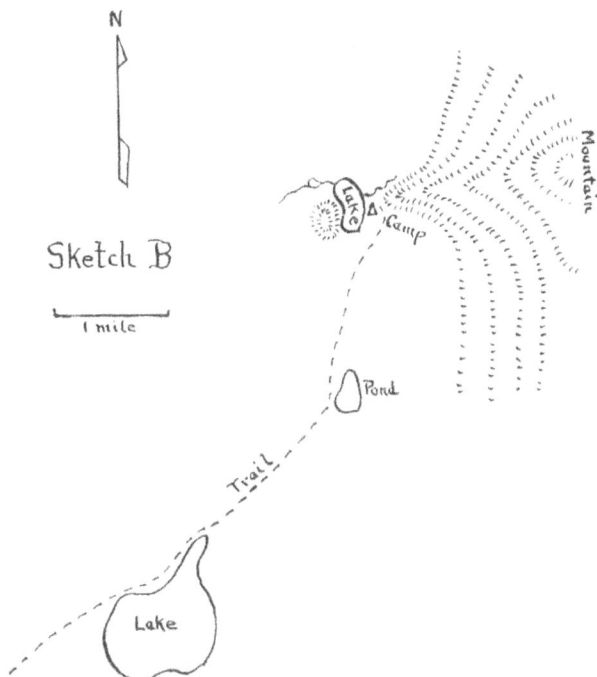

Sketch B

1 mile

is nothing in the appearance of most of them to make them stand out as clear and unmistakable landmarks. Thus finding one's way through eastern mountains is not essentially different from any rolling, wooded country. One November I went moose hunting in eastern Canada with a companion and his guide. We hiked a whole day from the settlements over tote roads and trails, and in the dark of evening we came to our lean-to camp on the shore of a little lake, too late to see anything. All we knew that night was that we were in a camp on the east shore of a lake, that a little stream flowed into the lake alongside

the lean-to, and that back of the camp there was a hill. Sketch
A shows this stage of our knowledge. I was to hunt alone, and
it was a new country to me, so the next morning the first thing
I did was to make almost a complete circuit of the lake to get
some landmarks. On the opposite side of the lake from camp
was a poplar knoll, and from it I saw that the hill back of the
camp was a fair-sized mountain and with recognizable shape,
and that from its summit a sharp ridge ran down almost exactly
to the lean-to. Further on I located the outlet of the lake, and
I also noted its kidney shape. Thus at 7 a. m., my knowledge
of my surroundings is shown by sketch B, a copy of a page in
my notebook. I now decided that I would hunt to the west,
making a circuit of the country in that direction, and I felt
that with sketch B I could surely find my way back to camp
again. First I struck a high ridge running southwest and northeast just north of the lake, and from a cliff on its south face I got
a good view of the surrounding country. I descended from the
ridge and followed down the stream which was the outlet of the
lake, investigated three little beaver ponds on it, ran into an
alder swamp, sidestepped it and went through a flat of pines for
a long distance, struck the trail by which we had come into camp
the evening before and saw our tracks on it, and also recognized
a large beaver pond on it, came to the mountain to the east of
camp, and followed its base to the lean-to. That evening Sketch
C, also a page from my notebook, shows my knowledge of the
country after my first day's hunt. As this map gradually extended
in various directions I of course quickly had as good a knowledge of that piece of the woods as though I had lived in it all my
life, and there was never a minute when I did not know exactly
where I was. Incidentally I might remark that I got no information from my companion's guide. Guides are not always
infallible, and this one, although excellent in every other respect,
had a poor eye for country. That is, he never had developed the
habit of making a mind-map of the country as he went along,
but depended entirely on recognizing localities or else of coming
home the way he went out. As a consequence he was always
getting lost, and several times my companion, who had common
sense and who made mind-maps, brought him back to camp.

A knowledge of the varieties of trees of a country helps a lot.
It keeps the country from seeming monotonous and all alike. A

ridge is recognized and remembered because of its beech trees, a beaver pond because of a bunch of balsam, a valley because of its stand of big white pines, and a certain small lake can always be told by a peculiar leaning cedar on its northeast shore—just more *observation*.

Now take our third case. I think that without exception the most difficult country to find one's way and keep one's location

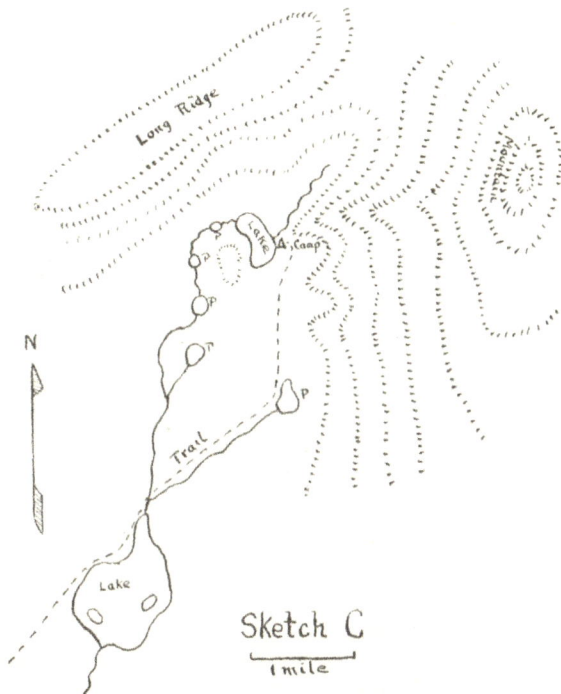

Sketch C

1 mile

in is the tropical jungle forests of Central and South America. Analogous to it is the flat cane-break country of our Southern States. In the jungle the country always looks the same. The big trees go up, almost without a limb, for 75 to 100 feet, and then spread out their verdure to nearly hide the sky. It is often difficult, particularly around noon, to tell the points of the compass from the sun, which you cannot often see through the leafy covering, and besides in the rainy season the sky is usually overcast all the time. Under the trees is a monotonous growth of palms, ferns, lianas, and creepers. You see so many peculiar looking trees that are entirely unfamiliar to you that your mind cannot remember them all and gets confused on trees. Above all, you cannot see over 50 to 100 yards in any direction. Even from the tops of the highest mountains as a rule you cannot see a thing until you have cleared off the top or cut a vista through the jungle in the direction you want to see, and this may take you hours. Even then all you get is a sea of jungle-clad hills, all almost exactly the same, and the far distance obscured in the tropical haze. I spent the better part of three years exploring and hunting in just such a country—Panama—and I soon found that the only way to keep located was to make a continuous map, and that in the thickest and hardest country it was often necessary to keep the map up to date every 200 yards. I made the map on a little sheet of celluloid which I carried in my shirt pocket—celluloid because paper would not stand the sweat of that hot climate. I used a compass continually to keep oriented. Every hour I would copy the sketch off the celluloid on to the big sheet in my rucksack, and wipe the celluloid clean for the next hour's mapping. Of course this necessitated a pause in the march every 200 yards to sketch in the ground one had just come over, and also pacing to determine how far one had come, but it was the only way. One winds around so much in the jungle to escape thick clumps of vegetation, steep hillsides, and other obstacles that otherwise it is impossible to calculate how far one has progressed in a straight line. The map was only a route sketch as nothing could be noted over a hundred yards from the line of march, but it would always enable me to retrace my tracks, and I always knew within a mile or so of where I was. Anyhow I never felt nervous in Panama because I always knew that by steering north I would strike the coast of the Caribbean Sea in three or four days, and what is this time in an interesting jungle full of birds and small mammals to a man supplied with rifle, knife, matches, machete, and a compass?

An experienced woodsman may sometimes lose his camp—in fact he probably does more often than he cares to admit—but he never loses himself completely. He always knows that if he holds a steady course in a certain direction he is bound to come out eventually. It may take a day or a week, but he is supplied with a rifle, ammunition, knife, a supply of dry matches, and a compass, or else he is not an experienced woodsman. He also probably has a fish-line and hooks. I have never yet seen a wilderness that did not contain enough animals, birds, reptiles, fish, fruit, or berries to supply a woodsman with food aplenty. Matches and a knife insure warmth and sleep at night. Such an experience to a woodsman is but an extremely interesting incident wherein he can show what he is made of.

In my younger days I started one morning after some goats which my companion had seen on high cliffs about 15 miles north of camp. He had not actually been to the cliffs, but had seen the goats with his field glasses, and he gave me sufficient directions. I failed to reach the cliffs that evening, and I bivouacked at a little alpine lake at timberline. I had a small tarp of waterproof silk, a little hand axe, and four or five elk-meat sandwiches. I set up the tarp as a lean-to, made a good balsam bed under it, built a fire in front, hauled in a big pile of dead trees and stubs for firewood, and turned in. At about 10.00 p. m. it started to snow, and by morning there was two feet of it and a raging blizzard was under way. I could not see 50 feet for the whirling snow. All I knew was that I had to get into lower and more sheltered country very pronto, and all I could do was to start blindly down the range. It was hard going at first, but pretty soon I got in a sort of a cañon that led downward, and where the wind was not so strong and penetrating, and the exercise of mushing through the deep snow soon warmed me up. I could not keep any sort of direction except that I knew that generally I was tending towards a western course. In the middle of the afternoon I reached a wooded and sheltered valley and made myself comfortable for the night and ate my last sandwich. I had not the faintest idea where I was except that I knew that about a day's travel southwest was a large river, and when I struck that I could surely find my way back to camp. Next morning it had stopped snowing, and that evening I struck the river, having shot a porcupine and two grouse on the way. That was a great experience and I would not have missed it for anything.

WHAT TO DO IF LOST

Anyone may lose his camp, or get pretty badly mixed up at times if he does not keep his wits about him. How badly depends mostly on how long he has let his mind go wool gathering, or how long he has been absorbed in something such as the chase of game which has taken his mind completely off of keeping track of his surroundings.   If 15 minutes ago you knew exactly where you were it is not so bad as it only means half a mile out of the way, and if you have memorized all the country near your camp and make a bee-line for it you ought not to miss it by more than a mile or so, and if you get within a mile of camp you should come to country you can recognize.   But it may be much worse than this, and if so you may have to take the long way out to be sure just as I did in the blizzard, and thus have an interesting experience.   This is only likely to happen in a thickly wooded country, although it might happen in open mountain country in a fog or blizzard.

If the tyro sportsman out by himself, or with an equally inexperienced companion, gets turned around and mixed up, and if there is a guide or woodsman back in the camp, he should sit down exactly where he is and cool off, light his pipe and take a smoke, and then light a fire.   If it is late in the afternoon he should make preparations for spending the night there, putting up a rude shelter, making a bed of some kind, and hauling in a huge pile of dead wood for an all-night fire.   Don't put off doing these things until dark.   Towards evening he should fire signal shots.   The guide or woodsman will usually find him that evening or the next day *if he does not move.*   To do so is child's play to a good woodsman.   But the best woodsman in the world may never find him if he starts to travel. First, last, and always, if you want to be found, DON'T MOVE!

The best system of signal shots to be fired in case one is lost or if an accident happens, is one shot, then an interval of about thirty seconds, followed by three shots in succession, these to be fired on the even hour if one has a watch.   The one shot fixes the attention of anyone within hearing, and they listen for the other shots which give direction and distance.   The time on the even hour shows that they are distress shots.   If your companions think you are lost or in trouble they will be listening on the even hour.   Arrange for such a signal with your guide or companions when you first start out on your hunting trip.   Also when you leave camp for the day's hunt tell your companions or guide or leave a memorandum as to the direction and country you are going to hunt over.

I should like to add three common-sense rules which I think everyone ought to observe when in an uninhabited country:

1. Never leave camp without the means of obtaining food (gun and ammunition or fish-line and hooks), a knife, a compass, and matches in a waterproof box.

2. Always keep an accurate mind map or sketch map of your route and the country you traverse.

3. If you suddenly realize you are lost, sit down, keep cool, and use your brain.

MAPS.

The hunter should always obtain and carry the best map possible to procure of the country in which he is going.

For the United States the best maps are those sold by the U. S. Geological Survey, Washington, D. C., at 10 cents for each quadrangle. By writing to The Director, U. S. Geological Survey, you can find out if these maps have been made of the region into which you propose going, and their names. The U. S. Forest Service, Washington, D. C., can also supply excellent maps of our National Forests which are often the best of hunting sections. If none of these maps are available for your region you can often obtain good maps by writing to the State Surveyor, the State Forester, or the Game Commissioner at the capital of the State. Railway folders are usually unreliable because they often are distorted to show the railroads in straight lines, but the general passenger agent of the railway can often supply you with good maps of a certain region, particularly that of which they are getting out publicity matter with a view to attracting sportsmen.

In general the same conditions pertain to Canada. The Director, Canadian Geological Survey, Ottawa, Canada, or the National Resources Intelligence Branch, Department of the Interior, Ottawa, can usually supply survey maps, or else sketch maps of more remote regions which are made from time to time, by the geological exploration parties that are being constantly sent out to cover the less known portions of Canada. The printed reports of these parties will also be of great value in the more remote regions of the North. The Provinces of Alberta and

British Columbia also publish maps of their own, and excellent ones too, which can be obtained from the Publicity Commissioner, Edmonton, Alberta, Canada, or the Provincial Bureau of Information, Victoria, British Columbia, Canada. If your country lies adjacent to the Canadian Pacific Railway, or the Canadian National Railway, write also to the general passenger agents of these lines, or to their agents in the larger cities.

For Mexico and Central America about the best maps that I know of are those published by the National Geographic Society, Washington, D. C. In the absence of better maps the sheet from an ordinary atlas is far better than nothing.

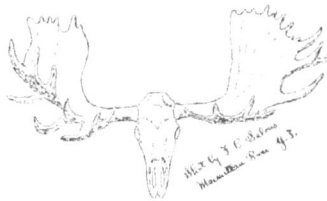

CHAPTER XVIII

CLOTHING AND PERSONAL KITS

In choosing clothing for a hunting trip, particularly in the northern part of the United States or in Canada in the fall of the year, many sportsmen make the mistake of selecting garments that are entirely too heavy. The temperature, even pretty far north into Canada, is delightful right up into the middle of November, and will not differ greatly from that in our northern cities. True, once in a great while Canada will treat us to a very cold spell with snow in the early fall, but then, as an old woodsman once said to me, "What's the use of being cold in a wooden country?" Big-game hunting, and the woods or mountain travel incident thereto, is as strenuous as a game of golf or tennis, and on occasions equal to football or rowing, and one would never think of bundling up in the heaviest mackinaws, in extra heavy high boots, with two or three pairs of the heaviest wool socks for a game of golf or tennis in November at home. Too often the sportsman is very much handicapped by just such clothing, which hampers his free movements and causes copious perspiration and chafing. Hunting is like home sports in another way, too, in that there are periods of inaction on the side lines in sport, and in canoes, resting on trails, on the windy shores of lakes, and on cold mountain tops in hunting, and there should be something for the hunter to slip on on such occasions, just as the track athlete has his sweater and the football player his blanket. But this warm garment is much too heavy to wear when hiking through the woods, or when climbing steep mountains. Above all, the hunter's clothing should be such that it does not chill one as soon as active exercise stops.

Everything in hunting in northern climates in the fall calls for medium-weight wool underclothing, light but durable wool outer clothing, light, comfortable non-slip footwear, and then some heavy wool garment carried on the back in a rucksack to slip on when one stops in the cold. Even in the high mountains of Alaska one will be perfectly comfortable when hunting or traveling in one suit of medium wool underwear, army wool breeches, an olive-drab flannel shirt, a pair of medium-weight wool socks, and a pair of light army shoes. But he should have a warm garment that is not heavy or bulky in his rucksack to put on when he stops for lunch, when he lies around camp, or when he sits down on the top of a mountain to look for game with an icy blast blowing. In our southern States the same thing holds true, only there the underwear may be a little lighter, and one's outer garments may need to be such that they will ward off thorns and burs. In the tropics wool is neither possible nor desirable, and khaki outer garments are the order of the day.

Breeches.—It is hard to improve on the olive-drab, wool Melton riding breeches of the U. S. Army. They are just right in color, weight, and texture, and are loose and free at the knee but fit tight below. They are perhaps best in the West where there is usually a lot of riding to do. For the northeast woods the typical form of golf breeches, made of similar material, is perhaps a little better cut. Old woolen trousers can easily be turned into golf breeches for hunting by your tailor. For southern countries where it is warmer and where there are lots of briars, thorns, and burs, the army khaki breeches are fine. They can be made as warm or as cool as is desired by altering the thickness and texture of the under-drawers. In almost all of the backwoods stores of Canada you can get a special heavy, dark-gray, long, woolen trousers intended for lumbermen's use. They are almost invariably worn by local woodsmen. These long trousers are particularly good when much snow is encountered. They keep the snow off the socks, and it does not melt on the socks and run down and wet the feet, as it will with almost any other combination. For very cold climates perhaps the best leg covering possible is a pair of golf breeches made of Loden, a heavy, dark-gray, almost black wool cloth woven in Switzerland and the Austrian Tyrol. It is extremely warm without being bulky, and is more nearly shower-proof than any woolen garment I have seen. Mackinaw is much too heavy for trousers as it bunches up so much in the crotch that it chafes on a long hike. For still-hunting one should particularly avoid breeches that creak or that scratch audibly when going through brush.

Shirts.—The very best are the olive-drab flannel shirts of the army, or heavy gray flannel shirts made on the same pattern. They are warm and comfortable, and the best for any climate, even for the tropics. One or more can be worn according to the temperature. I reinforce the elbows of mine with chamois skin—quite a convenience and comfort when one lies around on the ground much.

Stag Shirts.—A heavy coat is a confounded nuisance in the wilderness. It is heavy, bulky, and always in the way, and is suitable only for use in camp or when riding horseback or in a wagon. A mackinaw stag shirt, made to button all the way down in front so it can be put on and taken off like a coat, is the best garment. It would be too heavy to wear while actively hunting, but it is just exactly what you want to slip on when stopping for a rest or lunch, on a mountain top when you pause to search for game with your binoculars, or on a lake-shore calling for moose. You carry it ordinarily in your rucksack, where it is out of the way, but ready to don when needed to keep you from getting chilled. A good mackinaw will shed a heavy rain for a whole day, and with two olive-drab flannel shirts and a medium-weight wool undershirt under it it will keep a normal man warm in a blizzard. Sweaters are not much good in the wilderness. They tear easily, catch all the burs and briars, get very dirty, and the wind blows right through them. In very cold climates, however, they are excellent when worn under a drill parka.

Underwear.—The best for almost all use is the purest wool you can get of medium weight. The lightest weights are not durable enough, and the heavy weights are too heavy, and anyhow if it comes to a matter of warmth two suits of medium weight will keep you much warmer than one of heavy due to the dead air space between. I always take two or more suits. On return to camp from a day's hunt the suit worn is always damp from perspiration. Take it off at once, take a rub down with a rough towel, and put on the dry suit. This will increase one's comfort and warmth a lot, and insure a far better sleep than if one turns in in his damp underwear. Anyhow it is nasty and unhealthy to sit around in damp, clammy underwear. Flannel pajamas, however, are the best sleeping garments for camp. Some men advocate wool underwear even for the tropics. I have never been able to wear it there. It is entirely too hot, and I have always worn the lightest cotton that I could get that was durable. Some cotton undershirts are so flimsy that even the straps of a rucksack will tear them in a single day's travel.

Hats.—Any good felt hat with a fairly wide brim will do. I like the typical Stetson hat such as is worn in the Northwest, with a fairly wide brim for any climate. It shades the eyes, keeps the rain from the face, guards the spectacles if you wear them. In woods and brush laden with snow it keeps the snow from falling down the back of your neck inside your shirt. If you have ever traveled through jack-pines after a heavy snow, and when the snow was melting a little from the sun, and had a nice, big gob of wet, half-melted snow fall right down inside as you stooped to go under a bush you will appreciate this latter quality in a broad-brimmed hat.

Socks.—In the Army wool socks are compulsory. Cotton socks can be worn only by permission of a surgeon. And there is a reason. Long years of experience has shown that when there is much walking to do the feet can be kept in condition only in wool socks. This is entirely apart from the matter of getting one's feet wet. In any climate the sportsman should wear wool socks exclusively. If leather shoes are worn they should be of light wool. If moccasins or rubber shoes are worn they should be of heavy wool to better cushion the foot. For hunting and for hard footwork it is much better to wear stockings about the height of golf stockings, than socks. The stockings can then be pulled up over the outside of the riding breeches, or to meet the cuffs of the golf breeches, and answer in lieu or leggings. Leggings are not needed or desirable when hunting in the North. They are all entirely too noisy, and much too heavy for active foot work. In the tropics, however, and in most of the South leggings are a necessity on account of the brush and thorns, but they should never be worn in the North. In snow long trousers will keep the legs much dryer than any leggings.

Footwear.—The matter of footwear needs pretty thorough treatment because the average sportsman makes grievous mistakes in the selection of his foot covering, and he is usually more handicapped by foot troubles than by any other one thing on a hunting trip. What I have to say here is not only from my own experience, but represents the views of the Infantry of the Army after an experience of over a hundred years where walking of long distances over rough ground has been a profession. *The kind of boots or shoes most advertised for sportsmen are exactly the kind you should avoid.* The kind that the clerk in the shoe or sporting goods store tries to sell you as just the right thing are just the kind that will most handicap you on a hunting trip. The heavy boots with tops coming half way up the calf are just exactly the kind of boots you should not wear.

There is no place that weight tells as much as on the feet. Add a pound on each foot and you very considerably slow yourself down, decrease your mileage, and decrease your climbing ability, but particularly you greatly increase your fatigue. In the city you are used to shoes that come up only an inch or so above the ankle. Above that is the Tendon Achilles at the back of the leg, which is the most essential tendon in your body and absolutely necessary in walking. The experience of centuries has shown that it should be free and not bound, and moreover that if it is bound it quickly sets up a most painful inflammation in its sheath known as Synivitis. Unaccustomed to any pressure here, you put on high-topped boots and then proceed to do more hiking·than you have for months or years. The top wrinkles just above the ankle, puts pressure on the tendon, and in a day or two, or perhaps sooner, you are entirely incapacitated for walking. These tops weigh about a pound apiece, and they will slow you down from three and a half miles an hour to about two and a half miles an hour, and will make your limit about ten miles instead of about twenty. To travel long distances easily you need some spring in your feet, and you cannot get this with thick, unbending soles. Moreover the last on which these so-called sportsmen's boots are made is usually all wrong. The forward portion of the sole on the inside tapers outward to make them look fashionable, and also so as to crowd the great toe outward to cause bunions and deformities, whereas the great toe should turn inward if anything to give the normal and the best stride and foot action. Lastly, the shoe clerk has not the slightest comprehension of how to fit a pair of shoes to a man for active walking over rough ground.

I know of but one last which is correct for the active

outdoor man with a fairly normal foot, and none others that are even approximately so. This is the Munson U. S. Army last, the last that is universal in our Army. For general outdoor work the regular Army field shoe cannot be beaten. The type I mean is made of an oil-tanned leather, is leather lined, and has a rather thick sole. Some shoe makers catering to the sportsmen's trade also make shoes on this same last which are of finer and more durable leather, and more nearly waterproof, as well as much more expensive. When a man has to figure the maximum wear out of his shoes some of these are better than the standard Army shoe.

When a man walks over uneven or rough ground he uses every muscle in his feet most vigorously, which calls for a greatly increased blood supply. The whole foot swells in a way that is never experienced in the city or even on a golf links. By actual measurement the average foot becomes a quarter inch longer and a quarter inch wider, and very much larger in circumference after an hour's walking on a rough road or trail. A forty-pound pack on the back will more than double these increases. The shoe must fit this enlarged foot or cramping, chafing, and foot troubles will ensue. Also heavy wool socks take up more room in the shoe than do the cotton or silk ones you wear in town. Only experience will tell the exact size of outdoor shoe a man should wear, but, generally speaking, the first pair one buys should be a size longer, and at least two sizes wider than city shoes.

After you get your shoes, proceed to break them in before you jump off into the wilderness. This is quickly done by soaking them in water for a few minutes, then put them on and go for a two-hour walk over fairly level ground. At the end of that time they will be dry and perfectly moulded to your feet. Then oil them liberally with neatsfoot oil. Also take a can of boot grease with you on your trip and apply it every two or three days.

The Munson Army shoe is fine for long-distance walking, particularly over country roads. But for hunting, or the woods and mountains it slips too much. The remedy is hob-nails of which more hereafter.

Bearing in mind the above, the other important essentials in hunting footwear are noiselessness in shoes intended for the woods, and security against slipping in those to be used in the high mountains. For hunting in the woods stiff soles are not the proper thing, although a pair of this type of army shoes might be taken for traveling over trails and tote roads. The still-hunting shoe should be noiseless, and it should not slip on roots or rocks, or on a steep hillside lightly covered with wet snow. Soft, oil-tanned moccasins with single or double sole and no heel are largely worn, but while they are noiseless they, are very slippery. Your guide will often wear them, but you must remember that he is light and sure-footed to a degree you can never hope to reach, and he has probably worn such footwear from boyhood. The best shoe that I know of for woods hunting is the lumberman's leather-topped rubber, known under many names. The lower portion is of rubber, with a heavy corrugated rubber sole and the uppers are of soft, oil-tanned leather. Get it big, not over 7 inches high, and with a heel so as not to unduly strain your tendons, which are not used to shoes without heels. To avoid the clammy feeling and the perspiration which comes from wearing rubber, and to prevent bruises, you wear these shoes with felt insole and two pairs of heavy wool socks, and you get your shoes big enough to take all these and fit well. One pair of the socks should be full length like golf stockings which you will pull up over your trouser tops and use instead of leggings.

For mountain work you want entirely different footwear. In alpine hunting you do not, as a rule, approach so close to the game as in the woods, and absolute silence is not as essential. But these shoes must not slip on rock, shale, snow, or ice, or serious injury, if not death, may result. There will be much slipping and sliding, and digging in of heels and toes, and the uppers as well as the sole should be quite durable. So you want good, oil-tanned leather shoes, not too heavy, with a flexible sole just thick enough to hold hob-nails, tops not over seven inches high, made on the Munson Army last. Order them with medium-size, round-headed, steel hob-nails riveted in as shown in A in the accompanying cut, these being about the only kind of nails you can get from the average shoe dealer. These nails are not for security, but only to prevent the leather wearing out quickly on the slide rock and shale. Now break your shoes in well to conform to your feet as previously suggested, and then proceed to add the security hob nails as shown in B in the cut. The large square solid black nails are "heavy edging Swiss hobnails." The small round solid black ones are "Sharp pointed wing screw calks." Both these types of nails can be had from the large sportsman's outfitters in our largest cities, and sometimes in stores in mountain districts. The wing screw calks are screwed into the sole with a little wrench. One or two of them will come out every day and must be replaced. They should also be replaced when they become very dull. This gives you a sharp edge to your sole with which you can stick on anything, and not enough nails have been added to appreciably increase the weight of the shoes.

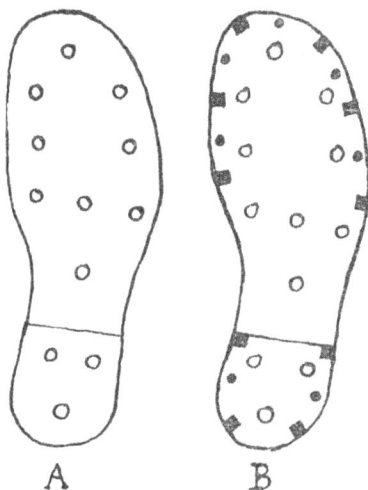

A   B

Belts.—Usually the sportsman will wear a belt to keep up his breeches, but this goes around the waist above the pelvis bone, that is around the tender part of the abdomen, side, and small of the back, and nothing should be hung from it. Some kind of a hunting belt is generally considered n e c e s s a r y to carry a few things on that one may need in a hurry. This hunting belt should be wide so that it will not cut into the flesh and impede circulation, and it should be worn low down below the crest of the pelvis or hip bones. A belt about 2 inches wide of soft leather, with a dull buckle is about right. Do not carry much on this belt or it may impede the circulation even if worn low. About three pounds is the very limit. Above all, do not carry anything on it that is long and dangling, and that bumps against the legs at every step, like a hand axe for example. On the hunting belt you want only those things you may need in a hurry, usually only a few cartridges and your field glasses, and perhaps sometimes a small camera.

Cartridge belts are not good.   Cartridges are hard to get out of the loops quickly, they corrode and get dirty, and the thin soft points of modern spitzer bullets are liable to get deformed.   The best contrivance for carrying cartridges on the belt is a little oiled leather cartridge box just the right size into which to slip the pasteboard carton in which twenty big game cartridges are always packed.   Take the cover off the carton and slip it into the box, carton and all.   Each cartridge lies in a paper partition in the carton, does not rattle, and can be gotten out quickly.   The leather box has loops at the back through which the belt passes, and a cover which fastens down with a stud, not a buckle, so you give it a tug and it comes loose instantly, making available the twenty cartridges, each in its pasteboard partition.   I usually carry ten high-power cartridges in the front row of the carton, and ten small game or short range cartridges in the rear row.

Sometimes when I am expecting chances at photographing game I carry my little No. 1 Kodak Special camera on my belt, but usually it reposes in its little heavy leather, chamois lined holster in the rucksack.

Rucksack.—The rucksack is a really necessary and a most convenient piece of equipment for all seriously minded hunters. In it you carry your mackinaw stag shirt when you are actively exercising, and have it ready to slip on when you stop in the cold.   The rucksack also takes your lunch, camera, extra films, extra ammunition, a skinning knife, tape measure, note book and pencil, maps, and a small supply of matches.   Also sometimes it may carry a kettle for tea, a hand axe, tripod for the camera, etc.   Do not get a cheap rucksack such as the boy scout models selling for a couple of dollars.   They wear out in a day or two of real work.   If you must economize make your own of stout canvas and leather.   A good bag should have stout oiled leather shoulder straps.   The under side of the sack which lies against the back should be of heavy waterproof duck so that it will not wear out quickly from friction.   The outer side should be of some softer waterproof material which will not squeak and scratch when branches and twigs rub against it.   If you are hunting by your lonesome without a guide your rucksack should be big with a wide mouth, so you can pack heads, skins, scalps, and meat back to camp in it.   Mine has gores which permit it to open out very wide, and then grommets at the top through which a small rope passes, puckering it in again and taking the weight of the contents off the seams of the canvas. There are two pockets on the outside for the camera and small odds and ends. Also there is a small piece of woven webbing with two eyelets in it sewed to the outside of the cover to which can be fastened a hand axe, Army canteen, or a machete, using the same carriers and fasteners as are used in the Army for attaching these articles to the cartridge belt of the soldier. Many times in Panama I packed the small deer of that country back to camp in it, their backs down and feet sticking out the top, the weight being 50 to 75 pounds. Often it has carried heavy sheep heads and scalps, or a big load of meat, and once I came proudly into camp with a grizzly bear skin hidden in its depths.

Knives.—For quite ninety per cent of the work that a hunter has to do with a knife a sheath knife is entirely too large and clumsy. A large pocket knife is far better in every way for whittling, all odd jobs, and for skinning and cutting up game. A sheath knife is good only for the same jobs that a butcher knife is used for, and for these—cutting bread and meat, and kitchen work generally—a good small butcher knife in the cook kit is much better. The pocket knife should be rather heavy, and fairly large, and should have two blades, one with a sharp point for fine work, and the other with a more rounded point for skinning. It should be of excellent steel, soft rather than hard so that it can be sharpened quickly and will not nick. The Remington Arms Company make a hunting knife that is of most excellent steel and ideal in every way.

The knife should be kept sharp to be of any use at all, and for this purpose a small whetstone should always be carried either in the pocket or in the rucksack. It will not do to have the whetstone back in camp for in skinning an animal the knife dulls with most remarkable rapidity, and even on so easily skinned an animal as a deer, has to be sharpened two or three times during the process. You can cut wood and whittle for hours with a knife and not dull it half as much as two minutes in skinning a large animal.

Match Safe.—Precaution dictates that every sportsman going into the wilderness should carry on his person a waterproof match box filled with matches. There are several good makes on the market. Keep it filled, and never use from it unless necessary, carrying a supply of matches loose in the pocket for ordinary use.

Contents of Pockets.—There are some things that you use often enough to make it advisable to carry them on the person at all times, but you seldom want them in a hurry, so you do not carry them on your belt. The pockets are the place for these articles, and a well-thought-out list might comprise the following: Watch, compass, pocket knife, waterproof match box filled, loose matches, pipe, tobacco pouch, whetstone, handkerchiefs, extra spectacles if you use them.

Spectacles.—For those hunters who are compelled to wear them, the best type of spectacles are those with large, round, toric type of lenses, and with rustless frames. Spectacles of this type are largely sold to rifle and shotgun shooters. The lenses should be of the toric type as such lenses have the same correction for vision at the edges as at the center of the lens, and therefore the sportsman will obtain his full correction in the portion through which he aims. It is well to have two pairs in case of an accident to one. The pair commonly worn should be of medium amber glass as this will reduce glare in bright sun or on the snow and will give better vision. But amber glasses are useless at night without artificial light, and the hunter coming back to camp after dark will find himself greatly handicapped with them, if indeed traveling over the rough ground is not absolutely dangerous. Therefore the other pair should be of the regular colorless glass, and should be carried in the pocket.

Toilet Articles.—Every man has his own pet list and kind of toilet articles. These might include hair-brush, comb, steel trench mirror, tooth brush, tooth powder or paste, safety razor, shaving brush, cake of soap in metal box, face towel, and bath towel. All of these except the towels should go in a little kit roll which may be of khaki so that they will be all together in the pack. Where transportation facilities are limited, as in backpacking or with canoe, the kit should be as small and compact as possible. Hair-brushes, shaving brushes, and tooth brushes are now to be had in very small and compact form, either folding or fitting into small cases, which are fine for small kits. It is well also to take a can of talcum powder and another of foot powder for the early days of the trip when one's skin will be more or less tender.

Repair Kit.—On all but the shortest trips some kind of a kit to make the necessary repairs to equipment and clothing is almost a necessity. Breaks, tears, rips, etc., occur very frequently in the rough life of the wilderness. As a suggestion my own full kit taken when I have plenty of transportation comprises the following:

Small tool holder, with awls, gimlets, screwdriver, etc.
Needles, darning and triangular glovers for leather.
Heavy linen thread (shoe thread).
Rivets and burrs.
Extra hobnails.
Assorted wire nails and tacks.
Buttons, safety pins.
Scissors.

Only a few of each article are taken, and the whole go in another little khaki kit bag. Sometimes a flat file for sharpening the axe is very desirable. The whetstone is carried in the rucksack or pocket, and a special folding screw driver for the rifle is included in the rifle cleaning kit.

Medicine Kit.—Whenever one goes over a day's journey into the wilderness some kind of a medicine kit should be taken along as a precaution. The clean and unspoiled wilderness is such a healthy place that this need not include much more than a laxative, dressings for serious axe wounds, and the special medicine for the treatment of any special weakness that some men have. Some men are addicted to colds, others to stiffness and rheumatism, and others to sprains and strains. In the tropics quinine may be very necessary, as well as iodine to treat all skin abrasions, and in some localities a snake-bite kit may be advisable. Usually the special travelers' kits are too bulky and heavy. They contain many articles which will never be used in the woods or mountains. It is better to make up one's own kit and pack it in a small tin box or pressed top waterproof can.

As the novice looks over the catalogue of a modern sportsman's outfitter, he will see many other articles which might appear to him to be advisable to take "because they might come in handy," but every additional article means more weight and bulk to be handled over portages or trails, and one more thing to take care of, and the old timer has found that it pays to go as light as possible, and cut out everything but the absolute essentials. There are, however, a few other articles that might be included. Among these are an electric flashlight and an alarm clock, both useful aids to getting one to the hunting grounds very early in the morning, and back again after sunset, so that the best hours can be spent in hunting. A small alarm clock will get you up two hours before sunrise, so that you can make your toilet, cook and eat breakfast, wash the dishes, and with the aid of the flashlight be able to start out for the hunting country while it is still dark, so as to arrive there in time for rosy dawn, that best hour of all for hunting. But avoid all patent gimcracks and all flimsy articles easily broken or torn. Such have no place in a wilderness outfit. Some articles it might be well to take two of, unless one is doing a lot of back-packing and has to travel very light—a pipe and a pocket knife, for example. Remember that the cardinal principle of wilderness outfitting is to go "light but right."

Packing.—All of the personal kit included in this chapter, with the exception of that worn or carried on the person, should be contained in some receptacle. On a back-packing or canoe trip they may be packed in the rucksack or packsack. When pack horses are used the sportsman should see that he has a pannier or alforjas reserved for his personal kit and perhaps his photographic kit. If the bulk of the personal articles are too big to go in such a container, then the clothing and underwear may be conveniently packed in a waterproof canvas bag. For back-packing and canoe trips this canvas bag can be one of the long, round ones, about 9 inches in diameter and 22 inches long such as is sold by sportsman's outfitters for this purpose, but for packing on a horse one shaped like an ordinary 50 pound flour sack or gunny sack is very much more convenient, also it can be used as a pillow. In these containers the articles should be packed with those less frequently required at the bottom. Right at the top of the pack should be the toilet kit, towels, rifle cleaning kit, repair kit, one suit of extra underwear, pair of extra socks, and the camp shoes or slippers in the order named. When camp is made these might be taken out and placed alongside the bed, and are then at hand without having to hunt all through the pack for them. They will be needed practically every day. Little things like this count in reducing the camp work to a minimum when one returns tired after a day's hunt or travel.

We have dealt so far with the ideal clothing, but as a matter of fact the sportsman will often extemporize clothing which he happens to have at home, and rightly so, in many cases, because well-broken-in and comfortable old clothes are more satisfactory than many new and perhaps poorly fitting garments. I well remember, as a young man, hunting for four months in a frock coat—the tails of which I had doubled up underneath and sewed into game pockets—overalls, and a pair of heavy knee-high boots I got by mail-order from Montgomery Ward. And I also remember several years ago starting out in a pair of new riding-breeches, and having all the seams rip and all the buttons come off in the first week, so that I was in a mess indeed. It pays to wear clothing that has been broken-in and tested beforehand.

CHAPTER XIX

CAMP BEDS AND BEDDING

"I go camping to have a good time, and one-third of that time is spent in bed."—Chauncey Thomas.

We go hunting and camping to have a good time, to accomplish a certain object, and to return with increased health and energy. Success in all of these depends very much on what kind of a bed we have. It is very easy for a sportsman, particularly an elderly man, to work so hard during the day that a sleep which is the least bit restless will fail to build him up again, and thus he may actually wear himself out and do damage to his system that it may take months to repair. On the other hand, it is extremely unlikely, no matter how hard the trip or task that the sportsman sets himself, that anything but better health and increased energy will result where one "hits the down" early, and is utterly oblivious until the next morning.

The first requisites of a good bed are that it shall be comfortable—that is soft enough and large enough. One should be able to turn over in it without getting all tangled up, and without waking up. It must be warm enough, but not too warm.

Secondary requisites are that the bed shall be light and lack bulk for packing, and that it shall be shower-proof.

Warmth in a bed depends upon insulation. There is nothing in a bed which gives warmth. The object of the covering is to keep in the warmth of the body. The best insulation is obtained by *dry air* confined in or between the fibres or layers of the covering. Closely woven blankets of a certain weight thus do not keep in as much warmth as a lighter comfort or quilt. Materials vary in conductivity of heat, cotton being poor, wool good, and fur or feathers the warmest of all.

It is necessary that the air contained in the covering be dry.

Damp air or damp covering conducts the heat away very rapidly. Cotton absorbs moisture readily. The body gives off much moisture during sleep, but under certain circumstances this moisture may rise through wool and escape without imparting much dampness to the wool. Going to bed with underclothes wet with perspiration means a cold and uncomfortable night. It is better to spend an hour by the camp fire drying clothes and bedding than to go to bed damp. It is better still to put on dry underclothes or dry pajamas.

These are the principles upon which your bed should be built. We will discuss first the covering, and then the methods and devices for making the bed soft. Comfort depends both upon the softness and upon the arrangement of the covering.

Blankets.—Blankets are almost obsolete for camp bedding in cool or cold climates. If woven closely enough to be durable they will not contain enough dry air to keep in the body warmth. When enough are taken to keep one warm they weigh much more than some other forms of covering, and bulk larger. It takes much time and labor to make a comfortable bed with them on the ground. Arranged as a camp bed they are either easily thrown off as one turns over in his sleep, or they tangle all up about one's limbs, neither of which are conducive to a sound sleep. The advantages of blankets are that they can be aired and dried easily, that they are convenient on a camp cot, that they are suitable in warm climates where only a light covering is necessary, and that often they can be taken from home thus making it unnecessary to go to the expense of purchasing special camp bedding. I have used blankets in camp, sleeping on the ground for an aggregate of approximately twenty-two months, and I would not willingly go back to them if I could get better forms of covering.

Sleeping Bags.—The original sleeping bags were merely blankets sewed lengthwise into bag form, and covered outside with a waterproof canvas cover. The bag was usually about 3 feet wide by 7 feet long, and you crawled in the top, one side being slit down about two feet to facilitate this operation. The advantages of the bag over the loose blankets were that you could not kick the blankets off, nor were they so liable to tangle up, that your bed was ready made at all times and that all you had to do was to lay it on top of your mattress, and finally that blankets in the form of a bag were warmer than separate blankets as there were not so many seams and cracks for the cold air to come in. But a hunting trip in the North where the thermometer went to freezing every night required that the sleeping bag be made of four blankets, giving four layers of blanket above and under the sleeper, and these together with the waterproof canvas covering brought the weight up to about 25 pounds, and the bulk was considerable. Various forms of camel's hair and llama wool blankets, very light and very loosely woven, have been tried, and this reduces the weight and bulk for equal warmth, but such blankets are not as durable as desired.

The ultimate development of the sleeping bag is one made with a wool comforter or quilt, the wool being quilted between a light, all-wool flannel, thus taking advantage of the non-conductivity and insulation of the loose material. The cover, too, instead of being of heavy waterproof canvas, is a very light cravenetted material which is fairly shower-proof, but which permits the moisture given off by the body during sleep to arise and evaporate in the air, thus keeping the quilt dry. Such bags combine the advantages of warmth, light weight, and small bulk, and are very satisfactory coverings for camp use. My own, which I have used for approximately an aggregate of twenty months in camp sleeping on the ground consists of a wool quilt with flannel lining weighing 5½ pounds, a thin wool blanket in bag form weighing 2 pounds, and cravenetted covering weighing 1½ pounds, total weight of 9 pounds. It measures 7 feet long by 3 feet wide, and it rolls into a bundle 3 feet long by 8 inches in diameter. When I first obtained it it contained only the wool quilt, but I found that this was not quite warm enough when the thermometer went below freezing at night, so I added the light wool blanket bag inside the quilt. I have often used it for many nights at a stretch when the temperature varied between 10 above and 15 below zero, and it is perfectly comfortable provided one's bed is sheltered from the wind, as inside a tent. This bag provides a very good compromise, and is adjustable for almost any temperature. Thus in warm weather one may use the wool blanket only, or even the cover only. When it gets a little colder just the wool quilt inside the cover is exactly right, while in the coldest weather the entire bag is sufficient. However, as I am notoriously warm blooded, and always sleep with much less covering than my companions, I think that this would be too cold a covering for the average man, and that he will be better advised to have his bag composed of two flannel-covered quilts, one about six pounds and the other about four pounds, together with the cravenette cover. Several of our large sportsmen's outfitters are now making up such sleeping bags.

It is often said that sleeping bags cannot be properly aired. The components of a modern sleeping bag are held together by tie ropes running through small holes at the four corners, and it is only necessary to loosen these ropes to take the bags entirely apart. Also the entire bag can be aired very well by laying it out in the sun and propping the inside open with small sticks. The only drawback about a wool quilt bag is that if it gets thoroughly wet it takes a long time to dry it.

Robes.—When the temperature gets much below minus 20 degrees it is almost impossible to sleep warm in a wool covering. Hunters, prospectors, and trappers in Alaska all use fur robes, single sheets about 8 feet square with the hair on one side and lined with light canvas on the other side. The robe is so large that it is unlikely that it will be kicked off during the night, and it has body enough to lie flat when one turns over. The warmest and most satisfactory fur is the hide of caribou which is the choice of the Eskimo. Robes are also made of wolf skin, mountain sheep skin, and moose skin, while the lightest of all but now very expensive, is one made of the hide of lynxes. Further south in British Columbia the hides of marmots or woodchucks are also largely used for robes.

But these robes are decidedly winter coverings for the Far North. They are entirely too warm, and also too expensive for covering on the ordinary hunting trip, even the trip pretty far into the North and pretty late in the fall. As a substitute for them, and more adapted to slightly warmer climes, the eiderdown robe has appeared on the market in the last few years. This is a rather thick quilt filled with the feathers of the eider duck, or often and practically as good, with goose feathers. On one side it is lined with an all-wool flannel, and on the other with a light, waterproof cotton or a light, cravenetted material. They are usually made in two sizes, about eight feet square, and about 7 feet by 6 feet, and have patent snap buckles along two sides so that they can be converted into a bag if desired. They are decidedly the best camp bedding ever devised for rather cold countries like Canada and our Rocky Mountains in the fall where the temperature at night will practically always be below freezing, and from that to thirty below. They are not as warm as fur robes, but have even been used with good satisfaction in the arctic. Their disadvantage is that there is only one thickness, and if that is too warm you are not comfortable. But in cold weather they keep in shape better than sleeping bags, they are lighter for their weight, although a little bulky, and one can toss around and turn a lot in them without waking up, they keeping put very much like one's bed at home with its mattress and its blankets tucked in all around. For hunting trips in Canada and the high mountains of our West they certainly are the most comfortable and perfect covering I have tried, and although they are rather expensive, they pay for themselves in the fine night's sleep they give. Formerly they were made only in Canada, but now one New York outfitter has made one that is even better than the Canadian bag, and not quite so expensive, duty considered.

Pillows.—Many hunters content themselves with a coat, a stag shirt, or a bag of clothing wrapped up as a pillow. This is all right just so long as it is thoroughly comfortable and does not interfere with a good night's rest. Usually, however, a good feather or air pillow is best, the latter if you want to cut down on weight and bulk. In Panama where I was carrying everything on my back I used to carry merely a pillow-case which I filled with palm leaves at night, and closed with safety pins, and it did very well. I have also used a pillow-case stuffed with underclothing this being much better than a canvas bag filled with the same articles. But the air pillow with a clean pillow-case over it is by far the best arrangement. Don't get too small a one. One widely advertised sleeping bag has an air pillow about as big as a ten-cent piece, and one's head will not stay parked on it for forty winks.

Mattresses.—So far we have considered the bed covering only, and not the bed itself which gives the softness on which to rest one's weary bones. The common mattress in the North is balsam or pine or spruce boughs, shingled on the ground by the well-known method. This is fairly good, good enough to make the young and hardy man quite comfortable, particularly if some pains is taken in making the bed, and if it be reset and freshened up almost every day.   But it takes a lot of time to make a good bough bed, at least a half hour and commonly more, usually at the time day when one finishes his journey and is both tired and hungry.   Soon the bough bed gets mashed down, when it is little better than the bare ground.   The older man, particularly, will find much to complain of about it, and will seldom be able to get a really refreshing sleep on it, certainly after the first night of sleeping on one.   But a balsam bed is romantic and it smells deliciously.

Further south, where balsam, spruce, and pine do not grow, one is harder put to it to make a good, soft bed from the materials at hand in the forest.   Horace Kephart used a bed-tick, merely a sack 6 feet long by three wide, which he filled with leaves or any kind of browse obtainable.   It was placed on ground smoothed over, and with hollows dug for the shoulders and hips.   Every day it can be taken up and shaken to stir up the matted leaves. It does fairly well, but it too is really comfortable only to the younger man, or to the old moss-back who is thoroughly hardened.

In the tropics it is best to go the limit and use a folding canvas cot wherever the transportation facilities will permit. A cot keeps one up out of the way of ants and other insects, and the mosquito bar, usually an absolute necessity in this country, is easily set up in conjunction with a cot.   In South America the hammock is almost universal, but we must remember that the native who uses it seldom camps away from the thatched shack, the supporting pillars of which he uses to tie his hammock to.   In the jungle trees do not always grow convenient for this purpose where one wishes to camp, and the hammock is often hard to pitch.   Also it is difficult to arrange the mosquito bar with one so that it will surely exclude all winged pests.   In Panama I used a thick pile of palm leaves placed on the ground for a mattress, and over it I staked down my little mosquito proof jungle tent with its light floor cloth on top of the leaves. This made quite a comfortable bed for the young man, but hardly so for the next older generation.

The air mattress is by all odds the best camp bed.   It gives one all the comforts of his home bed; often in fact it is much more comfortable to sleep on than any bed mattress.   It is light, easily deflated and packed, and is entirely suited for camp use. It is the bed of all others for the middle-aged or elderly man. Almost invariably the sportsman who tries one will never thereafter be without it willingly. It is not necessary to get the air mattresses the full size on one's bed at home. Thirty inches wide by four feet long is plenty large enough for use under a sleeping bag or robe. What you want is to get it under your head, shoulders, hips, and, perhaps, knees. A width of 30 inches enables you to utilize the full width of your 36-inch sleeping bag. The overhang of your feet at the bottom will not bother you any, and if it does all you have to do is to stick some boughs under there to build the bed up to the height of the mattress.

Not the least of the advantages of the blow bed is the ease, rapidity, and lack of labor in making your bed. Where a good balsam of spruce bed will require at least half an hour to build, the air mattress can be put in position and inflated ready for use in a couple of minutes. It should not be inflated tightly, but just so that when lying on it one can just barely get the feel of the ground under the shoulders and hips. This makes it most comfortable, and one is then not so liable to roll off of it. This degree of inflation is easily accomplished in a couple of minutes by lung power alone, but if desired the outfitters will provide you with a little, round pump that works like an accordion. There must be some arrangement for keeping the sleeping bag or robe squarely on top of the mattress, and to prevent it from sliding off during the night. This can be accomplished by laying two long logs about 30 inches apart, on the ground on either side of the bed space. Between these place a few boughs or some grass or leaves on the ground to keep the bedding away from the dirt and dampness. Shorter logs should also be placed at the head and foot of the bed. Between these logs in the bed space, and on top of the boughs or leaves, or grass, lay first your poncho or ground cloth, on top of that place your air bed and inflate it. Over all lay your sleeping bag or robe. This makes a very ship-shape bed. Or better still and less labor, you can have a light canvas or waterproof silk sack sewed on the bottom of your sleeping bag or robe to just contain the inflated air bed, and to hold the sleeping bag squarely in place on top of the mattress. Then all you have to do is to smooth off the ground a little with the back of your axe, lay the combined mattress and sleeping bag on top, and blow her up. However, there should be something between this combination and the ground like a poncho or ground cloth to keep dampness and dirt away from the mattress.

It has been said that air mattresses are cold to sleep on. I have not found them so, and I think that those who have have tried to lay blankets on top of the mattress as on a bed at home, with not sufficient bedding between the mattress and the body. Certainly the air mattress is never cold if one uses a sleeping bag or robe with it, having the same amount of bedding under one as on top. But if it still is cold a ready remedy is to place a folded blanket or a piece of skin with the hair on between the sleeping bag and the mattress. An air mattress 30 inches wide by four feet long will weigh about five pounds, and with a sleeping bag or robe of about ten pounds weight, makes a total weight for the entire bedding of about 15 pounds. Compare this with the old scheme of blankets or sleeping bag made of blankets, which for equal warmth required a weight of at least 25 pounds and gave very little comfort. By all odds the most satisfactory and comfortable camp beds one can obtain today are: For a climate where the nights are quite uniformly cold, an eiderdown robe arranged on top of an air mattress with a sack to contain the mattress sewed or otherwise arranged to stay with the robe; and for countries where one gets much range in temperature at night, a sleeping bag with several graded thicknesses of bags similarly arranged with an air mattress.

Packing the Bed.—For back packing the sleeping bag or robe, together with the air mattress, if one be taken, can be rolled in a round roll, about 3 feet wide, surrounded by a featherweight poncho or the light tent, and can then be carried as a single pack by placing pack-straps on it, or can be lashed on top of the packsack. For a canoe journey it is best to inclose this same roll in a round waterproof canvas duffle bag of the right dimensions, then if you get an upset your bedding does not get wet. On a pack horse it is best to fold the sleeping bag and air mattress once from top to bottom, mattress inside the bed to protect it, making a flat package about 3 feet square and three or four inches thick. Fold the poncho or ground cloth over it, and pass a light rope around it, still preserving the 3 feet square shape. Lay this on top of the horse pack just before the pack sheet is placed over the whole load, and then throw your hitch.

CHAPTER XX

SHELTER AND TENTS

A tent of some kind is the usual shelter and home of the big-game hunter. He needs first a comfortable, dry, warm place where he can get a good night's rest to recuperate after the exertions of the day afield, and second, his shelter should, if possible, be a jolly, attractive, temporary home. The important thing is to get the right kind of a tent shelter. If the camp is stationary and the transportation adequate, one need not skimp in the weight or bulk, nor need he consider the labor or time for pitching the tent, but can make himself perfectly comfortable with the many attractive goods offered by the modern outfitter. If, on the other hand, one goes the limit in the life of the nomad, he wants something that weighs next to nothing, takes but a couple of minutes to pitch, and is yet good for a three days' rain. Between these extremes there are tents whose weight need not be cut much as they are carried by pack-horse or canoe, tents for very cold weather, tropical shelters, and bug-proof tents to protect one where the bite of a single anopheles mosquito may mean deadly malaria.

If the hunter relies on his guide to supply the tent, the latter must provide what he can get in his out-of-the-way corner of the globe—usually a heavy wall tent, comfortable but a handicap in many ways on a trip where camp is moved every few days. But many sportsmen like to specialize on their outfit, and there are others who take a pride in going it alone, and these must needs figure everything—efficiency, comfort, weight, time, and labor. The following ideas present the views of a humble member of the latter class.

GENERAL CHARACTERISTICS OF TENTS

A tent of ordinary canvas, not waterproof, must have the roof made on a slope of at least 45 degrees or it will not shed a heavy rain. Even then drip will come through if anything touches the inside of the roof during a heavy rain. Sometimes even the touch of a finger to the roof is enough to start a leaking place. A fly over the roof remedies this trouble. Unwaterproofed tents must have the guys loosened in a rain for the canvas shrinks temporarily when it gets wet and will draw the pegs.

Tent material waterproofed by saturating with paraffine is good under most conditions, but it gradually loses its waterproof qualities if exposed to a very hot camp-fire or in tropical sun, and it becomes very stiff in cold weather. Decidedly the best material is duck with both warp and filling both double and twisted, or fine, closely woven Egyptian cotton, the material to be waterproofed by the green electric process which turns the goods a light green color.

The material must be strong enough to stand the strain of its weight when pitched, even in a strong wind. The very smallest tents for temporary camps should be made of nothing lighter than green waterproof Egyptian cotton which will weigh about 5 ounces per square yard. A wall tent 9 feet square should be made of canvas not lighter than 8 ounces per yard, and larger tents had better be constructed of the regulation 12-ounce, double-filled U. S. Army canvas. Such tents will stand the grief of the wilderness, and will last for a long time. The very light feather-weight materials are good for back-packing, where the weight must be cut to the last ounce, but they soon tear or wear through, and are seldom good for more than a single season.

A sewed-in floor-cloth, almost always of heavy, brown waterproof canvas, is advisable only in the worst mosquito countries, or when everyone uses air beds. Otherwise it is a confounded nuisance, and usually a positive handicap.

In figuring on the capacity of a tent, draw a floor plan to scale—1 inch equals 1 foot. For any degree of comfort you must allow a floor space not less than 3 feet wide and 7 feet long for the bed of each occupant, and there must be additional space for storing personal effects, rifles, packs, grub, and kindling wood. The roof should not come lower than 3 feet above the opening of the sleeping bag or it may be almost impossible to crawl into it.

The wall tent is the most common canvas shelter and it has stood the test of centuries. It is heavy and it takes time and labor to erect, but these do not count for much in a stationary camp. It is roomy, just right in shape where cots or stoves are used, and it is very comfortable. The roof is steep enough so that it sheds rain or snow well, and the roof does not sag. It

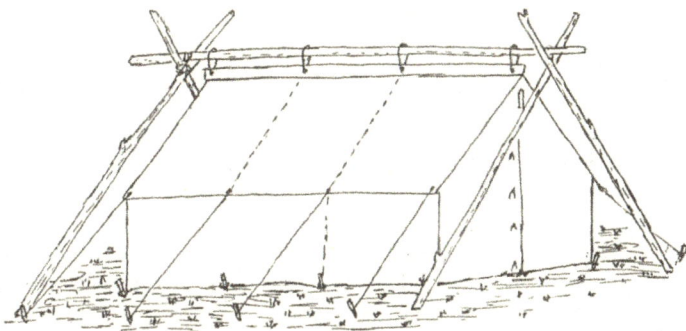

WALL TENT, SHOWING TAPE RIDGE AND MOST PRACTICAL METHOD OF PITCHING

should be made with a tape ridge with loops as shown in the illustration so that it can be erected with an outside ridge pole. (In fact this is an excellent feature for almost every form of tent). The walls should be made so that they can be rolled up and tied in hot weather. For the tropics there should be a door at each end. 7 x 7 feet on the ground with a height of 7 feet at ridge and 2½ feet at walls is about the smallest tent of this type that will be really comfortable for two men. It will weigh 10 pounds made of green waterproof Egyptian cotton, or about 15 pounds if of 8-ounce canvas. If you are to use a tent stove for warmth or cooking, figure your ground plan to determine the size of the tent so that there will be nothing inflammable within 18 inches of the stove. The stove-pipe ring through the roof must be of asbestos or tin, and the pipe should rise at least 6 inches above the peak of the tent outside or a heavy wind will blow sparks right into the roof.

A wall tent with a board floor, with fly over the roof and extending 6 feet or more in front as a porch, with "Gold Medal" cots, mattresses, a tent stove, and all the fixings of the big outfitters, is thoroughly comfortable in rain or shine, winter or summer, in any climate. Usually it is possible only for the hunter who camps in one locality, and who can get back again after each day's hunt. This is camping "de luxe," and not very different from living in a cabin or shack.

THE LEAN-TO

Decidedly the best form of tent for the hunter who moves camp every few days, who has to figure on weight and bulk, and on time and labor of pitching, is some form of lean-to. Such a tent is cheerful and warm with a fire in front. If it is properly made it can be pitched in a few minutes in a dozen different ways, accommodating itself to the ground and the facilities in poles and trees at the chosen camp-site. There are a great many forms of lean-to tents. Perhaps the most common is the "Baker" or shelter tent with a sloping roof, vertical sides, and a vertical back wall. I do not like it at all for a temporary camp. It takes more time and labor to pitch it right than a wall tent. The roof is not steep enough to either shed rain well or to reflect the heat of the camp-fire down upon the occupants and beds as it should. Snow makes the roof sag horribly. The "Forester" type of tent, especially when made with a hood in front, is a very satisfactory type. It is erected quickly with a tripod of poles, and reflects the heat well. I used one for a number of years and found it very comfortable and convenient. But I like something which will accommodate itself better to the problem as outlined by the particular place at which you stop to camp. It is often much easier to cut one pole and tie it to two trees for a ridge than to cut the three poles for the Forester, or to stretch a rope between two trees, or to jab one end of a pole into a tree and the other into the ground. A heavy snow storm may make it advisable to erect a strong ridge pole and lean other poles up against it to strongly support the roof. For all these purposes it is hard to beat just an ordinary tarpaulin of green waterproof Egyptian cotton. For two men it had best be a rectangle 8 feet wide by 12 feet long, with grommets every 2 feet around the edge, and weighing about 3½ pounds. It can be pitched in a dozen ways, but perhaps the most common and best is with a ridge about 6 feet long, the 8 foot length extending

TWO OF AUTHOR'S LEAN-TO CAMPS IN HUNTING COUNTRY, MADE
WITH SIMPLE LIGHT TARP, 8 FEET BY 11 FEET

HUNTER'S LEAN-TO TENT, FRONT AWNING THROWN BACK FOR FAIR WEATHER

HUNTER'S LEAN-TO TENT, FRONT AWNING STRETCHED OUT FOR RAIN OR SNOW

back to the ground, and the long ends brought down to the sides as shown in the illustration. Such a tarp is always most useful in camp to cover stores, as a canoe cover in heavy seas, as a fly over the tent or the cook fire, etc.

My pet lean-to, however, is a tarp cut and shaped as shown in the accompanying sketch. It has a 6-foot ridge and triangular sides which can be brought down to the ground. There is a tape ridge for quickly tying to any form of ridge pole, and a little front awning which will shelter from rain or snow driving into the front. As it spreads out perfectly flat it can be used in every case just as well as the plain rectangular tarpaulin. Any handy-man can make one up himself, or any tent maker can make it to order. The size given is about right for two men. In designing one figure on the floor space you want, and then cut the tarp out of stiff paper, 1 foot equal to one inch, and get the dimensions just right before you start to make it up.

In a lean-to, or before a camp fire, the best way for the sleepers to lie is lengthwise, with side toward the fire, and not as is usually done with feet to the fire. The idea that a man sleeps warmest with his feet to the fire comes from the pernicious habit of going to bed with wet feet or damp socks. To sleep warmest before a camp fire one should have his vital organs, his abdomen and small of the back, nearest the fire. The feet will be perfectly warm if one takes the trouble to put on dry socks before turning in. Sleeping in damp socks or damp underwear is a bad habit, and is not conducive to a good night's rest or the best health in camp. A daily bath may not always be possible in the cold of late fall in the woods or mountains, but at least one can take along a change of underwear and socks, and after he reaches camp, usually in a more or less perspiring condition, a strip, rub-down with rough towel, and the clean, dry clothes will be as good as a bath, and will insure a warm, comfortable evening and night's rest, as well as greatly preventing stiffness. Flannel pajamas also are fine for sleeping outdoors.

PLAN OF LEAN-TO TENT

Most comfortable size for one man but will hold two nicely. Figures give dimensions in feet. Weight when made of green waterproof Egyptian cotton, 5 pounds.

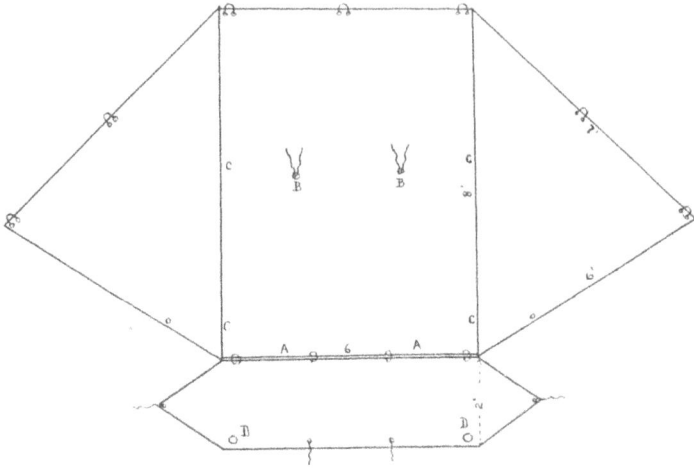

PLAN OF HUNTER'S LEAN-TO TENT, SHOWING CONSTRUCTION

A.—Tape ridge with grommets and four cord loops for ridge pole.

B.—Tie tapes sewed to roof to take belly out of roof.

C.—Tape loops inside roof to tie mosquito bar to.

D.—Large size grommets for poles to hold out front awning. Under apex of ridges are two tape loops through which a stick is thrust for hanging clothes, etc., on to dry.

THE TEPEE

The tepee or Indian lodge is one of the two great inventions or developments of the American Indian which that race has handed down to posterity, and which will endure for all time; the other being the light, portable canoe. The tepee in its perfected form is the product of the Indians of the Northwestern plains and the Rockies from the Colorado to the Liard. In this form it has never been improved on, and is far superior to any other type of cold-weather tent. The tepee is not a light tent, and in certain localities it is difficult to get the proper poles for its erection. But in any country where fairly straight poles can be found or cut, and where the transportation is adequate—pack horse, canoe, or team—it is by far the most satisfactory winter

TWO OF AUTHOR'S TEPEE CAMPS IN THE NORTHERN ROCKIES

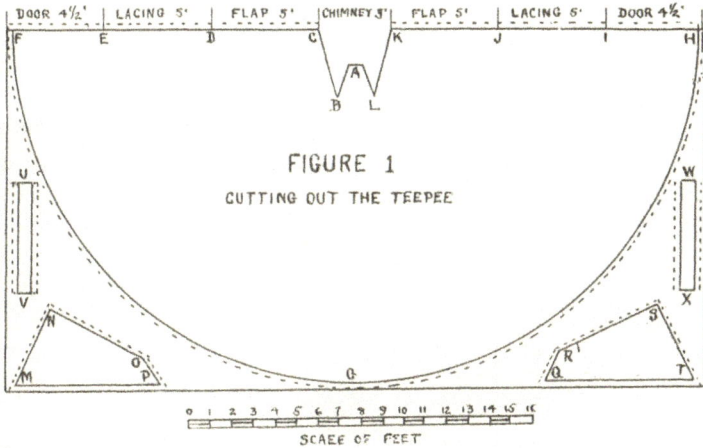

FIGURE 1

CUTTING OUT THE TEEPEE

SCALE OF FEET

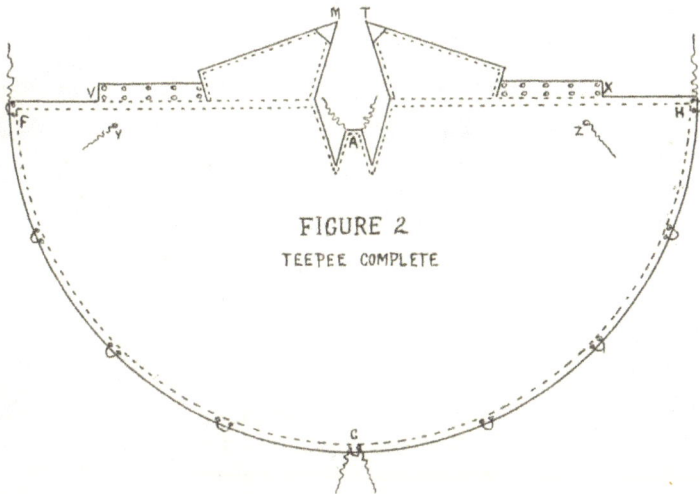

FIGURE 2

TEEPEE COMPLETE

tent. It seems to be the fashion among certain writers to condemn many things on hearsay evidence, and it is true that the tepee has been much maligned by those who do not know it. To be satisfactory it is necessary that it be constructed right, pitched right, and managed right.

Strange to say, very little has appeared in print on this essentially American type of tent. Several writers have described its construction, and several have written much rubbish on how to run it. Ernest Thompson-Seton first described its construction. Others who have written on how to make it have merely copied Seton's description without giving him credit for it. Seton knew how a tepee should be made. He got it exactly right, but he described it only for boys, and his diagrams show it only in

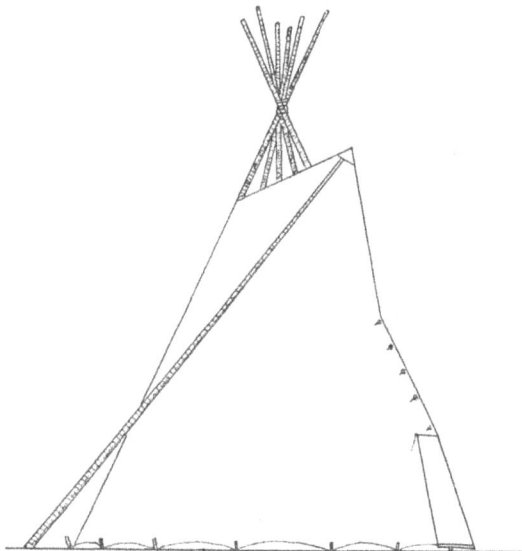

FIGURE 3

boy's size. It is quite amusing to note that writers who have thus plagiarized Seton have made their descriptions for men, but have adhered to the small tent Seton designed for boys, thus recommending a shelter so small as to be ridiculous.

I wish here to acknowledge the assistance I have received from Seton's writings. But on the subject of the proper pitching of the tepee, or on its management, all writers are either entirely silent, or else their descriptions have been so altogether wrong as to indicate that they had no practical knowledge of their subject. The novice who followed their instructions would very shortly declare the tepee and its fire to be absolutely impossible.

Pitched and operated right, the tepee is under all conditions of cool or cold weather the most satisfactory temporary or portable home imaginable. You come back after a day afield in shine or rain, snow or bitter cold, and in five minutes you are sitting dry, warm, and comfortable, with a cheerful open fire in front of you, the wood crackling, the sparks and smoke going straight up, the cheerful warmth radiating everywhere, and the light from the fire, reflecting on the canvas, illuminating the whole interior.

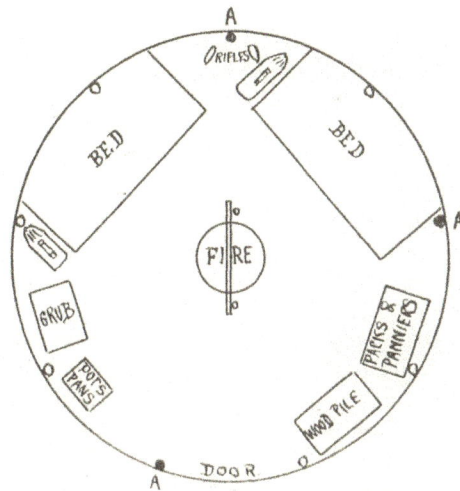

FIGURE 4

AAA - THREE INITIAL TRIPOD POLES

FIGURE 5

Cooking is a real pleasure over such a fire because the smoke goes straight up, never in your eyes or nose, and it makes no difference if it is raining cats and dogs outside. After the day's work it is a real luxury to lie back on a comfortable bed or couch and watch the glow of the wood fire. It is a thousand times more cheerful than the unromantic sheet-iron stove, and easier to run. It is never too cold or too hot, as the temperature can be regulated exactly by the size of your fire.

With proper pitching of the tepee and proper management of the fire, there is no smoke nuisance, notwithstanding popular opinion to the contrary. In the morning you do not get up and dress in the cold or crawl out in the rain or snow to build the fire; you reach one arm out of your sleeping bag or robe, lay a bundle of previously prepared shavings and kindling wood on the fire-place, touch a match, and ten minutes later you arise in a warm, light, and comfortable home. On a recent trip of two months Stanley Clark and I pitched our tepee twenty-three times and we never took over fifteen minutes to do it. In the two or three instances where we did not find poles already cut at our camp sites, it did not take us over three-quarters of an hour from the time we stopped the pack train until we had the tepee up and a fire going in it.

The best size for the tepee is 16 feet in diameter. This size permits two men to sleep, cook, and live in it in perfect comfort and to store in it all their packs and duffle. It will accommodate three men with scarcely any crowding. The 16-ft. size permits of the best management of the fire. In a country where lodge poles are usually found at all camp sites they will be just right for a 16-foot tepee. The following instructions have, therefore, been written for this size. A 10-foot tepee will just barely accommodate one man, and the fire will be a little difficult to manage well, being so close to the bed that often its heat will be uncomfortable. A 14-foot tent is the smallest that can be recommended for two men and there will be little room in it for duffle. Larger than 16 feet makes a rather unwieldly and heavy tent, difficult to pitch and hard to transport.

The best material for the tepee is 8-ounce duck. Thinner and lighter materials can be used, but the light material is liable to be punctured or worn by the little knots on the poles. Made of 8-ounce canvas or Egyptian cotton, tepees will weigh about as follows:

Diameter	8-oz. canvas	Egyptian Cotton
10 ft.	13 lbs.	7 lbs.
12 ft.	19 lbs.	10 lbs.
14 ft.	30 lbs.	16 lbs.
16 ft.	50 lbs.	28 lbs.

It is not at all necessary that the cloth be waterproofed. The steep pitch precludes any leaking in of the rain and almost all waterproofing depends more or less on paraffin, and paraffin will not stay in the canvas on account of the heat of the fire. It is also advisable that the canvas be white, not khaki or tan color, for if white the light of the fire will afford perfect illumination at night and makes the use of a lantern or candles entirely unnecessary.

The professional tent-maker will probably cut his canvas so as to utilize the full width of the strip at the bottom or ground edge of the tent, and taper the strip up to the peak. The method is hardly practicable with the amateur, and he had better first sew his canvas in a rectangle and then cut out the pattern as shown in Fig. 1. In this way the construction is simplified and very little canvas is wasted because the few spare pieces are used for reinforcements. For a 16-foot tepee you first sew your canvas into a rectangle 32 feet 4 inches by 16 feet 2 inches, approximately; a couple of inches more or less makes little difference. Using a point in the center of the longest side, describe a semi-circle with a radius of 16 feet 2 inches. The tent is to be 16 feet on the slope from the peak to the ground, the 2 inches being the allowance for a hem around the bottom. Mark out, also, the cuts at the peak, the two smoke flaps, and the pieces for the front lacing as shown in Fig. 1, leaving margins for hemming as shown by the dotted lines. The scale accompanying Fig. 1 indicates the measurements of the various parts where not given.

Sew the two smoke flaps and the front lacing pieces to the semi-circular main piece exactly as shown in Fig. 2, which shows the complete tent. Note the reinforced hemming and the seams as shown by the dotted lines. The reinforcing at the peak "A" which is tied to the back pole and keeps the tent up tight should be particularly strong. At "M" and "T" triangular pockets are sewn in the peaks of the smoke flaps into which the smoke poles are inserted. These pockets should be double canvas on both sides, and very strongly sewed so that the poles will not poke through. The lacing holes in the front pieces should be in series of two. The two holes are about 3 inches apart, and each series of two is a foot apart. These holes should be made with buttonhole stitch, and should be of such size that a lacing pin ½-inch in diameter can be inserted through them. They serve to pin the front of the tent together after it has been erected and wrapped around the cone of poles. Grommets and peg ropes should be provided around the bottom of the tent, nine of them, spaced as shown.

To certain points of the tepee should be strongly sewed heavy oil-tanned, rawhide belt laces or thongs, as follows: To the bottom of each smoke flap thongs about 4 feet long, to the bottom of the door at "F" and "H" thongs about 18 inches long, to the grommets at "G" two thongs 12 inches long, to the peak "A" two thongs 18 inches long, or rather one thong passed through the re-inforcement and projecting 18 inches on either side, and to the points "Y" and "Z" through small grommets, two thongs a foot long. This completes the tepee, and as will be seen, it is very sim-ple, the only thing involved being a lot of sewing and a little but-ton-hole work. Your best girl will show you the button-hole stitch. Any sail or harness maker will insert the grommets for you with a little machine he has. In a pinch you can do away with the grommets and simply sew in rawhide laces as the Indians did. Rawhide belt laces can be had at any large hardware store. Get those about twice the thickness you use for laces in your sporting boots. They hold very much better and last longer than ropes, and are easier tied and untied.

To pitch the tepee you need eleven poles. They should be as straight as possible, about 20 to 22 feet long, 3½ to 4½ inches in diameter at the butt, and 1 to 2 inches in diameter at the tip. In the Northwest the lodge pole pine or jack pine makes perfect poles and is the tree that the Indians used for this purpose. In localities where this tree does not grow it may take some time to find eleven straight trees of the requisite size. For this reason in the East the tepee is usually confined to more or less per-manent camps, as it takes too long to find and cut the poles every move.

All through the Rocky Mountains from Montana northward tepees have been used for hundreds of years, and usually at every good camp site you will find sets of these poles stacked up all ready for use. Sportsmen should never cut these poles up for smaller tents, or use them for firewood—remember the other fellow coming to that camp site tired and hungry, perhaps in vile weather, expecting to find poles all ready. When you are through with a set of poles, stack them up so they will not rot. I have often come to very old Indian camp sites that I know had not been occupied for forty or fifty years, and found the poles nicely stacked up and most of them usable.

Place three of these poles on the ground, close together and parallel, the butt of the center one six inches below the butts of the outside ones, as shown in Fig. 5. Over these poles lay the tepee, inside down, the back tent peg loop ("G" in Fig. 1) at the butt of the center pole, and the peak "A" pulled out as far as it will go toward the tip of the center pole. Tie the tent at the back tent peg loop "G" to the butt of the center pole, using the two thongs at "G." Tie it tight as close to the very end of the butt as possible. Stretch the center of the tent tight along the center pole, and tie the peak "A" tight to the center pole. With a lash rope, halter shank, or other strong piece of rope, tie all three poles tightly together at a point $2\frac{1}{2}$ feet above the point where the peak "A" is tied to the center pole. These three poles are to form the tripod upon which you lean six other poles to make the cone of nine poles around which the tent is erected and wrapped.

Erect these three poles as a tripod, butts about 14 ft. apart. The butt of the center pole, with the tepee tied to it, should be placed just about where the back of the tent is to come. One of the other poles is to be placed with its butt where the side of the door will come and will form one of the door poles. The third pole is placed in the circumference of the 14-foot circle, equidistant between the other two poles, making a firm tripod. Against this tripod you now lean the remaining six poles, butts equidistant around the 14-foot circumference, one of these poles being located for the other door pole, as shown in Fig. 4.

Around this cone of poles you now wrap the tepee, the peak of which has already been stretched to its full height, by being attached to the back pole. To get it approximately high enough you take hold of its upper portion and just fling it up on the poles. The two door ends, "F" and "H," come around to the butts of the door poles. To assist in getting the tent high enough on the cone you may take the tenth and eleventh poles (which should be about a foot longer than the other 9 poles, and need not be as straight or heavy), insert them in the pockets of the smoke flaps, and poke the peak of the tent upward as shown in Fig. 3. Next, you tie the front of the tent at "F" and "H" to the butts of the door poles. Then you cut five little pins from a bush, about ½ to ¼ inch in diameter, about 6 inches long and slightly pointed at the ends, and with these you pin the front of the tent together above the door, poking the pins through the holes in the two sides of the tepee, and out through the other two of the series of holes. This keeps the front of the tent together.

Your tepee is now up, but it is a rather baggy, sad-looking thing because the circle of poles is only 14 feet in diameter, and you have not adjusted it into shipshape form. Go inside the tent, and a pole at a time, move them all out about a foot until the canvas is all taut and smooth. You may also have to move the poles a little to one side or another, particularly the back pole to which the back of the tepee is tied, to make the canvas smooth all around. Also the door poles may have to be spread a little bit, or brought closer together. Usually these door poles are about 4 feet apart, and the other poles about equidistant around the circumference of the tent. Raise the smoke flap poles enough to make all smooth about the peak of the tepee. Then go outside, cut nine tent pegs, and pin down the bottom of the tepee all around, but do not pin it down tight to the ground. The sides must be up a little off the ground to allow air to get through, or the fire inside will not draw. If the canvas is an inch above the ground at each peg, and two to three inches above midway between pegs it will suffice. For a one-night stand in calm weather the pegging down of the tent is not necessary. Also it is always possible, if in a hurry, to erect a tepee on a tripod of poles only, like a lean-to, and build the fire in front.

The tepee should be pitched so that the door is at right angles to the prevailing winds. Winds usually blow up or down a valley, so the door should be pitched facing one side of the valley. In the East, in open country, wind usually has either an easterly or westerly direction, seldom, if ever, coming from due north or due south, therefore the door should face either due north or due south. The only time you will ever have any trouble with smoke is when the wind blows straight into the door, and then only when the door is open. As stated above, the sides of the tent must not meet the ground by from 1 to 3 inches all around. This is absolutely necessary, and must be looked to particularly when it is snowing, as the tent may have to be dug out to preserve this air space.

Take a pack cover, or any small tarp or piece of canvas, most convenient size 4½ feet square, and tie it by its two upper corners to the two tie cords or thongs at "Y" and "Z," Fig. 2, letting the tarp hang down over the door opening, thus closing the opening. Tie a short pole along the lower edge of this tarp or door. This will weight the bottom of the door and keep it down and in place. The door usually must be kept closed while the fire is going to keep it from smoking, although there are certain conditions of wind when the door does not need to be kept closed.

Usually the fire will draw correctly no matter how the smoke flaps are arranged, but if there is any difficulty raising the flap on the side from which the wind is blowing, lowering the flap on the other side will correct it. If the wind blows straight from the back of the tent raise both flaps up high, but prop the poles outward at the top so that there will be an opening between the smoke flaps in the front of the tepee. If the wind comes straight toward the door raise the flaps and bring their peaks around so that they lap in front and completely close the front of the peak, and also keep the door tight shut.

The fire is built in the center of the tepee, and occupies a space not over 2 feet in diameter. In front and rear of the fireplace are driven forked sticks, fork about 2½ feet above the ground, and on these is rested the cross-piece from which are hung the usual pot hooks for the kettles. The fire is built cone-shaped by setting up the wood pyramid fashion, highest in the center. Only dry wood should be used and it should be cut in lengths of from 12 to 15 inches and split. Split some of it small enough to use for kindling wood and to encourage a blaze until the fire burns down to a good bed of coals. As a usual thing try to get wood that does not throw big sparks, as the beds are placed very close to the fire and a sparking wood is liable to burn holes in the blankets unless one is constantly on the watch. It is good to have a little pitch pine to put on the fire as soon as supper is cooked, as the flames from this wood make the interior of the tepee as light as day.

The firewood is piled up on one side of the door as shown in Fig. 4. On the other side are the pots and pans and the grub sacks. The beds occupy positions as shown, logs being staked down to confine them and their pine-bough mattress. The personal duffle bags are placed at the head of each man's bed and the rifles are stood up in rear of the tepee, their muzzle through a rawhide loop tied to a pole. Rawhide laces may tied from pole to pole about five feet above the ground and make convenient places to hang extra clothing and wet socks. Each man's hunting belt with the field glasses, hunting knife, and cartridges is buckled to a pole above the head of his bed. Fig. 5 also shows where packs and panniers are placed if desired. When the camp was in shape I usually placed my toilet, repair, and rifle-cleaning kits, each in its little moose hide roll, on the side of my bed, between the bed and the wall, and thus I had everything needed right at hand. The axe and wash basin are placed outside against the tepee near the door. Saddles are hung up on a pole lashed between two trees where they will be out of the way of knawing porcupines, weasels, and rabbits.

A draft comes in under the walls of the tepee. This is necessary to make the fire draw, and it keeps the air fresh inside. Twenty-nine days in the month this draft is not noticed. About once a month heavy wind will make it unpleasant as one lies or sits on his bed. The remedy is to take a pack cover, or any other piece of canvas, tarp, or piece of clothing, tie it to the poles about two feet above the bunk, and let it droop down as a curtain, tucking the bottom under the bedding. So long as half the circumference of the tepee is up from the ground the fire will draw well.

Some writers have asserted that the Indians placed a curtain all around the tepee in this manner. This is a mistake. It is not necessary, it seldom was done, and I doubt if the fire would draw well with such an arrangement. The draft could not get at the bottom of the fire where it is needed. I asked Dr. George Bird Grinnell about this feature, knowing that he knew more about the old tepee Indians than any living American. He said that he had never seen such a curtain, although sometimes if the wind was strong the Indians would hang up a blanket back of their bed as described. The Indians usually make one bed at the back of the tepee, placing the fire about a foot or so toward the door from the exact center of the tepee, but the arrangement of beds and fire as shown in Fig. 4 is best for white men.

If the tepee is pitched, arranged, and run as described it will be found the most comfortable home imaginable. Lean-to tents with a fire in front are nice for a time, but they involve too much labor in getting the wood for the large fire that is required to make them even passably warm in cold weather, and they cannot be kept comfortable in a wind. Moreover, the smoke nuisance, particularly when one is cooking, is dreadful. Also there are often times when it is impossible to keep the lean-to free from smoke. In a rain cooking is very difficult and disagreeable. As for a closed tent with tent stove, while it is comfortable, the stove is very unromantic, and an abomination to pack. It usually does not give out enough heat, or it roasts one out and gives no light. It is not to be compared with the cheerful tepee open fire with its flame, glowing embers, and genial warmth. Of course, the fire gives out smoke, but when managed as described this smoke is entirely confined to a column immediately above the fire, and it does not spread out until it reaches a point about $5\frac{1}{2}$ feet above the floor. A man cannot stand straight up in a tepee when the fire is 'going, for his head will be in the smoke. He should walk in stooped over, and then sit down, and when he moves around he should bend over or go on hands and knees.

I do not advise a tepee for the eastern United States or Canada, except for a permanent camp, because it takes too long to find, cut, and trim the necessary poles. But for a permanent camp it will be ideal in our North woods, being a much healthier abode than the little, stuffy, poorly ventilated, and dirty log cabins usually found throughout the hunting country of New Brunswick and Ontario. In the Southwest, also, straight poles are entirely too difficult to obtain, and in a warm country, of course, the fire would soon roast the occupants out. In summer, the Indians built the fire out in front of the door of the tepee, and they rolled the walls of the tepee several feet up the poles, much as we raise the walls of a wall-tent today in hot weather. With the walls raised in this way the tepee is very cool in hot weather, because the hot air ascends through the open top instead of accumulating inside as it does in closed-top tents. It is in the Rockies, from Colorado northward, where straight lodge-pole or other pines and spruces abound, that the tepee is at its best. There, whenever one has a canoe or pack horse to transport it, it is the best of all tent homes, and is even satisfactory in the middle of winter.

Once two of us weathered a blizzard in the far Northern mountains in a 14-foot tepee. We were in a valley of dead jack-pines. The thermometer dropped way down, and for three days it snowed and blew a gale. We had plenty of good firewood, and a pack cover apiece hung up back of our bunks kept all draft out. Did we suffer? Not much. If the truth must be told, four or five days before we found a number of old magazines at an old camp site, and the whole three days we lay on our bunks in perfect comfort reading and getting up only to cook some most delicious meals, including steaks and liver of a young grizzly I had shot several days before.

CHAPTER XXI

BIG-GAME RIFLES

There is no article of sporting equipment to which so much attention and specialization has been given as the big-game rifle. American sportsmen are not content with choosing their rifles from among a number of standard models, but are deep students of the whole subject, including even design, construction, and manufacture, and of late years many of them have come to having their rifles made to order, and writing the specifications themselves down to the most minute details. Every sportsman's magazine in the United States and Canada devotes a complete department to the subject, and the writers are legion. Every man, no matter what his experience or his lack of experience, feels perfectly competent to discuss the matter in all its phases, and some editors print practically everything that they receive on the rifle. Indeed some of the so-called experts, whose efforts in this line we see appearing in print every month, have never been in the big woods and have never shot a head of big game in their lives. From among all this mass of matter it is very difficult for the sportsman looking for the best advice "to take the corn and leave the chaff behind."

THE CARTRIDGE

It is important that we start our discussion with the cartridge, for on its choice depends most of the important characteristics of the big-game rifle. We will regard the older, lower power cartridges as obsolete and divide our modern cartridges into three classes, the *small bore* (.25 caliber and under), *medium*, and *magnum* (very heavy) cartridges. There would seem to be just two requirements: First, that the cartridge have sufficient killing power to dispatch the game neatly and humanely, with an absolute minimum on the number of cripples that go off to die a lingering death. Any cartridge short of this is decidedly un-sportsmanlike. Second, that the cartridge be such that the rifle using it shall have sufficient accuracy, flat enough trajectory, and a moderate enough recoil so that the sportsman can place his bullets with sufficient degree of accuracy. It is only the shots that strike well into the vital areas of an animal that will kill quickly and humanely. The very heaviest cartridge that can be fired from a shoulder rifle will not kill humanely if it does not strike in a vital area.

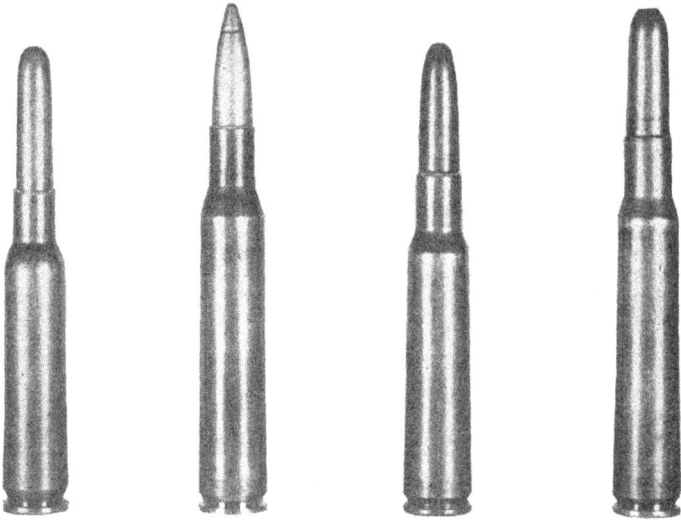

THE BEST BIG-GAME CARTRIDES. LEFT TO RIGHT: 6.5 MM. MANN-LICHER, .270 WINCHESTER, 7 MM. MAUSER, AND .30-06 U. S. GOV-ERNMENT

Killing power.—From this standpoint there are two types of modern cartridges. First, the ultra high velocity type with light bullets, giving a muzzle velocity of 2,700 feet per second and over. These give remarkably quick kills in a majority of cases, but until very recently the bullets for them were made very light and were almost always constructed with too thin jackets and of such type that they opened up or expanded much too easily and readily on heavy bones or heavy muscular tissue, and hence they frequently failed to reach the vital organs at

which they were directed. Some of these ultra high-velocity
bullets will often actually fail to penetrate through six inches of
heavy muscular tissue. I have had the bullets remain in the
bodies of woodchucks, otter, and beaver. Such cartridges give
a chance for failure. If possible the sportsman will wish to
eliminate any such chance. Second, the medium high-velocity
type of cartridge using a heavy bullet, and having a muzzle velocity of from 2,300 to 2,500 feet per second. This type kills
well, although undoubtedly it does not give the proportion of
absolutely instantaneous kills that the first type is noted for, but
they practically never fail when properly directed. Many sportsmen have preferred this type because they feel that if they
do their part correctly they will experience no failures, although
some of their animals may go one hundred yards or so before
dropping. Decidedly the best cartridge seems to be a compromise between these two types, but with a more modern bullet
than either contains. The bullet should be quite a little heavier
than those seen in the ultra high-velocity type of cartridge, it
should have a jacket about three times as thick as the usual
jacket, and there should be only a pin point of lead exposed at
the point, or else just a small hole drilled through the jacket
into the point of the lead core, but this hole should not enter
the core any appreciable distance. Such a bullet can be given
a muzzle velocity of 2,700 feet per second or over in many
of our modern cartridges. It gives the instantaneous kills of
the first type without failures. It practically always carries its
path of destruction through bone and heavy muscular tissue into
the vital organs.

Accuracy.—Let us liken the vital area which presents itself
to aim on a big-game animal to an 8-inch disc or circle. Then
a cartridge is suitable for hitting the vital areas of big game only
up to that range at which all its shots, when fired by a good
marksman, can be contained within this 8-inch circle. Some
cartridges will do this only up to about 150 yards, others to 200,
and a few to 300 yards or over. One would hardly choose one
of the 150-yard accuracy cartridges for mountain sheep or other
game which frequently has to be shot at very long range. Other
things being correctly attended to, the accuracy of a cartridge
and the rifle adapted to it depends upon the fit of the cartridge
and bullet in the chamber of the rifle so that the bullet passes

from the case, through the throat, into the bore with the minimum deformation to itself. Decidedly the most accurate cartridges are those of the modern military type having long bullets which project a considerable distance beyond the mouth of the cartridge case and have much of their bearing exposed. It is possible to chamber a rifle for such a cartridge so that the bullet fits accurately in the throat ahead of the chamber. Thus the bullet is trued up by the throat so that its axis coincides with the axis of the bore before firing. Such cartridges in rifles chambered in this manner give the maximum accuracy at short, mid, or long range.

Trajectory.—Any modern rifle firing a fairly long and pointed or semi-pointed bullet, and having a muzzle velocity of 2,400 feet per second or over has a sufficiently flat trajectory to make it unnecessary for the hunter to estimate the distance up to 200 yards. With such a rifle a sure hit can almost always be obtained up to 300 yards by aiming slightly higher on the body of the animal above a vital area if the hunter believes the range to be longer than 200 yards. In practice such rifles have been found to be all that is desired for shots up to 300 yards, which may be regarded as the extreme sporting range for the modern big-game rifle in the hands of a good shot. Therefore the bullet should be long and pointed or semi-pointed, and the muzzle velocity should be at least 2,400 feet per second to obtain the desired trajectory—that is, a height of trajectory at 100 yards of not more than 3.5 inches when the rifle is sighted for 200 yards.

Recoil.—Some men can stand more recoil than others without affecting their fine sense of coordination which permits accurate aim, steady hold, and correct trigger squeeze, those three primary essentials of good marksmanship. The more experience in rifle shooting a man has had the heavier recoil can he stand up to a certain point. A very moderate recoil will often so disturb the tyro that he cannot shoot a heavy-charged rifle without flinching, and hence cannot make hits with it. Experience has shown that a majority of experienced marksmen can readily withstand the recoil of the heaviest hunting loads made for the .30-06 cartridge in an 8½-pound rifle, and that there are very few that can stand more recoil than this and still do really good work, particularly in rapid fire. There are quite a number of light or less experienced sportsmen who cannot even stand the recoil of the

.30-06 cartridge and do good shooting. Once again, it is only the shots that strike well into the vital areas of big game that count.

Small-bore rifles.—There is a certain class of men in the United States called "small-bore cranks." They advocate the use of .25 caliber or even smaller rifles of high velocity for big game. They seem to think that there is something reprehensible about carrying larger rifles "when the little rifle will do the work." I admit that experience has shown that some of these small-bore, high-velocity rifles will kill deer quickly and humanely, but they are not satisfactory in these respects for larger game, and I consider their use on game larger than deer as extremely unsportsmanlike. If a hunter uses such a rifle, very often instead of killing his game instantaneously or within a few seconds at most, he gives it a lingering or painful death by firing many shots into it before he brings it to bag, or he merely wounds it and it goes off to die after hours or days of suffering while the mighty hunter armed with his tiny weapon proceeds to wound and ultimately kill another or several other animals until he actually brings to bag the one or two head permitted by his license. This is not humane, it is not sportsmanlike, nor does it tend to conserve the game.

Magnum cartridges.—The pilgrimages of many of our sportsmen to African game fields, and to the habitat of the big, brown bears of Alaska, and their writings on the subject of hunting the animals of these regions, has lately introduced still another type of cartridge into the United States—the Magnum. It is rather hard to define or limit a "magnum" cartridge. Generally it is one of extremely high power, medium or high velocity, and heavy bullet. Such cartridges range in size from those intended for medium-sized big game to those designed for use only on the thick-skinned dangerous game of Africa, including the elephant. Among certain of our hunters, particularly the very wealthy class, these cartridges are attaining a certain degree of popularity because they are so high in the scale of killing power. But they one and all are characterized by very heavy recoil, and there are very few marksmen who can shoot even the lightest of them without flinching. For the third time, it is only the shots that strike well into the vital areas of an animal that count. We have many excellent cartridges of moderate recoil that will kill every time on any American game when they strike in the vital areas, and no cartridge can do more. Magnum cartridges, by reason of their heavy recoil, are usually not as satisfactory as rifles of slightly lighter recoil, and however their killing power may be needed for certain classes of African game, they are not necessary nor desirable for any American game.

The best cartridges for American big game.—I regard the following cartridges as being the most suitable for use on all American big game, considering killing power, recoil, accuracy, and flatness of trajectory:

256 Mannlicher or 6.5 mm. Mannlicher.—Used in Mannlicher-Shoenauer and Mauser bolt-action rifles. The best bullet is the long one, weighing from 150 to 160 grains, and giving a muzzle velocity in a rifle having a 26-inch barrel of from 2,250 to 2,300 f.s. This long bullet drives well through heavy bones and muscular tissues, and is much better than the lighter bullets which in this cartridge cannot be given that ultra high velocity which would make them kill well. This cartridge with the heavy bullet has been used so extensively on our big game for the past thirty years that there is no doubt as to its efficiency. The recoil is very light. It is the lightest cartridge that I would consider suitable for all American big game.

.270 Winchester Center Fire.—Used in Winchester Model 54 bolt-action rifle. This is the newest cartridge of the lot, so new that it has not at the present writing been tried on big game. But I venture to predict that it will be found one of the best. The standard cartridge fires a pointed, easily expandable 130-grain bullet at the very high muzzle velocity of 3,160 f.s. I believe that if this cartridge were modified to use a 140-grain open-point bullet, with copper jacket almost twice as thick as the standard jacket, muzzle velocity 3,000 f.s., it would prove one of *the best cartridges* for all American big game. The recoil is moderate, very slightly less than that of the .30-06 cartridge.

7 mm. Spanish Mauser.—Many rifles of high efficiency and of American manufacture, with Springfield or Mauser bolt actions, are now being made to order for this cartridge. Two good bullets are now available. One of 175-grains weight can be given a muzzle velocity of 2,400 f.s., and the other of 150 grains can be loaded to about 2,700 f.s. with permissible breech pressure. Either cartridge kills well on all American game, and both give extremely fine accuracy. The recoil is very moderate, and I think that this cartridge is most excellent for the sportsman who desires a light rifle of light recoil.

.30 Caliber Model of 1906. The Springfield cartridge.—So well known that it hardly needs description. It has been developed in accuracy and reliability far above that of any other cartridge in the world. It is seen at its best in Springfield and Winchester Model 54 bolt-action rifles. Two most excellent big-game loads are sold in this caliber to suit the ideas of both the ultra high-velocity advocates and the reliable heavy bullet admirers. These are loaded with a 180-

grain, open-point, boat-tail bullet at a muzzle velocity of 2,725 f.s., and a 220-grain soft-point bullet at a muzzle velocity of 2,350 f.s. Either of these cartridges is extremely reliable on any American game, and on the thin-skinned game of all other countries as well. The killing power, accuracy, and reliability is really superb. The recoil is such that the majority of sportsmen, and all trained marksmen, can fire rifles adapted to this cartridge without any tendency to flinch.

There are a few other good cartridges which might have been included in the above list, but they are none of them superior to those listed, they are older cartridges, and they are getting more and more obsolete every day. When a cartridge begins to get obsolete the cartridge makers manufacture it only at long intervals, or cease its manufacture altogether, and the stocks of it on dealers' shelves begin to get very old. Old cartridges are liable to develop certain defects, notably season cracking of the necks of the brass cases, these defects rendering them less reliable than newer ammunition.

Deer cartridges.—I am not unmindful that many of my readers may be so situated that they can hunt only deer. The vast majority of our citizens will never get a chance at any game larger than deer, and it is probable also that in a few years deer will be the only big game obtainable without long and expensive journeys. But it is also likely that white-tailed deer will continue to furnish us excellent sport for generations to come. These animals are easily killed, and are almost always shot at very close range. Such high-powered, long-range, extremely accurate cartridges as those just listed are not needed for deer alone, although they will do for deer as well as any other cartridge. Among the cartridges which have ample killing power, accuracy, and flatness of trajectory for deer, and which give moderate recoil, may be mentioned the following:

.38-40 W.C.F.	
.38-55 W.M.&S.	In either low or high velocity
.44-40 W.C.F.	
.250-3,000 Savage	
.30-30 W.C.F.	
.30 Rem. Auto.	
.32-40 H.P.	
.32 Win. Special	In high-power loads
.32 Rem. Auto.	
.33 W.C.F.	
.35 Rem. Auto.	

These cartridges have been used to such an extent on deer that there is no doubt whatever as to their suitability, but I would not recommend most of them for game larger than deer. Most of them are adapted to light, short-barreled, rapidly operated, and handy rifles which are most suitable for still-hunting deer in thickly wooded country.

THE RIFLE

The sportsman is no longer restricted to certain standard factory makes of rifles. We now have a number of high-class rifle makers in this country who are prepared to make rifles to order and to their customers' exact specifications, subject only to the limitations that it be mechanically possible and safe. The design of our rifles has gone hand in hand with the great improvement in our marksmanship, and as a result we seem to have developed a type of rifle in the United States which appears to meet the views of our most expert rifle shots and our foremost sportsmen, and which in its performances seems to surpass anything that the world has known before. In this type every little detail has been given the utmost attention. If the beginner wishes to become a really good shot I think that it would be well if he adhered as closely to this type as possible, for as he improves in his shooting he will most certainly gravitate towards it, and he will scarcely reach top notch unless he adopts it almost in its entirety. Another remarkable fact is that this type appears to be the same whether the weapon is to be used for target shooting, hunting, or war. Indeed it should be so, for there is practically no difference in the requirements or essentials for any of these forms of shooting. The highest grade of target shooting is accurate rapid fire at neutral colored objects at unknown ranges, and the same may be said of hunting or of warfare. Durability is also an important attribute in a rifle for any purpose.

Weight.—Our pioneer forefathers used to carry rifles weighing ten to fifteen pounds all day long over steep mountains or through trackless forests and think nothing of it. But they knew no better, and probably they considered it a necessary evil, for in those days it was thought that rifles had to be that heavy to be safe and accurate. But weight is always a handicap, and particularly in the very strenuous sport of big-game shooting. A man will travel farther, hunt over more country, have a better

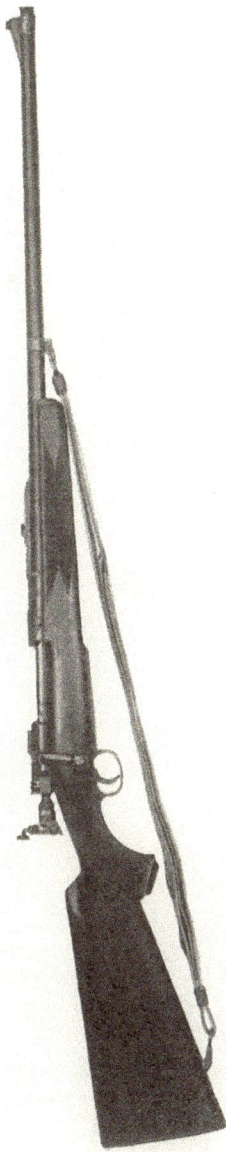

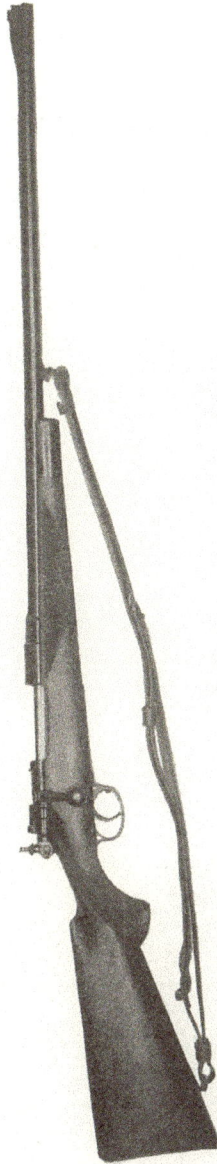

UPPER—SPRINGFIELD SPORTING RIFLE, SPECIAL BARREL, SHORT RIB, LYMAN NO. 103 REAR SIGHT, RAMP FRONT-SIGHT BASE. LOWER—AMERICAN-MADE RIFLE WITH MAUSER BREECH ACTION, 7 MM. RIBBED BARREL, LYMAN SIGHT ON COCKING PIECE

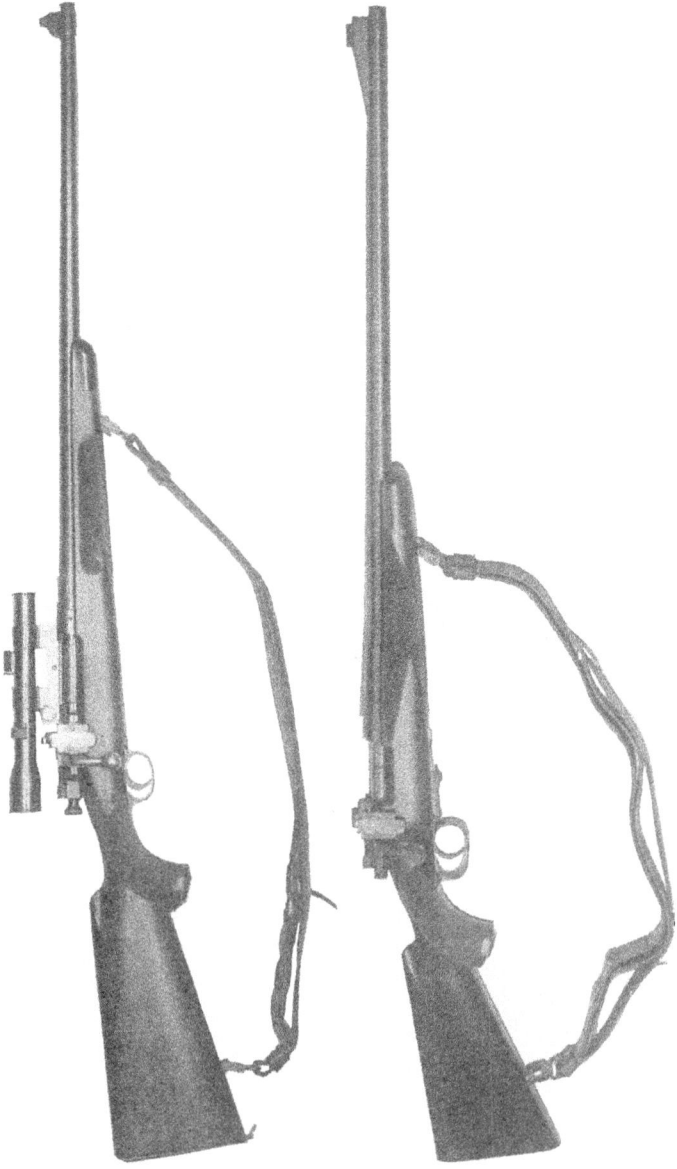

UPPER—SPRINGFIELD SPORTING RIFLE WITH HENSOLDT TELESCOPE SIGHT, AND WITH DETACHABLE NOSKE MOUNT-ING. LOWER—AMERICAN-MADE RIFLE WITH MAUSER BREECH ACTION, LYMAN NO. 48 REAR SIGHT, RAMP FRONT-SIGHT BASE

chance of coming on game, and be in better condition when he does if his weapon is light. But it is easily possible to have a rifle so light that it lacks the essentials of accuracy and light recoil. So the matter of weight must be a compromise, and experience has shown that for the cartridges we have been discussing as suitable for all American big game the happy medium is seven to eight pounds. Rifles for these cartridges can be made within these weights and still maintain sufficient weight and distribution of metal in the barrel to give the desired accuracy. If, for some special purpose, very light weight is desired, it ought to be obtained by shortening the barrel to a minimum of 20 inches, by hollowing out the butt-stock, and by using light fittings, rather than attempting to decrease the diameter of the barrel, or cutting metal from the breech action.

Breech actions.—The handy and quick American lever action was designed many years ago in the time of black powder. It was afterwards found that many of these actions could be satisfactorily adapted to cartridges of more modern smokeless, high-velocity types giving breech pressures of from 36,000 to 38,000 pounds per square inch. We have many such rifles still in use, of which the famous .30-30 is a good example. Many of them are excellent for deer rifles, but it should be remembered that they are really obsolete, and their limits should be understood. They are not satisfactory, many of them are unsafe, with modern high-intensity cartridges. Their durability, life, and safety margin decreases as the breech pressure of the cartridges used ascends.

Modern big-game cartridges give a mean breech pressure of about 50,000 pounds per square inch. To successfully withstand such pressures the breech block or bolt should lock at its head. The various parts should be made of properly heat-treated alloy steel. The proper heat treatment of any alloy steel is necessary to develop its strength and toughness, to resist strain and shocks, and hardness of surface to resist wear. The alloy steel bar as it comes from the steel mill, the alloy steel forging as it comes from the giant hammers, or other alloy steel part which has just been machined, does not have these essential characteristics any more than if made of cheap carbon steel. And many of our older breech actions are just made of ordinary carbon steel forgings.

It is a great advantage to use a breech action so designed that it cannot possibly jam. It is also a great advantage to use one with which the greatest power can be exerted to insert a cartridge which may be slightly over-size, or to extract a fired case which may stick. Another advantage is the ability to dismount and assemble the entire mechanism without tools for cleaning or repair. It is generally recognized that the Mauser type of bolt action possesses all of these desirable features to a degree not found in other types. Besides the genuine Mauser breech action, the Springfield, Remington Model .30, and Winchester Model 54 actions are of this type, and all of them have had a great deal of attention paid to the selection of the proper alloy of steel and its correct heat treatment. There is not space here to explain all the reasons why, and only the bare statement can be made that from the standpoints of safety, durability, functioning, accuracy, and suitability, the above types of breech action are far superior to any others so far known.

The proper assembly of a Mauser type of breech action and its adjustment and regulation is an art by itself. Many gunsmiths or individuals attempt this who know nothing whatever of the matter, and as a result we see many bolt-action rifles which are decidedly inferior to many of our cheaper and older lever-action arms. The bolt action at its best is seen in the Springfield rifles which have been specially selected and adjusted for National Match shooting, and in the Winchester Model 54 rifle. The sportsman should see that the assembly and adjustment of his rifle does not fall short of the standard set by these.

Barrels.—Our old-time rifles, including many of comparatively recent design, had barrels of conventional weight, shape, and length. Slots were cut in them for the attachment of sights and forearm fastenings. They did well for black powder cartridges, but when high velocity came and pressures began to rise it was found that they did not vibrate evenly, and the vibrations with the more powerful cartridges amounted to so much that the desired degree of accuracy was not attained with them. The modern barrel for high-intensity cartridges should have a certain weight, distribution of metal, and a certain contour from breech to muzzle, and it should have no weakening slots of any kind cut in it. Such a barrel at its best is that seen on the Winchester Model 54 rifle, and the standard Springfield sporting

THE HOWE-WHELEN REAR SIGHT FOR SPRINGFIELD AND MAUSER BREECH
ACTIONS, ADJUSTING TO MINUTES OF ANGLE. BRINGS APERTURE NEAR
EYE FOR RAPID SHOOTING

rifle, the weight being kept as low as is possible considering a high degree of accuracy and reliability. The modern barrel should be made of alloy steel. Perhaps the best is a nickel steel containing about $3\frac{1}{2}$ per cent nickel and 0.30 to 0.40 per cent of carbon, and made by the acid, open-hearth process.

Our older black-powder rifle barrels used to be made with the bore quite a little larger than the bullet, the lead bullet expanding to fill the grooves. But it has been found beyond a doubt that far better accuracy and life of barrel is attained with modern high-power ammunition if the groove diameter of the bore be made the exact size or just a trifle smaller (about .0002-inch) than the diameter of the jacketed bullet. The throat of the chamber should be so cut that it accurately fits that portion of the bearing of the bullet which projects beyond the mouth of the cartridge case, and the ogive or curve of point of the bullet should almost impinge upon the start of the lands at the throat. This method of boring and chambering will usually result in the greatest accuracy and the longest barrel life.

Sights.—Many years ago Mr. William Lyman designed a type of rear sight which bears his name. It consists of a large aperture placed relatively near to the eye, and the rim around the aperture is thin so that when aiming the sight appears like a slightly blurred but thin circle in the center of which the bead of the front sight is seen. This sight presents very little interference with the game and its surroundings. It avails itself of the well-known ability of the human eye to center objects with great accuracy. No one has been able to improve much on this form of rear sight for hunting purposes. With almost everyone, after a little practice to become accustomed to it, it can be used with greater accuracy, can be caught quicker, and can be seen in poorer lights than other forms of rear sights, and particularly than the very obsolete open sights.

A few years ago an experiment was tried with two riflemen of international reputation as expert shots. They were given the same rifle, ammunition, and their sights were adjusted the same, and they were told to aim and fire at a target 100 yards away, aiming in the normal and standard manner. Their groups on the target were six inches apart. This is true to a more or less extent with any two men. How, therefore, can one man adjust the sights on a rifle correctly for another man except by the merest chance? If an expert shot be using one make of ammunition in shooting at a certain range, and he then change to another make having the same weight bullet, and the same muzzle velocity, it is probable that he will find that the second ammunition requires an entirely different adjustment of the rear sight in order that the bullets may hit close to his point of aim. This may also be true of two lots of ammunition, same weight of bullet, and same manufacture, but made at the factory on different days. The moral of all this is that the rear sight should be capable of accurate and positive adjustment for both elevation and zero or windage in order that the sportsman may be able to regulate the sight so that his point of aim and point of contact may coincide at the desired range. Preferably, one graduation on the rear sight should move the point of impact one inch for each hundred yards of range, this being called a "minute of angle." The scales on the sight should be numbered so that they can be read and a record made of the sight adjustment. After being set, the sight should be capable of being tightly clamped so that there is no danger of its adjustments being changed or jarred out. Only with such sights can the highest degree of marksmanship be attained, and only with such can the sportsman always be sure that the rifle is sighted to strike exactly where he aims. A number of such rear sights having the Lyman type of aperture are now available for modern rifles.

The front sight should have a brightly colored bead which can be readily seen even in poor lights. Such a front sight is not quite as accurate as one which presents a dead black silhouette like the target front sight, but it can be caught and aim taken very much quicker than with the black sight, and that is a very important consideration in a hunting rifle. The bead should not be of silver for that would glisten too much in sunlight and would blurr the vision. A dull gold bead is the best. Ivory is good also, but gold has the advantage that it can be blackened in the smoke of a candle or burning camphor for target shooting. The best diameters for this bead are 1/16 or 3/32 inch.

Stocks.—The butt-stocks and forearms usually seen on American factory-built rifles are made in accordance with standards established before the development of our present efficient methods of marksmanship. They are seldom a proper fit for any man, and one trained in modern methods of shooting will usually find them a most decided handicap. A properly designed stock, made of such dimensions that it will fit the sportsman exactly, is well worth while on a big-game rifle. It greatly increases the accuracy and rapidity of fire. The exact dimensions depend somewhat upon the build of the individual, his breadth of shoulders, length of arms and neck, his muscular development, and no rule can be laid down for determining these dimensions. It must be a matter of fit and trial, and the sportsman should have a certain amount of experience in shooting before he will be able to determine if a certain dimension of stock does or does not fit him. When he brings his rifle to his shoulder in any of the many firing positions the sights should, almost automatically, come into alignment with the object at which he is to aim. The butt should not catch on the clothing, but should snuggle comfortably against the shoulder. The comb of the stock should support the face so that there is no difficulty in holding the eye steady in the line of aim. If a bolt-action rifle, the length of stock should be such that it is easy for the right hand to grasp the bolt handle for rapid fire in any position without removing the butt from the shoulder. It has been found that the following dimensions of stock will fit about ninety per cent of American sportsmen very excellently, these dimensions being for rifles intended for shooting mainly in the standing and sitting positions, but capable of efficient use in the prone position also. The drop is measured from the line of 200-yard sight.

	Inches
Length from trigger to middle of butt-plate	13.50
Drop at comb from line of sight	1.62
Drop at heel from line of sight	3.00
Middle of trigger to front of pistol grip cap	3.37
Pitch (angle of butt-plate)	3.00

The butt-plate should be of the usual shotgun type, never of the crescent rifle type, and should be full man-sized, not the boy-sized butt-plate often seen on factory-made stocks. It should be about 5.1 inches long, 1.6 inches wide, should be of sharply checked steel to prevent slipping or breaking when used in mountainous countries, and it is very convenient to have a trap door in it so that an emergency cleaning kit can be kept in a recess in the stock. The illustrations show the type and the excellent lines of stocks made on these specifications.

Every big-game rifle should be equipped with a sling strap which is properly designed for either carrying or for shooting in the prone position. The standard prone position using the gunsling is a very decided advantage, and it can be used in perhaps ten per cent of shots in mountain hunting. But more important yet, the sportsman seldom gets his rifle sighted in with absolute accuracy, seldom develops real nail-driving marksmanship, and has nothing to assist him in holding steadily when his heart is thumping away with muscular exertion or buck fever, if he has not a good shooting gunsling on his rifle and knows how to use it to insure steady holding.

ACCESSORIES

Cleaning kits.—If the bore of the rifle be not properly cared for within a few hours after firing, it will begin to deteriorate through corrosion or rust, and within a day or two it will begin to deteriorate to such an extent that the accuracy will suffer. A rifle can be completely ruined in a week or two through neglect. The evidence of rust can be removed, but the damage caused by it is beyond repair. The only solvent for the fouling of modern cartridges is water, or solutions containing water. Oils or solutions containing oil, no matter how widely they are used or advertised, have no effect in removing the corrosive products of the combustion of the primer. Modern cartridges, the bullets of which are jacketed with gilding metal or copper, cause no metal fouling, and the bore of the rifle may be perfectly cleaned by first swabbing with water, then while the bore is wet run a brass wire bristle brush through the bore twice, swab with water again, dry the bore thoroughly, and finally oil the bore.

For such care a little cleaning kit is needed, and the smaller and more compact the better. One firm makes a most excellent steel cleaning rod with joints only 6 inches long. It has a jagged tip, and also a tip for holding the brass brush. It goes in a little bag containing also an oil can, a supply of cut flannel cleaning patches, and a pocket screwdriver. It is all that is needed for the perfect care of the rifle.

Most practical sportsmen also like to have a small, light, emergency cleaning kit in the butt-stock of their rifle, under the trap of the steel butt-plate. It comes in useful when one spends a night away from the camp and the regular cleaning kit. The usual emergency cleaning kit consists of a very short jointed steel cleaning rod, or else a thong pull-through, a brass brush, a very small one-drop oil can, and a small supply of flannel patches.

Rifle covers.—Many of the rifle covers one sees are of canvas lined with some kind of flannel. They are very bad, for in a damp climate or almost anywhere in summer or outdoors, the flannel absorbs moisture and will rust the rifle. The very best covers are those made of heavy, brown, waterproof canvas, reinforced at muzzle and over the breech action with heavy oil-tanned leather. They protect the rifle, will not cause rust, and they are easily dried if they should become wet. Such covers usually have to be made to order by any house dealing with camp equipment.

Saddle holsters.—These are necessary in mountainous countries where one travels on horseback. The style seen in the West is excellent. They should be made of very heavy leather, almost sole leather, which has been made waterproof and pliant by a thorough soaking in neatsfoot oil. The saddle holster is best slung on the left side of the saddle, the body of the holster passing between the two thicknesses of the stirrup leather, and fastened to both pummel and cantel, muzzle slightly depressed, and butt coming almost, but not quite, as high as the top of the pummel. There is usually a certain height that the scabbard should be hung on the saddle so that it comes just in the hollow inside the knee in riding, and its presence is then not felt when one is in the saddle.

REVOLVERS AND GROUSE GUNS

I have often been asked what caliber and make of revolver I would advise for a hunting trip. A revolver of any make, except a .22 caliber target revolver in the hands of an expert revolver shot, is an absolute incumbrance on a hunting trip, and one will have no use whatever for it except for shooting at a mark. Unless the sportsman is a well-known and expert revolver shot, and takes his gun along because he cannot be happy without it, the carrying of a large-caliber revolver or pistol on a hunting trip almost always marks one as a tenderfoot.

Throughout almost all of the hunting localities in Canada grouse are very plentiful, and they are so unsophisticated that it is easy to obtain standing or sitting shots at 10 to 15 yards. My experience has been that practically every day I see three to five of them, sometimes literally hundreds. They make a most toothsome addition to the sportsman's meals in camp, and are easily killed with a weapon using the .22 caliber long rifle cartridge. Such a weapon also has the advantage that it makes so little noise that it is not liable to alarm any big game that may be in the immediate vicinity. The grouse gun should not be so big and obtrusive as to be in the way. Something that can be carried in the rucksack when hunting, or hung from the pummel of the saddle on Western trails is very convenient. A .22 caliber target revolver or target pistol with a gold or ivory bead front sight is excellent for the sportsman who is an expert pistol shot, but it takes a very high degree of skill to shoot one of these weapons well enough, and where only three to five grouse are seen in a day even a fair shot will miss at least half of them with a revolver or pistol, and that does not give enough to make a good mess for the sportsman and his guide. A long-barreled .22-caliber target pistol with a little skeleton stock which fits in a dovetail in the end of the grip is excellent, or the Marble "Game Getter" gun with barrel not over 12 inches long, is just exactly the thing. With it one can bring to bag many additions to the mess without alarming the big game in the vicinity.

CHAPTER XXII

WILDERNESS MARKSMANSHIP

"The rifle is a noble weapon. It brings us pleasures that no scatter-gunner can ever know. A shotgun takes you into cultivated fields, or into those narrow wastes within sight and sound of civilization. But the rifle entices its bearer into primeval forests, into mountains and deserts untenanted by man. To him in whom the primitive virtues of courage, energy, and love of adventure have not been sapped there is scarce a joy comparable to that of roaming at will through wild regions, viewing the glories of the unspoiled earth, and feeling the inexpressible thrill of manliness sore tested by privation and hazard, but armed and undismayed."—*Horace Kephart.*

Basic.—Good shots are made, not born. An untrained man instinctively does the wrong thing in firing a rifle. He gives the trigger a sudden pressure, a pull, or jerk when ready to fire, which causes the shot to go wide of the mark by disturbing the alignment of the rifle. The instinctive dread of recoil increases this tendency, and also causes flinching. But with proper instruction any man who is physically fit to hunt big game can become an excellent and reliable rifle shot. Intelligent and educated men can develop themselves with little assistance into first-class marksmen by following the Army training regulations on this subject as a guide,* and by practice in conformity with the principles laid down in these regulations. Study of these regulations, a little home practice, and about ten afternoons on a rifle range or in the country will perfect most men to such an extent that they are far better shots than the majority of sportsmen and guides. But there are some men who cannot learn practically from printed instructions, and for such an individual coach is necessary.

---

* "U. S. Army Training Regulations No. 150-5, Marksmanship, Rifle, Individual," and "U. S. Army Training Regulations No. 150-10, Marksmanship, Rifle, General." Procurable from Superintendent of Documents, Government Printing Office, Washington, D. C. Price 10 cents each, stamps not acceptable.

The essentials of good shooting are that the individual must know (1) how to hold the rifle with a fair degree of steadiness in each of the firing positions; (2) that he shall know how to aim accurately and consistently; and (3) that he shall know how to squeeze the trigger without disturbing the steady hold and accurate aim. Furthermore, he must learn by practice how to coordinate these three essentials—holding, aiming, and trigger squeeze. He must also master the functioning of his rifle and the "Mechanism of Rapid Fire." Until a man has mastered these he is still in the beginner's class, and is not prepared to undertake practical shooting of any kind.

It is easier to teach a man to shoot who has never previously had a rifle in his hands than a man who has done a lot of promiscuous shooting without a guide or intelligent instruction, and who has developed many faults. Some faults in rifle shooting, particularly those concerned with the three essentials, are absolutely detrimental to progress and very difficult to overcome. A sportsman should never start rifle practice without a proper guide or a qualified instructor.

The ultimate object of all instruction and practice with the rifle is to develop in the individual the ability to hit small, indistinct targets at unknown ranges, and to hit them quickly and repeatedly, even though they be moving.

I have often seen it stated in print that a good target shot is seldom a good game shot, and vice-versa. This is not true, and men who state such things are neither one nor the other. Exactly the same qualifications, skill, and knowledge are required for hitting a target as for hitting game, and once a trained marksman has become accustomed to his surroundings he will do as well in one form of shooting as the other. But it is first necessary that he be basically trained, and the instruction in this is given in detail in the Army training regulations. It is true that the so-called "target shot" who has never done any shooting except slow fire at a bull's-eye target is often too slow and deliberate for success in shooting at game. But such a man is not a real target shot. He has never proceeded beyond the A.B.C. of target shooting. He is still in the beginner's class, for his basic training has not been completed. Basic training includes the rapid functioning of the rifle, the mechanism of rapid fire, the learning of a quick but perfect trigger squeeze, and requires considerable practice at rapid fire.

Today we see more and more tendency to confine target shooting to the prone (lying) position only. This is to be deplored. A man should be able to shoot well and quickly in any position. In days gone by in the Army we were required to practice and qualify at rapid fire in the standing position. The target was silhouette of a kneeling man at 200 yards, and it appeared in view for twenty seconds during which time the marksman was required to fire five shots at it. Similar practice was had in the kneeling, sitting, and prone positions, but the basic position for rapid fire was standing. I know of no form of shooting better qualified to teach really practical rifle marksmanship. When a man can "stand up on his hind legs" and hit a kneeling silhouette five times in twenty seconds at two hundred yards he is a first-class game or target shot. Such skill is by no means beyond the capabilities of any man, although it does require almost a season's practice. But before one can profitably indulge in such practice he must have acquired the ability to put 80 per cent of his shots in the regulation 10-inch bull's-eye at 200 yards, slow fire. The trouble with the so-called target shot is that he pursues the system so far, and then instead of proceeding to practical shooting, he confines all his future practice to trying to put 99 per cent of his shots in that bull's-eye, slow fire, one minute per shot. Bull's-eye shooting is a fascinating game, but it is not practical rifle shooting, it is not military target shooting, and it is of little use in game shooting. It is like learning to say the alphabet forward and backward but never learning to read. A man who has mastered slow-fire target shooting only is not a target shot. A hunter who has never mastered the basic essentials of good marksmanship is not a game shot, although he may be living in that delusion caused by one or two lucky or fluke shots at game. The sportsman who desires to become a good game shot with the rifle should obtain the Army training regulations and proceed to develop himself in all the essentials and fine points of slow and rapid fire by intelligent practice, or he should obtain the services of an experienced coach to teach him these things. After that he will have learned enough to enable him to perfect himself in any form of rifle shooting which he desires.

Accuracy of rifles.—No rifle or ammunition will shoot with absolute accuracy. The best rifle will not shoot well with poor ammunition, nor will the finest ammunition shoot well in a poor rifle. A good rifle with good ammunition, when fired from a machine rest or from a muzzle and elbow rest by an expert shot, should group all of its bullets inside a 3-inch circle at 100 yards, or a 6-inch circle at 200 yards, or 9 inches at 300 yards. Some excellent rifles and ammunition will average about one-third smaller than this. Certain of the older types of cartridges may come up to this standard up to 150 yards, but not at longer ranges.

Aiming and Sight Adjustment.—More consistent and accurate aim can be taken at a bull's-eye target by aiming with the front sight below and almost touching the bottom of the bull's-eye, than by aiming at its center. The sights are then clearly silhouetted against the white portion of the target and appear clear and distinct. If one were to aim at the center of the bull's-eye the front sight would merge with the black bull's-eye, and it would require very good light and very excellent eyes to tell if one were aiming at the center, top, bottom, or side of the bull. On a bull's-eye target, for accurate and consistent results, aim should always be taken at the bottom of the bull in the prescribed manner.

The marksman shooting for a record or for competition, who desires to make the highest possible score on the bull's-eye target, aims his rifle in this way, but he sets his rear sight for increased elevation, so that when so aimed the bullets will strike in the center of the bull's-eye. His shots thus strike at a point a few inches above where the front sight is aligned on the target. But in game shooting it is very much more practical and convenient to have the bullets strike exactly where the top of the front sight is aligned. Therefore if one is adjusting the sights of a hunting rifle for a certain distance, using a bull's-eye target for convenience and to obtain accurate and reliable results, he should aim in the orthodox manner at the bottom edge of the bull's-eye, but should adjust his rear sight so that the bullets will strike, on an average, not in the center of the bull, but at its lower edge.

For example, we will say that we have a rifle shooting the .30 caliber Model 1906 Springfield cartridge. The particular make of this cartridge that we choose for big-game shooting is

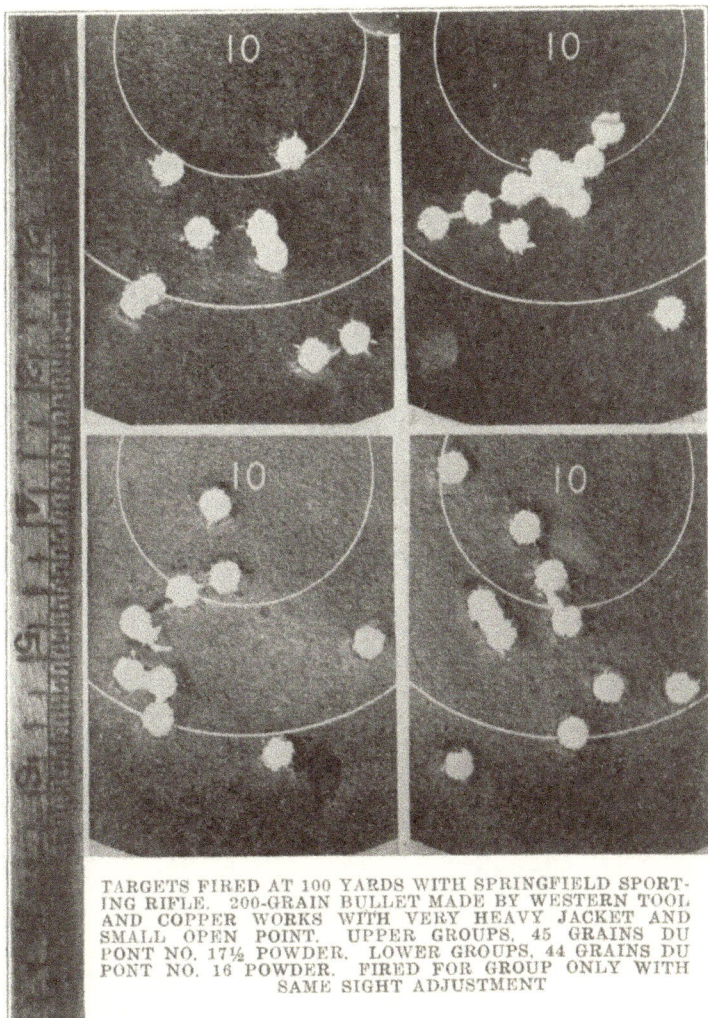

TARGETS FIRED AT 100 YARDS WITH SPRINGFIELD SPORT-
ING RIFLE. 200-GRAIN BULLET MADE BY WESTERN TOOL
AND COPPER WORKS WITH VERY HEAVY JACKET AND
SMALL OPEN POINT. UPPER GROUPS, 45 GRAINS DU
PONT NO. 17½ POWDER. LOWER GROUPS, 44 GRAINS DU
PONT NO. 16 POWDER. FIRED FOR GROUP ONLY WITH
SAME SIGHT ADJUSTMENT

loaded 'with a 180-grain, open-point, boat-tail bullet. The muzzle velocity is 2,720 f.s. From the catalogue of the makers of the ammunition we see that this ammunition, when the rifle is sighted for 200 yards, will have a height of trajectory of 2.75 inches at 100 yards. It will be convenient if we adjust the rear sight on this rifle so that the bullets will strike the point of aim at 200 yards. The rifle will then overshoot 2.75 inches at 100 yards, but this is not at all excessive for a rifle intended for big game. If we aim accurately and squeeze the trigger properly we will not miss the 8-inch circle representing the vital area up to about 225 yards, and our mind will be entirely relieved from any problems of estimation of distance up to this range within which we will obtain 99 per cent of our shots. If we believe that the range is slightly over 225 yards we can aim with the front sight aligned at a spot just a little higher on the animal. If we think that the distance is very long, say 300 to 350 yards, we should aim at the top or backbone of the animal immediately above a vital area, and the bullet will fall to strike very close to that area.

The setting of the rear sight for the exact or estimated range after the game has been sighted is usually impractical in the hunting field. The estimate of the distance will not be any more accurate than the estimate of the amount to hold the front sight higher on the animal, and time is lost in setting the sight, and it takes one's attention from the game. It is much more practicable to set the rear sight for the longest range at which the height of trajectory will make no material difference as above, and then aim higher for longer shots. On this theory some have argued that the hunting rifle should not have adjustable sights—that non-adjustable sights are much simpler and stronger. But I fail to see how a sportsman can ever maintain his rifle with exactly correct sight adjustment for any range with non-adjustable sights, for ammunition and other factors are too changeable, and no one can develop real marksmanship with non-adjustable sights. With readily adjustable sights reading to minutes of angle the trained shot can sight his rifle in with exactness in about six or seven shots. But with non-adjustable sights this may require a number of boxes of ammunition, and perhaps several day's time, and with the present price of high-power ammunition the extra cost of adjustable sights is more than saved by the decreased ammunition bill.

Where to Aim.—The vital areas on a big game animal, where a hit will cause a quick and humane kill, are the brain, the spinal column, and the heart region. The latter area lies in the chest cavity just at the point of the elbow, and about two-thirds of the way down from the back-bone to the chest bone. It is much the best area to aim at because it is the largest and hence the easiest struck. If the sportsman's bullet hits a little too high it will still strike in an area where a fairly quick kill will result, or it may hit high enough to strike the spinal column and kill instantly. If the bullet strikes too far forward it breaks the shoulder and anchors the animal so that it can be dispatched immediately. If it strikes too far back it gets into the abdominal cavity where the explosive effect of bullets fired from modern high-intensity rifles almost always kills quickly. And if the bullet falls too low a complete miss is scored, and at least the animal does not go off to suffer a lingering death. An animal does not always present a broadside shot to the hunter except in artists' pictures. Indeed the most usual shot is at an animal bounding away and presenting a rear view. A shot intended for the heart area should be aimed for that area no matter in what position the animal may be standing or running, although in standing shots it will often be advisable for the hunter to wait a little in hopes that the animal may turn and present a more favorable attitude for the shot. If the bullet be a long, heavy one, and the velocity fairly high, or if it be of medium weight with very thick jacket, very little lead exposed at the point, and with ultra high velocity, it will almost always drive straight through bones and tissue into the vital area at which it has been directed, no matter in what position the animal may present itself.

Running Shots.—Most of the earlier writings on wilderness marksmanship contained elaborate instructions as to the lead necessary when shooting at running game. The amount of lead depends upon the speed of the animal, the angle at which it is running, the velocity or time of flight of the bullet and the distance. In the old days it was sometimes necessary to lead a running animal as much as five or six feet, but with extremely high velocity modern rifles such extensive lead and elaborate calculations are not necessary. If the animal be running at a right angle to the hunter, straight across his front, he should endeavor to fire just as the front sight touches the point of the chest or the shoulder in front of the heart area. If the animal be in the ascending portion of a bound try also to aim just a little high, and if in the descending portion, just a little low. This is easy to write but hard to execute. Running game in thick woods presents the hardest kind of target. Often all that one sees of white-tailed deer in thick forests is a wave or two of a white flag, and the animal is gone. Over half of the time in such hunting it is not possible for the sportsman to get his rifle to his shoulder, much less aim and fire, before the animal is out of sight, and one must expect to glimpse much game that will offer no shot at all. Under these conditions success is to be sought rather by superior still-hunting than good marksmanship, so that the hunter will see the animal before it has been alarmed and is running, or lying in its bed, or just rising out of its bed. In the New Brunswick woods in early fall, when the leaves are dry and noisy, I have hunted deer from dawn to dark and have seen a dozen white flags without time in a single case to even get my rifle to my shoulder. Under such circumstances one will often have better success by just sitting on a log as I had once. While so resting a buck ran right past me, passing to my right. He came so quickly that there was no time to rise and turn around for the shot, and I had to take it left handed. By luck the front sight swung on to his chest just right, and just before he would have disappeared in a thick clump of balsams.

One day many years ago in British Columbia I jumped a splendid mule-deer buck in the partially open country near timber-line. He bounded straight across my front at about 100 yards range. I was using an old .40-72-330 black powder rifle. With such a weapon considerable lead was necessary, and I was conscious that each time I fired the picture of the sights and deer looked exactly like the trade mark of Lyman sights showing the aim through these sights at a running deer. After going about a hundred and fifty yards the buck cleared a bunch of brush and fell on the other side. When I came to him he had three bullet holes in his hide just back of the fore-shoulder. These were ideal conditions, just as the artist would depict them, or as the novice imagines them, and just as we try to arrange them in our running deer competitions on the target range. I never expect to see them again in the hunting field.

The Standing Position.—In woods hunting one almost always has to take his shots standing. Usually there is no time to assume any steadier position, and if one did sit down or lie down the brush would almost always interfere with the view. The artist loves to depict the hunter kneeling, but almost all trained riflemen find that the kneeling position is much more difficult than to fire standing, and that it takes a comparatively long time to steady down to a good hold and aim in that position. So the kneeling position is seldom used by good shots. One day I was still-hunting moose with my old friend Charlie Barker. We had stopped for a short rest and were sitting on a log watching an ermine hunting mice, when suddenly my sub-conscious mind seemed to tell me that there was something off to our right. I whispered to Barker and got up and strolled over that way quietly. A few yards and I saw the gleam of a big pair of moose antlers appearing like old ivory and glistening above a bush a hundred yards away, then I made out the face and nose of the moose. At once, standing where I was I aimed where I assumed the point of the chest must be, and squeezed off the trigger. Instantly my hand flew to the bolt handle, and by that sleight-of-hand motion known to trained riflemen, I threw in another cartridge and caught the bull as he turned sideways to run off. Almost instantly I was ready to fire a third shot which caught the moose when he had turned tail and was about to leave. At this shot the bull reared up and fell down with a crash, and at my elbow Charlie Barker yelled, "You've got him by gosh, you've got him!" It was exactly like the old days on the Army Infantry Rifle Team, rapid fire, 5 shots in 20 seconds, at the silhouette of a man kneeling at 200 yards—only it was easier. In those days, which the Englishman would call "salad days," we youngsters on the team used to be willing to bet a dollar any time that we could make a possible (five hits) at this 200 yard rapid fire.

There is another little lesson for the beginner to learn from this incident. It pays to keep pumping in accurately aimed shots as rapidly as possible while the game remains on its feet.

The Sitting Position.—This is a good steady position, fine for rapid fire, and good for runnning shots. It is the best position when one has to shoot down hill. Dig your heels into the sod, sit down, and get a good rest for each elbow on your knees. Keep your elbows in contact with your knees even while operating the bolt in rapid fire. As an example of firing in this position, I surprised a Rocky Mountain Goat feeding on the tall, half dead flowers in a little mountain meadow. Before I could fire he disappeared over a rise, and beyond that rise was a mountainside of steep bluffs and precipices, around the corner of one of which the goat had disappeared when I arrived where I could see ahead. I started to climb along the bluffs after the goat, and came to a shelf which jutted way out from the main mountain from the outer edge of which one could get a view ahead. I crawled out on this and saw the white billy standing on a ledge about 350 yards ahead. I sat down, waited a few seconds to get my breath, lined up the front sight just touching the top of the hump of white hair above his withers, and carefully eased off the trigger. A half second and I heard that welcome thump denoting a hit, sounding as though one had struck a sack of grain with all his might with the flat of a shovel.

The Prone Position.—Every trained rifleman knows that the standard prone position, with the gunsling properly adjusted, is the steadiest and surest of all ways of firing. One can even aim with absolute steadiness when his heart and whole body are thumping and pulsating from exertion, as they often are in big game hunting. But this position can be used only when there is a fairly level or slightly up-hill place to lie on, and when the game can be seen from close to the ground, and when there is five seconds or more time to assume it. It can practically never be used in thick woods, but in stalking on fairly open Western mountains the hunter can often avail himself of its advantages as it means an absolutely sure hit every time. In the West I have been able to use the prone position and the gunsling for shots at big game a number of times. The occasion which stands out most vividly in my memory is the completion of the stalk on mountain sheep already described in the chapter devoted to that animal. On another occasion, when hunting mule-deer, I started to climb a big, table-topped mountain, on the long summit of which I expected to find a buck. The mountainside was wooded with large pines, an open forest through which one could see quite a distance. The route I took, instead of leading me up to the mountain itself, brought me out on the top of a little peak which stood out from the side of the main mountain, and I could look over about 350 yards to the slope of the main mountain. As I stood there watching I saw a couple of small animals descending the slope among the pine trees. They were quite a way off, much higher than the peak on which I stood. I had heard that an Indian nearby had some pigs, and at first I thought that these were some of his pigs. I did not have field glasses with me at the time. But as they came to a fallen log and jumped it I saw that they were deer. I therefore laid down prone, adjusted my gunsling, set my sights for 400 yards, and waited until the deer came as near to me as their course would bring them, and then started shooting at the leading deer. At the third shot this animal dropped and rolled down the hillside.

Shooting from a canoe.—Next to running shots in thick woods I think that the most difficult are those that have to be taken from a canoe. The canoe always rocks more or less and it may be moving forward also. There is usually no way to rest the elbows, although if one is sitting in the stern he can sometimes put his feet up on the rear thwart and thus get his knees up high enough so that he can rest his elbows on them, but then he has to be mighty careful that the recoil of the rifle does not roll him off into the drink—a sad and bitter ending to a shot at a noble moose. When the rifle is at the shoulder the front sight sways up and down or sideways in a most exasperating manner. To save his life the hunter cannot hold the bead on the animal for even long enough to jerk the trigger, much less squeeze it off properly. It must be purely snap-shooting of the most difficult kind. Sometimes it will be found that there is a sort of limit to the swing or sway of the front sight. It swings up, comes to rest for an instant, and then swings down. On one or two occasions I have found it possible to aim so that the end of the swing brings the bead to bear on the animal, and then to time the trigger squeeze so that the rifle will go off at the end of the swing. This is like snap-shooting at objects thrown into the air, where the marksman aims and fires just as the object reaches its highest point, and comes to rest an instant before it starts to descend. Perhaps practice at glass balls and blocks of wood thrown into the air may have its practical side in making one a better shot from a canoe. At least such shooting teaches very quick aim and quick trigger squeeze. If there are two men in the canoe, and the bow-paddler is doing the firing, the man in the stern should endeavor, when possible, to turn the canoe so that the hunter can fire to his left, or to the left of the bow of the canoe. If he has to fire to the right of the bow it makes the shot many times harder.

My first deer was shot from a canoe. I was only fifteen years old at the time, and was spending the summer at a hotel in the Adirondack Mountains. The deer season was on and many of the guests at the hotel had been going hunting with guides, and a few of them had brought back deer. My only weapon was a .22 caliber Remington single shot rifle, but I was crazy to get a deer. One morning I got up at 2 a. m., sneaked out of the hotel, got my canoe, and paddled four miles to an inlet between two lakes where I knew there were deer feeding in the pond lilies every night. Just at the grey of dawn a spike buck came down to the inlet and started to wade and swim across about fifty yards from where I sat in the canoe, paddle in hand. I fired at the buck's head as it was swimming, and missed it. The buck turned and started to swim straight down stream, and I seized the paddle and started after it. I was afraid to stop paddling to fire for fear that the deer would get too far off. It was a great race down that stream, the buck about 15 yards ahead of the canoe. Pretty soon we came to a place in the stream where there was a little island about ten feet in diameter. That darn fool deer swam up to the island, jumped up on it, and stood there looking at me. Just at this instant the canoe jammed between two snags and I could go no farther or I might have run the canoe against the island and jumped out on it too. When the canoe wedged between the two snags I seized my rifle and tried to shoot, but I had the buck fever so bad that the barrel was swaying around like a bunch of sumac in a fifty mile gale. Then I flopped down on my belly in the bottom of the canoe, rested the rifle barrel on the side, aimed right behind the buck's ear, and fired. That foolish buck came down like a ton of bricks and lay there. At that time I did not know how to dress or gut a deer, and after much labor and upsetting the canoe once, I managed to roll the deer into it. At 10 a. m., just as the finely dressed ladies and gentlemen were coming out on the porch after breakfast, I paddled my canoe up in front of the hotel and landed at the boat house with my deer aboard, the proudest kid you ever saw in your life.

Confidence.—A big-game hunter should have that confidence with his rifle which comes only through perfect familiarity with it. Only thus will he be able to use it with effect, particularly in moments of excitement. The lack of this confidence is partly the cause of buck fever and of those unfortunate incidents which can be related by every guide of experience which happen when the game is apparently within grasp. I have heard of hundreds of these incidents, among which the following will suffice to illustrate the point. A Montana guide lead his sportsman up to within 50 yards of a bull elk. Upon being told that it was an elk with a fine head and that he must shoot, the sportsman placed his rifle to his shoulder and pumped every cartridge out of it without firing! Another incident happened with a sportsman who was considerably familiar with rifles, but not quite enough so. His guide showed him a moose within easy range. The sportsman immediately got the bolt of his rifle tangled up in his belt and when the guide had untangled that he unlocked the rifle to fire, but immediately locked it again, and tried to pull the trigger but could not. However, after a while he got straightened out and killed the moose which had most accommodatingly waited for him to do everything wrong at least once. Incidents of this kind are most unfortunate, and they leave a black spot on one's vacation even if no one knows about them but the individual. And such an incident might, in fact, often does, happen on the one shot that the hunter gets on a hunt that he has perhaps planned for years. The point is that they scarcely ever happen to men who have made themselves perfectly familiar with their rifles by a dozen or so afternoons of range practice, intelligently applied, before starting out, and they do very frequently happen to those who neglect to take such practice.

Boot Jack.
Alberta, 1922.

CHAPTER XXIII

PHOTOGRAPHY

For an intelligent and practical discussion of this subject from the standpoint of the hunter and sportsman it is perhaps best to divide it into three branches: *Record Photography.*—The making of good, clear photographs of various incidents, persons, and places for preservation as a record in an album, or possibly for book and magazine illustrations. *Pictorial Photography.*— The making of attractive and artistic photographs of scenery, persons, places, and other matter with a view to enlargement and framing, or perhaps of entering photographic competitions. *Game Photography.*—That is of live, wild game in its native haunts, animals and birds, usually involving a careful stalk or a long wait in cover to get as close as possible, an instantaneous exposure, and long focus lenses in order that the principal object shall appear as large and in as much detail as possible on the plate. The three branches, for any measure of success, require radically different equipment, technique, and methods.

RECORD PHOTOGRAPHY

Almost all sportsmen use a camera, but comparatively few get really good results with one except under what might be termed ideal conditions. The outdoorsman usually desires good, clear, record photographs rather than artistic prints. Usually artistic photographs are the result of a study of the subject which may last several hours, days, or even seasons. But the sportsman's subjects are usually fleeting. The majority must be taken now or never, some opportunities are gone almost instantly. Conditions must be accepted as they are without waiting for better light, or direction of the sun, or let-up in the wind, and no photographer requires more versatility in his technique than does the outdoorsman. From the indoors of cabins and camps, to outdoor tropical sunlight; from speed pictures to long-time nature studies; the sportsman must be always ready, usually with but one camera and one plate. I am writing here not for the man who specializes on photography alone, but for him who takes up this subject together with the gun, rifle, rod, canoe, or horse, and I am supposing that my reader already has a knowledge of the instruction book that accompanies his camera; that is of ordinary "Kodak literature." The trouble with such literature is that most of it is entirely too elementary, particularly as regards the subject of exposure, and that which is not elementary deals almost exclusively with artistic photography.

The choice of the camera deserves our first consideration, and I shall approach it from a rather unusual angle. Portability and all-around efficiency are the most important considerations. The camera must always be ready. It is most readily available and least obtrusive if carried on the belt, and it is therefore desirable that it weigh less than two pounds. High speed photographs, that is, those demanding exposures shorter than 1/100 second, require focal plane shutters. But as a rule subjects requiring such speed are few and far between. In three years I have not taken a photograph which required a shorter exposure than 1/100 second. But I have taken hundreds that required 1/5 second, ½ second, 1 second, or short bulb exposures, and the focal plane shutter is not suitable for these because the jar of the shutter shakes the camera, even when on a very firm tripod, and a blur usually results. But high speed in the lens is very desirable, not to take speed photographs, but to permit of slow instantaneous exposures in poor lights. Suppose a subject which you particularly desire to take occurs in the dimly lighted woods when the wind is blowing the leaves of the trees. A 1/25 second exposure is usually required to stop leaf motion. You could take a time exposure were it not for the wind, but you must give at least 1/25 second, and unless you can open your lens up to f4.5, you will usually fail to get any results.

Many subjects will require great clearness and definition in all portions of the plate for record purposes. Great depth of focus is desired, and this is only obtained by stopping the lens down to a small opening and giving a time exposure. Therefore the shutter of your camera must have capacity. I have found that the exposures which sportsmen should use, in the order

EXPOSURE 6 SECONDS AT f-22, KODAK SPEED FILM, NEW BRUNSWICK, OCTOBER, DIFFUSED LIGHT, 3 P. M., NO WIND, CAMERA RESTED ON A LOG

of their frequency, run about as follows: 1/25, Time, 1/5, Bulb, 1/50, and 1/100 second. The shutter should be capable of all these exposures. If in addition it can be set for ½ and 1 second, so much the better.

Shall our camera use plates, film packs, or roll films? Plates are all but impossible for the wilderness hunter. Liability to breakage, weight, bulk, difficulty in guarding against dampness, necessity of a dark-room or night for changing, bulky plate-holders, are all against them, so we pass them up. Film packs must be handled carefully or they get deformed and do not lie in a perfect focal plane with the lens. It is hard to find a really waterproof container to hold them on rough wilderness trips. Hot sun is liable to make them stick. They require a dark room or night to place them in the film tank for development, and under some conditions field development is highly desirable. Roll films do not have any of these disadvantages.

As to size, postcard or 4" x 5", are the most popular. These are the best sizes for albums, they adapt themselves well to book and magazine illustration, and they enlarge to a pleasing size. But cameras in these sizes are both bulky and heavy. When made for roll films they cannot be had with a faster lens than f6.3. The slow speed and the bulk and weight almost call for their elimination, although these are most desirable sizes, and could one satisfactory in other respects be obtained with a f4.5 lens, I personally would prefer this size and would willingly stand both the bulk and weight. But the slow speed lens with which this size of camera is always provided, will make it impossible to take too many pictures. There is only the one size camera for roll films made in this country with an f4.5 lens, and with shutter of proper capabilities. This size is 2¼" x 3¼", and cameras for it weigh less than two pounds. The two models of American make obtainable are the "Kodak No. 1 Special," and the Ansco No. 3 Speedex. There are also a number of most excellent English and German cameras of this size and type now available on the American market. This is a very convenient size. Contact prints are not prohibitively small for the album. Enlargements from good negatives can be made as large as 6 x 9 inches which cannot be told from contact prints. It is a very satisfactory size for lantern slides. The short focus of the lens gives great depth of focus, and the long hyperfocal distance makes focusing easy and accurate. It can be carried easily and comfortably on the belt in a little leather case, which for protection should be made heavy and strong like a pistol holster.

For the various purposes of outdoor work there will be needed with the camera a ray filter, a sky filter, a portrait attachment, a Kodak self timer, flash powder, films and waterproof containers for them, and a tripod. It will probably cost the beginner the price of several metal tripods to learn that they are so unsteady as to be useless for the purpose intended. You will use your tripod for time and bulb exposures, and merely taking hold of the wire cable release of a light camera mounted on one of these collapsible metal tripods will set up a case of ague in both camera and tripod which will last a second or so. Get a firm, wood tripod like the Crown.

It is in the nature of getting the correct exposures that most amateur photographers encounter their greatest difficulties. Almost everything that one can see is takable if one only knows the correct exposure. The instruction books that accompany the camera are woefully lacking in practical information on exposure, and in some the instructions that are given are very misleading. To understand exposure one must first know something about his lens—focal length, relative aperture, speed, relation of aperture and length of exposure, angle of view, and depth of focus should all be understood. The firm of Bausch and Lomb will send you a fine little booklet on this subject, and half an hour of study will put you wise. Then you will need a reliable exposure calculator. One with complete text which explains everything is best, and for years I have used the "Wellcome Exposure Diary." Study this too, and you will get a lot of necessary information that is not in print elsewhere. The exposure calculator answers perfectly for normal conditions, and its use will greatly increase the proportion of good pictures. I never take my camera out without it; in fact there is a place in the camera case for it. But sometimes it fails, and this is where experience comes in.

On my first hunting trip in New Brunswick, Canada, my photography would have been a total failure had it not been for the knowledge that one of my party had of the exposure necessary under the particular conditions that we encountered. The light in the late fall hunting season in all of eastern Canada

MOUNTAIN IN CANADIAN ROCKIES. EXPOSURE 1/25 SECOND AT f-16, KODAK SPEED FILM, KODAK SKY FILTER, OCTOBER, 10.00 A. M., HAZY SUNLIGHT, CAMERA HELD IN HAND

is very weak, much weaker than the monthly time and latitude tables in the various calculators indicate. This, added to the fact that ninety per cent of the photographs on a hunting trip in this locality will be taken in the shadow of deep woods, makes it necessary to use very long exposure. I find as a result of two years' experience in this locality that the following exposures are about right for photographs in the woods, for near scenes, strong foregrounds, groups, etc., 9.00 a. m. to 3.30 p. m., October and November, Kodak speed film:

Aperture	Sunlight	Diffused Light	Cloudy
f4.5	1/25 sec.	1/25 sec.	1/10 sec.
f6.3	1/10 "	1/5 "	1/5 "
f8	1/5 "	1/2 "	1/2 "
f11	1/2 "	1 "	1 "
f16	1 "	1½ "	2 "
f22	2 "	3 "	4 "
f32	4 "	6 "	8 "

Increase the exposure for very dark places or very dark subjects. Use one-half the exposure if the sun fully lights up the principal subject.

The conditions one meets in the high altitudes of the mountains of northwestern United States and Canada are also radically different from those encountered in the settled portions of the United States for which the various exposure calculators are prepared. The rare air at 5,000 feet or over calls for a shorter exposure, but on the other hand one is often farther north where the light is weaker, and also there is far greater decrease in the actinic value of the light say between September first and November fifteenth than is indicated in tables for more southerly countries. With ordinary exposures snow-capped peaks will blend with the sky, and photographs will not show where one ends and the other begins, nor will it show the pleasing lights and shadows on snow, or the attractive clouds in the sky unless a ray filter is used and correct exposure given. Prior to a recent trip in the Canadian Rockies, Mr. F. H. Riggall, a most successful photographer of the mountains of Alberta, furnished me with an exposure table of his own which I used with the greatest success, obtaining fully ninety per cent printable negatives, with many excellent ones. The table is about right for the higher mountain country of Montana, Idaho, Washington, Alberta, and British Columbia, for the late summer and fall. It is based on a shutter kept set at 1/25 second exposure, but of course if one uses shorter or longer exposures he would vary the stop used accordingly. I have slightly modified Mr. Riggall's table below, based on my own experience, and to make it a little more self explanatory.

EXPOSURE TABLE FOR NORTHERN MOUNTAINS

5,000 to 9,000 feet

Kodak Speed Film. Shutter at 1/25 Sec.

Light	Snow capped peaks and clouds	Landscape with very open foreground	Landscape with strong foreground	Shade or very dark objects
Very bright sun, May to August }	f45	f32	f22	f11
Bright sun	f32	f22	f16	f8
Hazy sun	f22	f16	f11	f6.3
Dull, no shadow	f16	f11	f8	{ f5.6 or f8 with 1/5 sec.
Very dull, Nov. to Feb.	f11	f8	{ f6.3 or f11 with 1/5 sec.	{ f4.5 or f6.3 with 1/5 sec.

Correct for 10.00 a. m. to 3.30 p. m.   For earlier or later, use larger stop or give longer exposure. After October 15 it is best to use one stop larger than above. With Kodak ray filter give 5 to 7 times more exposure. With Kodak sky filter, double the exposure or use next larger stop. Mountains under snow or white clouds in blue sky require exposure as indicated in the table, but in both cases it is very hard to avoid an under-exposed foreground. The sky filter is much better than the ray filter in this case, as only the top half is stained and you get a good cloud or mountain peak effect, and also a well-exposed foreground. In fact, for all distant landscape it is well to use the sky filter.

Small cameras like the 2¼ x 3¼ are so light that unless the tripod is a very substantial one and placed on firm ground, the mere act of taking hold of the cable release to operate it will shake the camera so as to make it impossible to use any exposure greater than 1/25 second. It is easy to overcome this difficulty, however, by taking a flat, folded, colored handkerchief or a folded glove; cover the lens with this pad, using it as one would an old-fashioned lens cap; while the lens is covered, open the shutter in the usual manner, remove the pad, making your

WHEN THIS PICTURE WAS TAKEN, A WIND WAS CONTINUALLY RUFFLING
THE FEATHERS OF THE GROUSE, SO A TIME EXPOSURE WOULD HAVE
BEEN IMPOSSIBLE HAD I NOT ERECTED A TARPAULIN. (NOT SHOWN) ON
THE WINDY SIDE, AND ALSO BROUGHT THE TARP OVER THE GROUND
BELOW SO AS TO REFLECT LIGHT UP AND PREVENT THE UNDEREX-
POSURE OF THE LOWER PORTION OF THE BIRD. EXPOSURE ONE MINUTE
AT f-22, KODAK SPEED FILM, NEW BRUNSWICK, NOVEMBER, 10.00 A.M.,
DULL LIGHT

exposure in the old-fashioned way; replace the pad over the lens, and close the shutter. If care be taken to press the pad only lightly over the lens barrel the camera will not be disturbed during the exposure. A little instrument that I have found most useful is the "Kodak Self Timer." Not only does it enable the photographer to get in his own picture, but it will operate the shutter of a light camera for long automatic exposures like 1/5, 1/2, and 1 second, without imparting any movement to the camera. Thus it is possible to perch the camera lightly on branches, bushes, etc., for these relatively long exposures, and since obtaining this little instrument I find that I use it for about one-sixth of all my pictures taken in the open.

Objects close to the camera require very long exposures unless they are both bright in color and in bright sunlight. It is well to stop the lens down to a small aperture for such subjects, and give a long time exposure. For example, for photographs of beaver and grouse hanging on the side of a cabin, 10.00 a. m., cloudy, cabin fully exposed to the sky, portrait attachment, lens 3½ feet from the object, I used f22 and a full minute exposure. The results were perfect, crisp negatives with every feather and hair showing.

Camp-fire pictures are exceedingly attractive, and easy to take. Arrange the back-logs of the fire so that they shield the lens from the direct light of the fire. Set up your camera and focus in daylight if possible. Set the shutter for time exposure and f16. Have only a very small fire. Wrap a teaspoonful of Victor flash powder in a piece of paper. When night falls arrange your group around the fire so that they will more or less face it, open the shutter of your camera and take your place in the group. Then simply toss the paper containing the flash powder into the fire and await the flash, then get up and close the camera. The same amount of flash powder and the same aperture will answer for the interior of a cabin. For a tent interior use half the amount of powder or stop down to f22, because the sides of the tent act as reflectors to the flash. Always place the flash where its direct light will not enter the lens, and arrange your group so that the flash will be a little to one side of the faces so as to get shadow and relief, and avoid flatness.

The tropics, with its dazzling sunlight and its dampness, is a most difficult country in which to get good photographs. If one follows blindly the instructions in the manuals and calculators he will have half of his pictures under-exposed. The contrast between light and shadow is very marked in the tropics, and a picture timed for intense sunlight usually results in what the advanced photographer calls "soot and whitewash." The rule to expose for the shadows is very necessary in such a country, and the shadows are usually very dense. Where the instructions call for 1/100 second exposure I have usually gotten far better results by using 1/25 second, particularly on near views where details in the shadows are desirable. For distant views follow the calculator. It is in the jungle that the photographer will find his greatest difficulties. The light is so dim in the virgin big tree jungles of Central and South America that snap-shots are impossible, even with an aperture of f4.5, and one must resort to long time exposures. Such exposures, of course, require times when there is no wind to disturb the vegetation. If any part of the sky is in the picture, even if only a glimpse is seen here and there through the tops of the trees, it will be very liable to fog the picture because of its dazzling brightness. In such cases I have found that the Kodak sky filter is a great help in subduing the sky, and allowing one to give a correct exposure for the remainder of the picture. In some photographs of groups and camp scenes or vegetation in the jungle I have used as long exposures as 30 seconds, at f16, and in taking pictures of near objects of dark color, such as flowers, etc., I have used as much as three minutes at f22.

Please note that these remarks are by no means intended to cover the whole subject of exposure, but only to be used, together with a little common sense, in conjunction with a good calculator. A good working knowledge of the relation of stop to exposure, depth of focus, etc., as given in the Bausch and Lomb pamphlet on lenses, and of exposure as given in the Wellcome Exposure Diary, or any good pamphlet on exposure, are necessary to intelligently apply the tables given herein and use the calculators. But with a little study, experiment, and practice, the sportsman will find that he can solve almost any problem in exposure and get his ninety per cent of good negatives. To guard against dampness, in southern countries, in the tropics, or near the sea-shore, always purchase films in the sealed tin cans, and see that they are ones which have come from the makers already sealed, not

RUFFLED GROUSE AT NEST. KODAK SPEED FILM, EXPOSURE 1/25 SECOND, NEW BRUNSWICK. JUNE, 10.00 A.M., f14.5, MILD SUNLIGHT

those which have been on the dealers shelves in a damp city for several months, and which he himself puts into cans to satisfy your demand. Do not open the can until ready to place the film in the camera. Try to expose all the film during daylight and return it to the can before the night dampness comes on. This method usually works all right, and such films will usually be perfect if developed any time within two weeks. It is also possible to place the film, after exposure, in a can containing a small amount of calcium chloride which has just been made perfectly dry by roasting before a fire. The calcium chloride will absorb all the moisture in the sealed friction top can, and the next day, during the dryest hours, the can can be opened, the calcium chloride removed, and the can sealed up again with assurance that the film will keep perfectly in it for it has been made bone dry. It is always best, however, to develop the film the same day that it is exposed, and this is the only safe rule in the tropics during the rainy season. The original tin cans that the films come in, and which are sealed with electrician's tape, are not really waterproof, only fairly damp-proof. I found this out to my cost when a dug-out canoe in which I was journeying along the coast of the Caribbean Sea was capsized two miles out from land, and all the films which were in these cans were found to be full of water when I finally got ashore. This loss was a pretty severe one, as it included the entire photographic record of a long exploring trip in an absolutely unknown jungle wilderness. As a consequence of this and another similar experience where a packhorse fell in fording a river, I am rather a crank on having the camera and films in waterproof containers whenever going into risky places in a canoe or when fording deep rivers. One can always get a supply of big friction top cans to hold the smaller individual cans of films, but I have yet to find a real waterproof container for the camera.

Sometimes outdoor development of the films is highly desirable. This is so in the tropics to avoid the ruination of the film by mildew. Also in going into a new country if one can develop the first two or three rolls of films on the spot he may get a line on the correct exposure which may prevent a total failure of all his photographs. For field development of roll film all one requires is the film tank, two flexible rubber trays, half a dozen film clips, a thermometer, the necessary developing and fixing powders, a tin cup arranged as a measure for the solutions in lieu of the breakable glass graduate, and a film album to protect the films after development. Films may be washed in the strip by attaching a clip to each end and suspending them in the slight current of a creek deep enough so that they will not touch bottom. In the tropics or very warm countries there will also be needed a large water cooling bag, a lot of cheese cloth, and a hypo-eradicator, and perhaps a hardener for the film. In most cases tropical water is too warm as it is for development, but if placed in the water cooling bag in the evening it will usually be about the right temperature at sunrise the next morning. Films cannot be washed in the streams, but this work must be done in a pan, using the cooled water, and in order that the hypo may be thoroughly eradicated before the water gets so warm as to frill the film, a hypo-eradicator should be used. The cheese cloth is to surround the film while it is drying to keep insects from alighting on it. Enough fixing powder or hypo should be taken to permit of mixing a fresh batch each time, and it will be cool enough when freshly mixed. A chrome alum hardener should be used immediately after the hypo bath as this helps to counteract the bad effects of washing water that is a little warm. In some places where it has been very damp I have had to fan the film for an hour or more to get it to dry. The Kodak instructions on development are excellent, and one can follow them almost explicitly. I have never attempted printing outdoors.

PICTORIAL PHOTOGRAPHY

It usually happens that just as soon as the sportsman begins to dabble in record photography to the extent previously indicated, and by putting a little thought, study, and experiment into it and averaging really good photographs, he begins to wish to make still better pictures, and particularly artistic ones. Indeed, if he becomes very enthusiastic he thinks every picture he takes should be a work of art, or that it is not worth taking. With his hand camera and other equipment, and by following the methods I have already outlined, he will occasionally get a photograph that is quite artistic, but probably more on account of a lucky choice of subject than by perfection in technique. If he pursues the subject very far he soon finds that his little record camera and its roll films have very decided limitations when it comes to making really artistic photographs.

This is not intended to be a treatise on artistic photography. The subject is far too long and complex to be adequately treated in less than a complete book, and there are many excellent works on this subject. But rather I aim to show the direction which the sportsman's efforts should take in his attempts to improve his work. There are two phases to pictorial or artistic photography— the choice of the subject, and the technique. Not every subject will make a good picture. A certain subject may appeal to one on account of its associations, but to others it may appear commonplace and uninteresting. Perhaps our artistic sense is dormant and needs development and education. But there are certain pictures which appeal to almost everyone. Why they appeal may be unknown to those who have not had the training of the artist. It is because the subject has human interest or natural beauty, and also because it has been composed on the plate or canvas in conformity with certain well established principles of artistic composition, which principles are explained in books on the subject. Our first thought, therefore, is to choose a subject which has either human interest or natural beauty. Next we must compose it artistically. We can give persons, groups, or movable objects certain posings, arrangements, lightings, and backgrounds with this end in view. But with inanimate, immovable objects like scenery we must take another course. Here we select the place, direction or point of view from which we will take our picture, perhaps with reference to artistic composition, the details of the view, and the lighting given to the subject by the sunlight. We choose the time of day when the light and shadows will be just as we wish. Perhaps we may have to wait hours, days, or even weeks for just exactly the combination of light and cloud effect that we want.

In many cases we will find that it is almost impossible to compose our picture just exactly as we wish it, and to judge of its pleasing composition, unless we can examine it on the ground glass of a fairly large camera. Other efforts and corrections in composition will often require a rising or falling front, and a vertical swing adjustment to the camera, or both. Hence for really serious artistic photography we find ourselves compelled to give up our little hand camera and roll films for the much bulkier and heavier, but much more adaptable view camera and glass plates.

Light, shadow, and color add immeasurably to the artistic value of any photograph. To obtain these they must not only be present in the subject, but far more difficult, we must get them correctly rendered on the exposed negative. The ordinary lens and plate or film are not capable of rendering very nice distinctions between certain colors, or faint shadows and lights. Black, blue, dark green, red, and deep yellow appear much the same in an ordinary photograph. If we give enough exposure to get the details we desire in certain parts of our photograph, we find that the delicate shadows which promised so much in the subject are entirely absent, or the delicate cloud effects or light and shadow on snow, sand, or water, have failed completely to register.

The ordinary roll films or film packs are orthochromatic only to a certain extent. The use of a ray filter with them will improve the relative color values, the faint shadows, and the cloud effects to a certain extent, but hardly to the degree desired. Sometimes we get fairly good results, but oftener we get merely a good record negative, not an artistic picture. To obtain the best results one should use backed panchromatic plates and a correct ray filter for the particular plate chosen. For outdoor photography, particularly for that kind which the sportsman will usually wish to do, probably the Wratten panchromatic plate used in conjunction with Wratten K1, K2, and K3 ray filters, and particularly the last named K3 filter, will be found the best, or at least as good as anything. With such a combination we get the very best rendition of color values, light, and shadow. The exposure with the K3 filter must be about $4\frac{1}{2}$ times as long as that which we would give with an ordinary plate or film and without a ray filter. In record photography this long exposure would often be a distinct disadvantage in preventing the getting of a photograph under certain conditions of light, wind, or moving objects, but in artistic photography we often have opportunities to wait for conditions suitable to our equipment. Indeed, in most cases an artistic photograph is the result of much study, planning, waiting, and work. One must not expect to get results off-hand as he does in record photography. Panchromatic plates, being sensitive to almost all colors or lights, require development in total darkness, but in these days tank development has been so improved that this is no disadvantage at all. In the field plates can be transferred from their box to plate holders in the evening, inside the tent, head and shoulders completely covered with blankets to exclude all light. The boxes, plates, and plate holders are arranged in a certain methodical manner, and the operation performed by feel alone.

The amateur who will delve into pictorial photography with a view camera, panchromatic plates, and ray filters, has a surprise in store for himself, and with study and experiment, mixed with a little common sense and artistic ability, he will obtain results which will delight himself and his friends.

GAME PHOTOGRAPHY

The amateur who will delve into pictorial photography with perhaps the most difficult, and in some phases of it the most strenuous and red blooded sport in the world. It takes a lot more skill to obtain a really first-class photograph of an animal than to shoot it. The sportsman must not only find the animal, but he must stalk much closer to it than in hunting, and above all he must not alarm it. He requires first-class knowledge of the arts of woodcraft, hunting, and photography, and a good knowledge of the habits of the animal. And he must do the work himself for the chances are much against his guide having the photographic knowledge necessary. All this is coming to be recognized so well among the sportsmen that a first rate photograph of a wild animal is now regarded as a more valuable trophy to the man who has obtained it than a record head.

The best game photographs picture animals in their native surroundings, or they tell some story of the lives they lead. A bunch of rams may be pictured at their noon day nap high up in a patch of snow on the roof of North America, or the ewes and lambs may be photographed as they graze upward on the short mountain grass, keeping in the sunlight ahead of the lengthening shadow of the peak across the valley. The bull moose may be caught as he raises his head from the water, mouth full of pond lilies and water grasses, or later in the season as he browses on willows, as he hooks at branches with his antlers, stands in his wallow, or wanders through a high alpine meadow in restless search of a mate. There is no legal limit for the photographer, his only limits are his skill, the number of animals that he can find, and the time. Look at the illustrations of animals in any of our natural histories, and then imagine what is possible in illustrating each animal, the life it leads, and the country it frequents. The educational value of such photographs is very great, and in after years, if the particular species should become extinct the photograph becomes of inestimable worth.

The very nature of the game of wild animal photography requires rather highly specialized equipment. The exposure must be instantaneous, certainly nothing longer than 1/25 second being permissible as a rule. The light may not always be good, and a lens working at an opening at least as large as f6.3 is very desirable. The ordinary hand camera will not do for its limitations are too great, and it puts a sportsman under too big a handicap for him to obtain any results except as an occasional piece of very good luck. It is very seldom that one can get near enough for a good photograph with a hand camera, it is too hard to set the focus and make the exposure both accurately and quickly, and to catch the animal just right in the small finder.

It is desirable that if practicable the image of the animal be at least ¾-inch high on the negative. Such size of image will give us a negative which, if properly focused and exposed, can be enlarged to show the details and expressions of the animal in a very satisfactory manner. Using a postcard size camera with a focal length of about 7 inches one must needs get within about 25 feet of the animal to obtain an image about ¾-inch high, assuming that the actual height of the animal is about three feet. If, however, we use a long focus lens, or a modern telephoto lens of about 14 inches equivalent focus, we will only have to stalk to about 50 feet of the animal to obtain an image on our negative about ¾-inch high. The shorter focus lens will give a much wider angle of view on our small plate, but this is not of much moment for we are taking an animal, not scenery.

Big game photographs are obtained in a number of ways, not counting the wonderful accidental chances that sometimes occur. A camera may be set up on a tripod, concealed by brush or otherwise, close to a game trail or other locality where it is known that the game may pass, or where it may go if driven by a companion. The photographer hides himself close by and operates the shutter of the camera from the short distance by means of a string when the animal comes to the exact spot on the trail at which the lens is trained and focused. Many of the wonderful photographs of Colorado big game taken by our pioneer big game photographer, Mr. A. G. Wallihan, were obtained in this manner. Or one may take flash-light photographs at night, the camera and the flash being operated by a string stretched across a runway or attached to a bait so that when the animal pulls the string it operates the flash and takes its own picture. The camera can be set up in the bow of a canoe with the flash powder in front of a reflector placed above and slightly in rear of the camera. The paddler in the stern silently brings the canoe as close as possible to the deer or moose feeding on the shore of lake or stream, and at the proper moment the sportsman in the bow swings the camera to aim at the animal, and with a special device opens the shutter and discharges the flash powder. Many hundreds of wonderful flash-light photographs of big game have been made and published by Mr. George Shiras, who has developed the equipment, technique, and art of this form of game photography to a very high degree.

For all these methods of big game photography a view camera with long focus or telephoto lens will suffice. The longer the focus and the quicker the lens, the better. Mr. Shiras has developed a type of combined camera and flashlight apparatus which is waterproof, and which can be left for days set up at the bait or the game trail.

The highest form of the sport, the form requiring the highest degree of skill, coolness, and knowledge, is where the photographer discovers the animal by still hunting or stalking, and then with infinite patience worms his way close enough so that he can get a satisfactory picture. For such work a reflecting camera similar to our Graflex is highly desirable, and it should have a long focus or telephoto lens working at least at f6.3. The sportsman can then quickly catch the animal on the ground glass, keeping it in view and constantly in focus as he advances, up to the very instant that he presses the button and makes the exposure. Also the focal plane shutter with which such cameras are equipped permits of making exposures about half as short as the ordinary shutters operating between the lenses, or conversely, permits of on exposure twice as long. Stalking was the method largely used by that prince of photographers, Mr. A. Radclyffe Dunmore, in obtaining his perfectly wonderful series of photographs of African animals, and he also used a very large, special, made-to-order reflecting camera for most of his work. He gives the following photographic hints in his book *"Camera Adventures in the African Wilds."*

"The sort of camera necessary for the work is one of the long-focus reflex type, equipped with convertible lens of high speed, and a telephoto lens of the greatest speed. The camera must be rigid enough to allow of the telephoto being used without danger of shaking. Plates or films may be used. The former are better and rather more reliable. Both keep well in inland East Africa (not Uganda), but should be kept in sealed tin cases, and be developed as soon as possible after being exposed. With tanks, the task of development in the field is easy enough, and the water for the purpose will be found quite cool enough if used early in the morning. Developing powders, ready-mixed and weighed, acid hypo, a fixing box, and a developing tank complete the outfit. In my work, every plate and film was developed within a day or two after being used. All your photographic outfit should be kept in watertight cases, and chemical of any kind must be in tins. For the camera, a soft sling case of canvas or pantasote is better than one of hard leather. It is both lighter and less noisy, and more compact when not in use, and unless the leather is really waterproof it has the disadvantage of holding the dampness. Plate-holders must be dusted frequently, as the fine dust stirred up when on the march finds it way into everything.

"Of course it is necessary to use a quick plate. Those I used were an American make, of double-coated orthochromatic. For all tele-photo work the double-coated plates are advisable, as they decrease the amount of halation very considerably. The orthochromatic properties are even more valuable as they give much greater vigor to the distant parts of the landscape than can be obtained by the ordinary plate, which is weak where there is a preponderance of blue, owing to the atmospheric conditions.

"It is well to take precautions against any mishap by carrying duplicate parts of any of your outfit which is liable to become broken, injured, or lost. For instance, the reflex camera is totally dependent on its mirror and ground glass, therefore extra ones, *cut to fit*, should be carried, securely packed between corrugated cardboard inside a wooden box. A small collection of various sized screws will also be found very convenient."

The 3A Graflex camera can be fitted with a telephoto lens working at f5.6 or f6.3 which has an equivalent focal length of about 17 inches, allowing us to get a suitable sized image of an

Photo by F. H. Riggall

PHOTOGRAPHING A ROCKY MOUNTAIN GOAT ON A RIDGE IN THE CANA-
DIAN ROCKIES. AN OPPORTUNITY LIKE THIS DOES NOT COME ONCE IN
LIFETIME. THIS GOAT WAS ENTIRELY WILD, AND NOT IN A PARK

animal if within about 65 feet of it. The telephoto lens has a long mounting and barrel, and the camera cannot be closed when this lens is in place. Nevertheless this is not very inconvenient, and this combination makes an excellent outfit for big game photography and general record photography as well. The ordinary f4.5 anastigmat lens which comes with the camera will answer for all record photographs, and one can carry the telephoto lens in a separate case in his rucksack or pack, and change lenses when he wishes to photograph game. This camera has the advantage also of using the 3A postcard size film, easily procurable anywhere, and easily developed. The camera seems rather large and heavy compared with a hand camera, being 10 x 5 x 6⅜ inches, and weighing 7 pounds, but a certain amount of bulk and weight is necessary with reflecting cameras. The telephoto lens arranged to fit on the lens board will probably weigh half a pound more. The outfit might be carried in a specially designed rucksack, permitting the hunter to also carry his rifle, and making a back-pack of about ten pounds, including the noon-day lunch. The Dallmeyer, Dallon Telephoto Lenses, Series XVIII No. 4, f6.5, and the Series VI, No. 4, are possibilities for use with the Graflex 3A camera.

The Naturalist's Graflex camera is also an excellent instrument for game photography. The size of the plate is 4 x 5 inches, and it is furnished with a special "telastigmat" lens with an equivalent focus of 24 inches, and working at f6.8. It has the longest focus of any speedy camera on the market, and very satisfactory images of big game animals can be obtained at 100 feet, which is a very great advantage. It is about the best outfit if the sportsman is going in strong for big game photography, wishes to get the maximum results, and cares little about hunting with the rifle. It is a big and bulky camera. Closed up it measures 20½ x 6¼- x 9¾ inches, and weighs 8 pounds without its case. To use films with it an extra roll holder will be necessary, but unlike the 3A Graflex, it has the advantage of being able to use plates, cut films, and film packs. All this is expensive, the complete outfit costing about $340.00. This camera is not adaptable to ordinary record photography, but is intended for birds and animals and nature studies only. If it is carried the rifle will probably have to be left in camp, but there is no question as to the excellent results it gives. It was with one of these cameras that Kermit Roosevelt obtained his wonderful elephant pictures in Africa.

Stalking game with the intention of photographing it is a very difficult procedure, and there are many pitfalls that have to be surmounted. Only experience will teach the sportsman how to overcome the difficulties and get around the tight places. One has not only to watch the wind, to keep out of sight, and to be sure that he makes no noise, as when hunting with the rifle; but he must also take into consideration the light and the direction of the sun, and the background. Usually he dare not alarm the game for, unlike the rifle, the camera will seldom give any results on a running shot. Above all he must get very much closer than is necessary with the rifle, and having gotten this close he naturally desires to remain as long as possible without disturbing the animal in order to get more than one photograph. In the excitement one must not forget to focus correctly, to have the animal well in the center of the plate, and to give the correct exposure. After one exposure has been made the photographer must not neglect to turn the roll to another film, or he may ruin the picture he has already taken. These cautions are very necessary for the excitement is intense when one is within fifty feet of a wild animal, the culmination of many days of effort. There is no thrill like it.

CHAPTER XXIV

PHYSICAL PREPARATION

"Allah reckons not against a man's allotted days the time he spends in shikir."

The physical preparation which you should undertake in advance depends upon why you go into the wilderness. If you are a tired business man, and you go for a rest, relaxation, quiet, and health you may not be able to do any training before you depart—you may not want to. Perhaps you are relying on Nature to cure you, to give you health and pep. She will do it too if you give her time in proportion to the length of time you have been disregarding her laws. Take it slow, very slow at first; don't overdo. If you are all tired out the best thing the wilderness has for you at first is rest, rest in the fresh, balsam laden air; and quiet disturbed only by the murmur of the brook, the rustle of leaves in the breeze, and the lap-lap of water on the lake shore. Afterwards should come gentle exercise, short at first, gradually getting longer and more strenuous. Perhaps after a couple of months you will be able to stand the big-game trails for a few hours.

But if you go into the wilderness with the idea of taking up at once active big game hunting, and of being successful at it, you must be in the very best physical condition, as hard as nails all over, with not a weak spot. The successful pursuit of big game is a strenuous athletic stunt requiring a sound constitution, a strong heart, good lungs, and the absence of excess weight. The two physical qualities most essential are endurance and light-footedness. Strength is also desirable. Not one city man in a thousand keeps in such condition. What I have here to say is for the man who desires to get in and keep in that superb condition of body which will permit him to hunt from dawn to dark, over trails that are long and rough and mountains that are steep, and do this day after day, thoroughly enjoying the sport and the strenuous exercise in the open air, and coming home at the end even better and stronger than when he started.

Our Creator made man to be a big, strong, fleet animal, and despite much abuse of our bodies we are still born with the living germ of those attributes in our bodies, latent, needing only to be developed in the right way. We cannot get or retain anything without work. Our achievements in anything are always in exact proportion to the amount of work—physical and mental —which we put into our effort. If you desire to get strong and healthy, and to keep so, and you take up calesthenics and setting-up exercises, and such light work, you can naturally expect to maintain a fairly healthy, supple body, and an erect carriage, but you won't get strength and endurance, nor real, vigorous energy. If you walk three miles every day it won't put you in condition to walk fifteen miles without fatigue, although your fatigue may be slightly less than if you had not walked at all. If you desire to teach a child to read you don't keep it constantly reciting the alphabet, saying it more times every day—you set it a *gradually increasing task, day after day making the task harder, more difficult, but not necessarily much longer.* In these words you have the whole secret of attaining and maintaining physical perfection.

The trouble with us is that we don't use our brains enough. We are content to follow a lot of cranks who have been telling us things on physical education which are not so for many generations, and when we think that we need exercise we turn to the so-called system of some crank who promises us that if we follow it we will become physical marvels in a couple of months. The chances are that it is a system of light exercise designed for tired business men and fat old ladies. It gets us only just so far. Perhaps after two weeks we feel a little better and we have a little more pep. If we keep it up we keep feeling just that well, and we have just that much pep, but we don't get any farther. All that we have done is to learn the alphabet. If, after using this light system for a month, and not getting what we hoped for, we follow a friend's advice and take up Professor So-and-So's system, which is a little more strenuous, we progress a little farther. We have learned to read "I see a cow." But we are still not getting what we want.

We know that big game hunting requires much walking. So we walk to and from the office, and on Saturday or Sunday we take a longer half day walk, or perhaps we play some golf, all on pavements or nice lawns. It makes us feel pretty good at first, but just so good. The chances are that we notice the improvement only the first month, after which we get used to our slightly improved condition. We stay in what a sedentary man would call good health for an office man. But if we go to the wilderness in this condition we find ourselves completely tired out after eight miles of rough going without a trail, and the next day we are so stiff we cannot hunt. If the city man attempts the kind of big game hunting described in this book with no other physical preparation than this, he will probably find, unless he is young and has wonderful recuperative powers, that his trip completely wears him out physically instead of benefiting him. What is the matter? Why you have just learned to read "The cow lives in the barn over the hill."

Man was created to be a hunter. When the meat in the larder began to get short he ventured forth into the wilderness on foot to obtain more. He caught his prey by his superior *speed* and *light-footedness;* he killed it by *brute strength* with his *bare hands* or with a *club.* He butchered it with a sharp stone. Then he *slung it, one hundred* or *two hundred pounds of it, across his shoulders,* and *strode* over *hill* and *valley* to his cave. If he had a family he did this every *two* or *three days.* In between he rested at home. *He did terrifically strenuous exercises every two or three days.* Thus he developed a wonderfully strong, muscular, capable, enduring body. If necessary he could work it for months at a time, as in war, with no damage, but the body was developed in peace by strenuous exercise at more or less regular intervals of two or three days. His woman, who did light exercise every day, developed an entirely different body—lithe, thin, soft, without strength, but with good endurance for her light tasks.

The heritage of ten million years cannot be wiped out by two hundred years of effete civilization. We still inherit the germ cells which will cause our bodies to develop into real men's bodies, strong, capable, enduring, God-like, if we give them half a chance, prescribing work for them similar in quantity and quality to that which gave our ancestors such physiques. The italics in the above paragraph will give you an indication of the nature of this work.

"But," you object, "a man cannot exercise like that at home and still attend to business." Quite true, but a method has been found which can be used at home by a business man, which will not take up undue time, and which will accomplish the desired results. It will, if persisted in, gradually make a man unbelievably strong, agile, swift, enduring, light of foot, capable of unheard of physical and mental work, gloriously healthy. With it there is a steady improvement which can be noticed from week to week, almost from every other day to every other day. It won't give the desired results in two or three months, but it will in eight months, from October to June, the exercise months. It takes half an hour every other day at home, a short walk every day, and five minutes' running or jumping every other day. During these periods the work is tremendously hard. It has to be to get results. It is no lazy man's or get-rich-quick method.

This is the so-called "double progressive method." You make a certain effort, or lift a certain weight, say five times. The next alternate day you repeat it six times, and so on up to ten. Then you go back again to five repetitions, but you make the effort slightly more strenuous, or you increase the weight a few pounds, and continue until you are doing ten repetitions, and so on.

If you wish to increase the strength of your thighs for mountain climbing you have probably been told to adopt the exercise known as the "deep knee bend," where you stand erect, then bend your knees until your buttocks touch your heels, and then straighten your knees again. Perhaps you start with ten repetitions and gradually increase to one hundred, and when you reach the latter figure you find you are devoting six or seven minutes to one exercise alone, and that it is deadly monotonous, leaving you tired out. Also you will notice some little improvement in the strength, size, and suppleness of your thighs. But the next time you get into the mountains there will be little if any improvement in your climbing ability because you have been lifting but half your weight with each leg, whereas in the mountains as you climb you are called upon to lift the entire weight of the body with each leg, plus the weight of a rifle and rucksack, and sometimes a heavy load of heads or meat besides. Climbing a thousand foot mountain is equivalent to doing the half knee bend two thousand times with a two hundred pound weight on the shoulders. No wonder you are tired and stiff the next day. But if you had done the deep knee bend in the ordinary manner for the first two weeks of your exercise, working up gradually from twenty-five to sixty-five repetitions, then the second two weeks held twenty-five pounds on your shoulders while you did exactly the same thing, third two weeks fifty pounds, then a gradually slower increase of fifteen to ten pounds every two weeks, by the time the next hunting season came around you would have thighs which would carry you up and down the steepest mountains from dawn to dusk every day with no fatigue.

A chain is as strong as its weakest link. You cannot have real strength and endurance without being strong in every part. Particularly you must have strength in the back, hips, and legs, for these parts are the foundations of a man's strength. Many a man has worked for strong, capable, 16-inch arms, and after many years of exercise for the arms found that he could not attain them until he had first strengthened his back, hips, and legs. It is common sense that Nature should not give us the very best of arms until our underpinning is strong enough to sustain what our arms pick up.

A series of exercises has been evolved, some twelve or fifteen in number, double progressive in character as described, which will gradually and steadily develop strength in the entire body, up to the ultimate limit of the individual, and do it surely.*

It makes super-strength far and above what the ordinary athletic man has, and it gives super-health as well. The beauty of it is that it makes a capable body, one that can turn from raising weights to climbing mountains, or hitting a rough and long trail with scarcely any breaking in process. The series of exercises take about half an hour every other day, giving much better results that way than if done daily. The little rest in between exercise days is used in building the body up. Your

---

* See "*Super Strength*," by Alan Calvert. Milo Publishing Co., Philadelphia, 1924.

cave man, you remember, did his strenuous hunting only every two or three days when the larder became low.

The original Swedish (Ling) System of Educational Gymnastics was very excellent and scientific in character. It insisted on this double progressive method. But it had two faults—it required a regular gymnasium with all its apparatus, and it was so complicated that it needed a trained instructor. The new method develops the same super-athletes as the Swedish system, but anyone can use it in his own bedroom, and he gets results quicker. The Swedish system insisted on walking, running, and jumping. Although not prescribed in the double progressive method, these should not be neglected.

In winter the walk to the office should be made just as fast and vigorous as you can possibly push yourself. If done right, this is walking enough, provided that the office is at least a mile and a half from home.

Three times a week one should run two or three hundred yards at a gradually increasing speed. In a large city you can use a deserted street in the evening without attracting attention.

On alternate evenings go out in the back yard and hop on one foot for a few minutes. Vary the way you hop, and make it continually more difficult and strenuous, until you are hopping on and off of a fallen log or rock.

As summer comes on, and the weather gets warmer, you will find that you cannot continue your indoor weight-lifting because it takes too much out of you in the heat. Also, the very fast walking to the office is usually almost impossible, for you would arrive in such a perspiration that bath would be needed before sitting down at the desk, and that is usually impossible, together with the change of clothes which would be necessary. So, instead, you adopt the afternoon after work as the period of exercise, and at this time of year there is sufficient light for this purpose well into the evening. Every other day you should take a couple of hours' work-out along the roads, or over the fields, or through the woods in the country, or in the park. Your car will quickly take you out to where you can do this, and take you back again to your bath and dinner. Gradually you make this more strenuous, and do it over rougher and if possible more hilly ground, and you combine fast walking with running and jumping. Your energy and strength now goes into your legs where you are going to need it in hunting, while the rest of the body still retains sufficient of the strength you built up during the winter and spring. So you arrive at the month of August or September, when you will leave for your hunting trip, in thoroughly first-class physical condition, hard as nails, with lots of endurance, energy, and light-footedness.

Such a method will gradually develop great strength, endurance, energy, glorious health, and a superb body. It will give a man the maximum efficiency for wilderness hunting, or any other kind of physical or mental work. It takes very little time, but that time must be used honestly, which means very, very hard work and the closest kind of mental concentration. It will work for men from twenty to fifty-five years of age, and it will accomplish perfect wonders in eight months.

APPENDIX A

CONVENIENT CHECK LISTS OF EQUIPMENT AND SUPPLIES

It is not intended that all of these articles should be taken, nor that others should not be taken, but most of those listed are usually necessary or desirable.

I

LIST FOR WOOD HUNTING
(Sufficient for one man for one month)

Worn on Person—
Stetson hat
Olive drab flannel shirt
Woolen breeches
2 pair heavy wool socks or stockings
Lumberman's rubbers, 7-inch tops
Medium-weight wool underwear
Hunting belt
Rucksack
Rifle

Pockets—
Pocket knife
Watch
Compass
Waterproof match box
Pipe and tobacco pouch
Loose matches
Handkerchief
Pocket whetstone
Map

Hunting Belt—
Cartridge box with 20 cartridges
Small camera and case (or else in rucksack)
.22 cal. pistol for grouse

Rucksack—
Mackinaw stag shirt
Small hand axe

329

20 rifle cartridges
50 grouse gun cartridges
Small aluminum kettle and cup
Spoon
Bags of tea and sugar
Waterproof match box
Tape measure
Note book and pencil
Camera and case (or else on belt)
Lunch
Gloves

Duluth Packsack—
Toilet articles
Towel
1 suit wool underwear
4 pair heavy wool socks or stockings
1 pair double-sole oiled moccasins
Can of boot grease
Rifle and pistol cleaning kit
Camera films in moisture-proof cans
Extra pipe
Toilet paper
Fish line, small snelled hooks, and sinkers
Tobacco
20 cartridges for rifle
100 cartridges for grouse gun
Housewife
Small medicine kit

Bedding and Shelter—
Light waterproof tent (Forester or Lean-to for 2 men)
Light waterproof tarpaulin (about 8x11 feet, wt. 3½ lbs.)
Sleeping bag
Camp pad or air mattress
Featherweight raincoat
Canvas bucket
Canvas basin

Supplied by Guide—
Axe
Guide's bedding
Guide's personal effects

NOTE: Guides often supply cooking utensils and tent, but these are usually very heavy and thus a handicap whenever moving camp. It is better for the sportsman to take his own light tent and aluminum cook kit.

II

(Sufficient for 1 man for 2 months)

Worn on Person—
   Stetson hat
   Mackinaw stag shirt
   Olive drab flannel shirt
   Wool riding breeches
   Hob-nailed Munson army shoes
   Heavy wool stocking (outside breeches)
   Medium-weight underwear
   Hunting belt
   Gloves

Pockets—
   Pocket knife
   Watch
   Compass
   Waterproof match box
   Pipe and tobacco pouch
   Loose matches
   Pocket whetstone
   Aneroid (?)
   Map

Hunting Belt—
   Binoculars and case
   Cartridge box with 20 cartridges

On Saddle—
   Rifle in saddle holster (magazine loaded)
   Camera in leather holster
   Grouse gun in holster and 20 cartridges
   Rain coat or pummel slicker
   Lunch

On Pack Horse, Top Pack—
   Sleeping bag
   Air mattress
   Air pillow with pillow case
   Heavy mackinaw or sheepskin coat
   In waterprooof canvas clothing bag same size and shape as 50-pound
      flour sack (not round duffle bag) carry the following articles, the
      bag going between the saw buck on top of load.
   1 wool undershirt
   2 wool drawers
   1 olive drab flannel shirt
   5 pair heavy wool stockings

6 handkerchiefs
1 pair light hobnailed alpine shoes
1 pair leather-top lumberman's rubbers

On Pack Horse, Side Pack in Pannier—
Bath towel ⎱
Rifle and pistol cleaning kit ⎰On top, first things to come out
Toilet kit ⎰
100 rifle cartridges
100 pistol cartridges
Camera films in moisture-proof can
Tobacco in waterproof bag
Diary and pencil
Rucksack
Toilet paper
Hand axe
Extra pipe
Tape measure
Tripod for camera
Light fur gloves (for cold weather)
Fishline, snelled hooks, and sinkers

Provided by Guide—
All saddle and horse equipment
Cooking and eating utensils
Panniers and pack covers
Large tent or tarpaulin
Axes
Guide's bedding and personal kit

III

COOKING UTENSILS

(For 3 men)

3 small aluminum kettles to nest
2 steel fry pans with detachable handles, 9-inch
1 sheet-iron Dutch oven or aluminum reflecting baker
4 aluminum plates
4 aluminum soup bowls
4 enamel-ware cups
4 knives
4 forks
4 tea spoons
4 dessert spoons
1 large spoon
1 butcher knife
1 wash pan, or wash basin
2 dish rags

2 cakes kitchen soap
Supply of matches in waterproof can
Add plate, bowl, cup, knife, fork, spoon for each additional man.
    For four men or over add one more kettle and increase diameter of fry pans to 12 inches

IV

GRUB LIST

(For 1 man for 1 month)

Flour	20 lbs.
Baking powder	½ "
Cereals as desired	10 "
Sugar, granulated	10 "
* Salt	2 "
Klim whole-milk powder	3 "
Beans, white navy	7 "
Bacon	7 "
Tea	1 "
Coffee, roasted and ground	2 "
Pepper	¼ "
Dried fruit	10 "
Crisco or lard	3 "
Butter, canned	3 "
Sweet chocolate	3 "
Maple syrup	1 quart
† Potatoes, onions, fresh vegetables, and fruit	?

Of course any other articles may be taken for which there is room. Every man has his own peculiar tastes and likes. The above is rather an old timer's list, where weight makes it necessary to pare down to essentials.

The sportsman should bring from home a number of waterproof cotton grub-sacks in which to pack the provisions. These come in 5 and 10 pound sizes, round, with tie string, and can be had from the larger sportsman's outfitters in New York, Chicago, and San Francisco.

---

  * More salt may be necessary for preserving skins.
  † The amount of fresh vegetables and fruit that can be taken is usually limited by the transportation. They cannot be carried in freezing weather, although when it freezes only at night they can be buried or covered up. The best substitutes for these are meat, bacon, and beans. Canned goods and dessicated vegetables are usually worthless as food, mere'y filling the stomach temporarily, giving no real energy, and usually injurious to the health.

APPENDIX B

ADDITIONAL DATA AND INFORMATION NECESSARY
FOR WILDERNESS HUNTERS

It has been thought best not to burden this work with such data and information, however necessary they may be, which are found in suitable and convenient form elsewhere. There is much in the science of Woodcraft, not contained herein, which the hunter should be familiar with. Happily almost all of it is contained in a single most excellent and comprehensive work, *"Camping and Woodcraft,* by Horace Kephart, The MacMillan Company, New York. This work is a masterpiece in its way. The wilderness hunter will be handicapped without much of the information which it contains. This recommendation is entirely unsolicited, neither the author nor the publishers knowing that it is being written. *Camping and Woodcraft* contains such excellent advice and instructions under the following heads (which are only a few of the subjects it deals with) that it would be presumption on my part to endeavor to deal with these subjects within these pages. I would have to repeat all that Mr. Kephart has said in his work, and could add very little in addition:

The Camp Fire
Camp Cookery
Concentrated Foods
Edible Plants of the Wilderness
Living Off the Country
Dressing and Butchering Game
Skinning and Preparation of Heads and Pelts
Field Taxidermy
Pests of the Woods—Flies, Mosquitoes, Snakes
Accidents, Emergencies, and Their Treatment
Axemanship
Cabin Building
Knots, Hitches, and Lashings

Camping and Woodcraft is indeed so valuable that many hunters would do well to take it along into the wilds with them, together with field books on the trees and birds, and also perhaps this modest work of mine might be judged worthy of a place in the hunter's pack. _

APPENDIX C—BIBLIOGRAPHY

Some of the best books on American big-game hunting and wilderness life, which have been of much assistance in the preparation of this work .

List of North American Recent Mammals, 1923.
GERRIT S. MILLER, JR.
Government Printing Office, Washington, 1924.

Life Histories of Northern Animals.
ERNEST THOMPSON SETON,
Charles Scribner's Sons, New York, 1909.

The American Natural History.
W. T. HORNADAY.
Charles Scribner's Sons, New York, 1904.

Mammals of America.
NATURE LOVERS' LIBRARY.
The University Society, New York, 1917.

The Conquest of Mount McKinley.
BELMORE BROWNE.
G. P. Putnam's Sons, New York, 1913.

Wild Life in Canada.
ANGUS BUCHANAN.
Frederick A Stokes Co., New York, 1920.

Lands Forlorn.
GEORGE M. DOUGLAS.
G. P. Putnam's Sons, New York, 1913.

Sport and Travel in the Northland of Canada.
DAVID T. HANBURY.
Edwin Arnold, London, 1904.

On the Headwaters of Peace River.
PAUL LELAND HAWORTH.
Charles Scribner's Sons, New York, 1917.

The Drama of the Forests.
ARTHUR HEMING.
Doubleday, Page & Co., Garden City, 1921.

Camp-Fires in the Canadian Rockies.
Camp-Fires in Desert and Lava.
    W. T. HORNADAY.
        Charles Scribner's Sons, New York, 1906-1908.

Out of Doors.
Let's Go Afield.
    EMERSON HOUGH.
        D. Appleton & Co., New York, 1915.

Camping and Woodcraft.
    HORACE KEPHART.
        Macmillan Company, New York, 1926.

In the Alaska-Yukon Gamelands.
    J. A. McGUIRE.
        Stewart and Kidd Co., Cincinnati, 1921.

The Secrets of Polar Travel.
    REAR ADMIRAL RORERT E. PEARY.
        The Century Company, New York, 1917.

The Happy Hunting Grounds.
    KERMIT ROOSEVELT.
        Charles Scribner's Sons, New York, 1921.

Hunting in the Arctic and Alaska.
    E. MARSHALL SCULL.
        John C. Winston Co., Philadelphia, 1914.

Hunting Trips in North America.
    F. C. SELOUS.
        Charles Scribner's Sons, New York, 1907.

Woodcraft.
    GEORGE W. SEARS (NESSMUK).
        Forest and Stream Publishing Co., New York, 1888.

The Arctic Prairies.
    ERNEST THOMPSON SETON.
        Charles Scribner's Sons, New York, 1911.

The Book of Woodcraft.
Rolf in the Woods.
    ERNEST THOMPSON SETON.
        Charles Scribner's Sons, New York, 1912.

The Wilderness of the Upper Yukon.
The Wilderness of the North Pacific Coast Islands.
    CHARLES SHELDON.
        Charles Scribner's Sons, New York, 1911-1912.

Big Game Fields of America—North and South.
DANIEL J. SINGER.
George H. Doran Co., New York, 1914.

My Life with the Eskimo.
The Friendly Arctic.
VILHJALMUR STEFANSSON.
The Macmillan Co., New York, 1913-1921.

Hunters of the Great North.
VILHJALMUR STEFANSSON.
Harcourt, Brace & Co., New York, 1922.

Camp and Trail.
STEWART EDWARD WHITE.
Outing Publishing Co., New York, 1907.

American Big Game in its Haunts.
American Big Game Hunting.
Hunting in Many Lands.
Trail and Camp-Fire.
Hunting in High Altitudes.
BOOKS OF THE BOONE AND CROCKETT CLUB.
Harper and Brother, New York.

Musk-ox, Bison, Sheep, and Goat.
The Deer Family.
AMERICAN SPORTSMAN'S LIBRARY.
The Macmillan Company, New York, 1904.

Packing and Portaging—Wallace.
Tracks and Tracking—Brunner.
Outdoor Photography—Dimock.
Winter Camping—Carpenter.
The Canoe—Pinkerton.
OUTING HANBOOKS.
Outing Publishing Co., New York.

Hints to Travelers.
The Royal Geographical Society, London, 1906.

Also numerous articles contained in the following magazines:
Journal of Mammalogy.
Natural History.
Forest and Stream.
The American Rifleman.
Outdoor Life.
Field and Stream.
Outdoor Recreation.
Rod and Gun in Canada.

E P
B M We hope you enjoyed this title
from Echo Point Books & Media

Before Closing this Book, Two Good Things to Know

1. Buy Direct & Save

Go to www.echopointbooks.com (click "Our Titles" at top or click "For Echo Point Publishing" in the middle) to see our complete list of titles. We publish books on a wide variety of topics-—from spirituality to auto repair.

Buy direct and save 10% at www.echopointbooks.com

DISCOUNT CODE: EPBUYER

2. Make Literary History and Earn $100 Plus Other Goodies Simply for Your Book Recommendation!

At Echo Point Books & Media we specialize in republishing out-of-print books that are united by one essential ingredient: high quality. Do you know of any great books that are no longer actively published? If so, please let us know. If we end up publishing your recommendation, you'll be adding a wee bit to literary culture and a bunch to our publishing efforts.

Here is how we will thank you:

- A free copy of the new version of your beloved book that includes acknowledgement of your skill as a sharp book scout.
- A free copy of another Echo Point title you like from echopointbooks.com.
- And, oh yes, we'll also send you a check for $100.

Since we publish an eclectic list of titles, we're interested in a wide range of books. So please don't be shy if you have obscure tastes or like books with a practical focus. To get a sense of what kind of books we publish, visit us at www.echopointbooks.com.

If you have a book that you think will work for us, send us an email at editorial@echopointbooks.com

www.ingramcontent.com/pod-product-compliance
Lightning Source LLC
Chambersburg PA
CBHW030531100426

42813CB00001B/219